"*Tonight at Ten* is a tender, compelling look at the competition and chaos of local news. It reflects the humanity of a veteran reporter."

Byron Harris, Veteran Investigative Reporter
and winner of Peabody, Murrow and DuPont Awards.

"*Tonight at Ten* is a must read for any TV news consumer. Steve takes us on a thrill ride by sharing a rare inside look into the fascinating and often bizarre stories behind the stories."

Walt Gray, News Anchor
ABC 10, Sacramento

"Through his own colorful and heartfelt recollections, Steve debunks the misconception that journalists are biased, cynical and uncaring. A must read for news junkies!"

Janet St. James, Former Health Reporter
WFAA-TV Dallas

Tonight at Ten

A TV News Reporter's Stories behind the Stories

Steve Stoler

To my dear friend Chris,
Thank you for your never-ending support & friendship. You are an exceptional police officer & person. You always make us Plano Proud! I hope you enjoy my book. c u 2 night @ 10!!

First published by Dog Ear Publishing
4011 Vincennes Rd
Indianapolis, IN 46268
www.dogearpublishing.net

dog ear PUBLISHING

ISBN: 978-1-4575-4939-7

This book is printed on acid-free paper.

Printed in the United States of America

Foreword

"There are no bad stories, just bad reporters," the late, great WFAA-TV news director Marty Haag once said to a newsroom full of reporters and producers. It was a pronouncement that got our full attention.

A reporter had just refused an assignment, and he made it perfectly clear to all within earshot that was *not* an option. Bottom line—reporters are storytellers whose job gives them a front row seat to history. Today's news is tomorrow's history.

But a good TV reporter is much more than a daily scribe. He or she generally has less than two minutes to capture your attention and get a few facts across before you move on to something else. The difference between a good reporter and a great reporter is empathy. The great reporter puts him- or herself in the viewers' shoes and answers the questions they want to know and why they should care. A compassionate reporter touches viewers in a way that moves them, stirs emotions—happiness, sadness, anger, indignation—and just maybe moves them to action. Perhaps the most rewarding part of being a reporter is doing a story about a destructive tornado one day and [seeing that] the very next day, homeless families have food, clothing, and shelter—thanks to stories that moved viewers to help. Steve Stoler is that kind of reporter.

Steve and I were working at competing TV stations in the Dallas-Fort Worth market when we first met. I had always admired his work, his affable personality, and the comforting tone of some of his best reports. I was moved when he shared the most personal of stories—his own battle with cancer Hodgkin's lymphoma. Once again, as he had many times before, Steve gave insight to a story that put the viewers' needs first. He could have kept his battle private, but he chose to share it so that maybe someone watching could be helped or maybe he could even help save someone's life.

Steve's book, *Tonight at Ten: A News Reporter's Stories behind the Stories* is an inside look at a reporter's notebook that viewers seldom see. You'll feel like you were on the scene of some riveting news events. The story of Baby Jessica McClure trapped in a Midland, Texas, backyard well for fifty-eight hours—the way the West Texas community rallied around her rescue—uplifted us all. There are stories of tragedy and triumph, and those that will touch your heart. It's all in a day's work for a TV news reporter but it's much more when that reporter has a heart, compassion, and a love of people.

So, if you like a good story-sit back and take in the stories and the backstories of a veteran ace reporter. You just might discover and learn to appreciate what makes a great reporter—a good person and a compassionate human being like my friend and former colleague Steve Stoler.

Gloria Campos
Retired, WFAA-TV Dallas-Fort Worth
1984–2014

Introduction

The Stories behind the Stories

It was 11:00 p.m. on my last night working at 41 News Central, in Macon, Georgia. My boss, Curt Smith, who was the news director had vowed to give me a test to determine if I was ready to take the next step of my career. I had no earthly idea what he was up to. I walked into the studio as I had every night Monday through Friday. I sat down at the anchor desk and started reading the nightly news off the teleprompter, but something about this night seemed very different. About ten minutes into the newscast, Curt walked into the studio and stood stoically next to the camera. I saw him in my peripheral vision but tried to block him out as I kept reading. I knew he was about to do something bizarre, but I still wasn't sure what—and so I read on. Suddenly, in the middle of a story, he turned around, dropped his pants, and mooned me. Miraculously, I kept my composure while seeing his exposed bare and extremely ugly butt. When we went to a commercial break, I started laughing hysterically. Curt proclaimed, "Nice job, Steve. You're ready to move on!"

Curt's unconventional test is only the tip of the iceberg of interesting stories I have to tell. In writing this book, I chose my most memorable stories behind the stories, reflecting a roller coaster of emotions. Some of these stories made me laugh out loud. Others brought tears of sorrow. There are stories that lifted my spirits and inspired me. Others challenged my faith in humanity. And in one very unusual twist, I actually became the story, sharing with viewers my personal battle with cancer.

Other stories, such as that of the falling bear, left me frustrated and shaking my head in disbelief. Imagine living in a quiet neighborhood and seeing a 300-pound black bear in a tree outside your front window. When residents in a quiet Asheville, North Carolina, neighborhood experienced this, some brave souls came out of their houses and huddled in small groups on the street corner. Someone in the neighborhood called all the local television stations. A small army of reporters and photographers, including yours truly, set up under the huge oak tree that the bear was in. My photographer, a newbie, had just changed positions at the station. He was a studio camera operator who wanted to be a photojournalist, and he was getting his chance. This was his first day shooting out in the field. I could tell he was nervous and uncomfortable.

The tree towered over the border of a picturesque golf course in the neighborhood. All eyes and cameras pointed upward. We could clearly see a huge black bear high in the tree. Apparently, he had come out of the mountains searching for food and ended up uncomfortably close to golfers and neighbors. It was a comical standoff. The bear curiously stared at us and we nervously stared back, hoping he would stay right where he was. We watched and waited patiently until two North Carolina game wardens showed up. We saw them get out of their pickup and load a rifle with a tranquilizer dart. This was going to be very interesting.

The game wardens moved us back about twenty-five yards, away from the tree. I could only wonder if the big burley bear would survive a thirty-foot fall from the tree. With anxious anticipation and cameras rolling, we looked on as one of the game wardens fired a blast from his rifle, hitting the bear in the side. Everyone jumped at the sound of the shot. Adrenaline rushed through my body. I could feel my heart racing.

The bear started feeling the effects of the tranquilizer. In a matter of minutes, he looked like he'd had a few too many shots of whiskey. He was slowly losing it. He lost his balance and began to slide downward off his perch on a strong, thick branch. He was hanging on with both front legs, but he was falling deeper and deeper into a trance from the drug. Soon, one of his legs came off the branch.

Now, he was only hanging on with one leg. Seconds later, that leg lost grasp too. He dropped down from the tree, upside down. I couldn't imagine how he could survive such a fall.

He crashed to the ground with a mighty thump, not moving. I thought he was dead. He was out cold, not from the fall but from the tranquilizer. I felt bad for the bear. From the exterior, he didn't look like he was injured badly; I could see only a small cut next to his nose. The game wardens assured me that with so much fat and cartilage in his body, the bear would survive the fall with just a few scrapes. They were right.

What an amazing sight. The image of the bear becoming groggy and then slowly falling from the tree was what we call the money shot in the news business. I remember that image as clearly as if it happened yesterday, even though it was more than thirty years ago.

When we arrived back at the station, I wanted to take a look at the video of the incredible fall, but I made a horrifying discovery. My rookie photographer made a huge error on his very first assignment. He hadn't brought any backup batteries. When the bear fell out of the tree, his camera had been running low on battery power. As a result, the video was so blurry, I could hardly see the bear falling. I was so angry, I threw my hands up in the air, and shouted, "Damn it!" The video looked so blurry, the earth-shaking fall that would have been our money shot was useless. All the other stations would have the money shot, but we wouldn't.

The photographer, desperate for video of the bear, drove deep into the woods in the Blue Ridge Mountains, where he met the game wardens. They allowed him to shoot video of them releasing the bear. He shot video no one else had, but it didn't come close to the drama of the bear's dramatic fall to earth. It was a shame our viewers never saw the fall, at least not on our news.

Television viewers rarely see what happens behind the scenes, or, as I refer to them in this book, the stories behind the stories. If you think all reporters are uncaring, callous, and shallow exploiters, then you don't know me. I hope that, in sharing my personal experiences, you will see the human side to television news, from the reporter's perspective. Perhaps along the way, these tales will entertain you and evoke the same gamut of emotions I felt while reporting them, though there is one particular emotion I sure hope you don't share with me as you read my book: utter embarrassment.

I'll never forget how an archaeological dig at the Texas–Oklahoma border led to such agonizing embarrassment. Dozens of Southern Methodist University students had worked long hours, braving intense triple-digit summer temperatures, using hand shovels and toothbrushes to unearth ancient Native American artifacts. When I arrived, the students looked worn out. Many of them were covered with dirt. Their shirts were sopping-wet with sweat.

I loved doing stories like this. It was a breath of fresh air from the daily news grind. New discoveries always intrigued me, especially when they provided a glimpse into the ancient past, from dinosaur bones to Indian artifacts.

Small groups of students worked in several different locations at the site. Each group surrounded a large square hole that it had dug to reach the artifacts. I was standing close to one of the holes that didn't have anyone around it. My curiosity got the best of me. I slowly inched my way toward the hole. I leaned over to glance into the four-foot-deep pit. I could see what looked like a single ceramic pot still partially buried in the soil at the base, and I wanted a closer look. I carefully moved even closer to the hole.

Then I got too close and the unthinkable happened. The hole collapsed and my leg went into the hole. I was mortified. The quiet, calm feeling that had permeated the dig site quickly transformed into sheer pandemonium. Everyone who saw gasped or screamed. The students and their professors came running, but they weren't worried about my safety—they were worried about the pottery. They were coming to see the damage I had caused. It looked like a stampede. Their sweaty faces were filled with horror—and you know who was to blame. These poor students had worked tirelessly for weeks in terribly hot conditions, attempting ever so carefully to preserve the ancient artifacts, but in a few seconds, I had managed to nearly destroy what had been preserved for more than a century. They were all shaking their heads, looking disgusted. I felt like a total idiot.

Fortunately, my clumsy misstep damaged one side of the hole, but not the pot. Somehow, it was intact and had never moved. When they saw the damage was to the hole and not the pot, the students lost some of their disdain for the news reporter responsible for the collapse and their horror subsided into relief. But I was still totally embarrassed.

As you'll see throughout my book, embarrassment seems to be a reoccurring theme throughout my career. Fortunately, viewers never saw the embarrassing story behind the story at the dig. In my thirty-four years in the business, I covered more than 8,000 stories. As you will see, all too often, the untold stories behind the stories are more fascinating than the reported stories.

I'm OK with being embarrassed in front of more than 100,000 people at a time, but I wasn't OK with the handful of people throughout my career who accused me of being biased and having hidden agendas. It got under my skin when I was called everything from a "damned liberal" to a "baby killer." The ironic thing about such views was my personal policy to *never* discuss politics or controversial social issues with anyone other than family and my closest friends. No one knew if I was a Democrat or Republican, a liberal or conservative, pro-life or pro-choice. That's how it should be when you're a journalist. Ethics mattered to me. Fairness mattered to me. Objectivity mattered to me. I wanted to build my reputation as a journalist based on who I was as a human being, and I tried to live up to those standards throughout my thirty-four years working at six television stations.

I.

We Can't; We're Broke

I got my first job in television news one month before I graduated from Mercer University. Of the dozens of Communications students at Mercer University, only two of us landed work at local television stations before graduating. On my first day of work, I left the campus at five a.m. in my Buick Regal with a nervous pit in my stomach. I saw no signs of life when I arrived at the dimly lit WCWB Channel 41 parking lot. I opened an unlocked back door into the studio, which was totally dark and eerily silent. I carefully navigated my way to the newsroom. My anxiety was growing by the minute because in less than two hours, I would be on the air. I couldn't find anyone to tell me what to do. I was on my own, literally. The only sound I could hear was the constant ticking of the Associated Press news wire machine printing stories.

I tore off a section of wire copy with Georgia stories, then found a pair of scissors, cut out the stories, and taped them to several sheets of script paper. At 7:20 a.m., five minutes before air time, I walked into the dark studio and sat down in the chair behind the anchor desk. I felt like an idiot sitting there, alone in the darkness. Was someone going to come in, turn on the lights, and run the camera, or was I supposed to do those things?

Finally, I saw life from behind the glass separating the studio and control room. I assumed it was the technical director, but he never came out into the studio. My nerves escalated. My heart raced. Sweat formed on my forehead. It was 7:23, two minutes before *I* would be live on the air. That's when the station's janitor, an elderly African

American man with no front teeth, walked into the studio and started flicking on the lights. He swept the floor for a few seconds, laid down his broom, then walked up to the camera. "You must be the new guy," he said. "Good morning. I'm Claude. I'm the janitor, and I'll be your camera guy for the morning news." I was surprised. I just couldn't believe the same guy who cleaned the floors and toilets ran the studio camera. This was small-market television and definitely what my professors meant by "entry level."

Fortunately, my first time on the air went off without a hitch. When it was over, I wiped the beads of sweat off my brow and walked back into the newsroom. I couldn't be happier. Not only had I gotten my first cut-in out of the way but I officially had a job in TV news.

All six members of our news team at Channel 41 shared one dreadful feeling: We knew we worked at the worst television station in the country. Technical problems were more common than commercials. Let me give you an example. Most television stations use two identical studio cameras. At Channel 41, we used two different makes of cameras, a Panasonic and a General Electric. These cameras produced images so vastly different that they made me look like two different people on the air; I could co-anchor a newscast with myself. The Panasonic camera made my navy blue sports coat appear dark gray. The GE camera gave me a darker skin tone, but at least my coat looked blue.

I'm sure high schools in Macon used superior equipment—but those schools definitely didn't have anyone like Joe the Engineer. Joe, a chain smoker, attempted to fix all the daily technical issues at the station. When our one editing system malfunctioned, Joe would open the top cover of one of the two video cassette recorders (VCRs) while smoking a cigarette. I would uncomfortably stare at his cigarette, waiting for his ashes to fall into the VCR. What a television station! For all of us, Channel 41's call letters, WCWB, represented our frustration. We came up with two slogans to match those letters: "We can't; we're broke" and "Why compete? We're beat."

Channel 41 matched its low quality in my low salary. I made only $40 a week. When I graduated from Mercer, I couldn't help but wonder if I could continue living on such abysmal take-home pay. That's when a coworker's forgetfulness turned into a new opportunity for me. The speaker of the Georgia House of Representatives came to the station on a Saturday to appear as a guest on the station's public affairs program.

All the on-air people took turns hosting the show. When Matt's turn came, Matt, who anchored sports, completely forgot about it. The interviewee showed up, but the interviewer did not. The frustrated speaker left the station without appearing on the show, and, needless to say, station management fired Matt. On that Monday, the news director, seeking Matt's replacement, asked me, "How would you like to do sports?" I told him I would love to. As a full-time employee, my salary more than tripled, to $150 a week.

I've got to admit, covering sports at WCWB was a little strange. Most of the biggest sporting events occurred on weekends, but unlike most television stations, Channel 41 didn't have weekend newscasts. Instead, we would shoot University of Georgia home football games in Athens when they were played on Saturdays. The highlights wouldn't air until Monday, two days after the game. So much for immediacy. We can't; we're broke.

When we added an eleven p.m. newscast, which I anchored, our general manager came up with a brilliant idea to promote the new newscast and attract viewers. Playing off the channel numbers, he called it the "4-1 and All" contest. For this contest, Channel 41 viewers would enter by mail. We would put their names into a spinning barrel and would draw a winner from the barrel. I hated the contest, not only because it disrupted my concentration during the newscast but also because the prizes were ridiculous. Once we went to a commercial, I would leave the news set and walk over to the contest area. After the first spot (commercial) ended, I would announce the contest live on the air: "Good evening, everyone. I'm Steve Stoler. It's time for the 4-1 and All contest. We're going to pick a winner now. Billy Bob Johnson, you are tonight's winner. You have forty-one minutes to call us and claim your prize, which tonight is a set of dentures from the Tom Hortman Dental Lab." *My God,* I thought, *did I just give away a pair of dentures on live television?* One morning after I had given out the dentures, one of my classmates at Mercer University walked up to me and said, "Stoler, did you really give away a pair of dentures on the news last night?"

Sometimes, the prizes were even worse. One local furniture store offered a glass ashtray for one of our lucky viewers. Yes, you read that right—a glass ashtray. Clearly, embarrassment was a staple at WCWB.

A few weeks into the contest, I walked into the general manager's office to vent my frustration. "How will the viewers ever perceive me as a credible news anchor when I'm giving away dentures and ashtrays on the air?" I asked. He laughed at me and told me he would try to bring in someone else to do the contest. He made good on his promise and hired Crys Quimby, who became the official host of the 4-1 and All contest.

A news director who received my resume tape wrote, "Your mustache and hair makes you look like you came to town with only the egg money."

Channel 41's awful reputation came, in part, from our rampant technical problems, which I mentioned earlier. One night while I was anchoring the eleven o'clock newscast, everything that could have gone wrong actually did. When it was time for sports, I tossed it to our sports anchor, saying, "A big win for the Atlanta Braves tonight. Here's Walt with Middle Georgia Sports."

But when Walt started talking, viewers couldn't hear him. His microphone didn't work. I unclipped the tiny lapel mic from my tie and handed it to him under the desk, but I accidentally hit the microphone on the bottom of the desk. Every little movement of the ultrasensitive mic made an explosive sound on the air. I couldn't believe this was happening. Why wasn't the microphone working properly? This was supposed to be a real television station, but instead, it felt like amateur hour.

After his sportscast, Walt handed me my mic back, and we went to a commercial, then came back to end the newscast with a final weather forecast for the following day. "Crys Quimby is here with a final look at our Middle Georgia weather. Crys, another balmy day in Macon today," I said.

Crys responded, but as with Walt, the viewers couldn't hear a single word she was saying. Her mic didn't work either. *What? You've got to be kidding,* I thought. Crys walked over to the weather map, even though no one could hear a word she was saying. Once the director changed cameras to the weather map, I got up and walked over to her with my mic, since of the three microphones on the set, only mine was working. As soon as I reached the edge of the map, however, I ran out of cable. The mic would stretch no further. I pulled and pulled on the cable, but it wasn't going anywhere. We had to solve this crisis. Crys looked into the camera, turned toward the only working mic, and said, "Folks, we're going to a commercial so we can regroup. We'll be back in a minute."

The director bolted into the studio from the control room. "Here's the plan," he said. "Steve, I'm going to show the Georgia map full-screen. Hold your microphone up to Crys off-camera so she can read the final forecast. When she's finished, move the microphone

Anchoring on the set at WCWB in Macon, Georgia, with weather anchor Crys Quimby, who started her career as a contest host. 1980.

back in front of you so you can wrap up the newscast by teasing Johnny Carson's guests on the *Tonight Show*."

At first, the plan worked. As I held my mic in front of Crys, seated to my left, she gave the forecast. I looked down on my notes to see who Johnny Carson's guests were, and suddenly, I heard Crys's voice crack. She started laughing. As I looked up at her, I couldn't help but notice her face turning red. Not knowing what was happening, I glanced at the on-air monitor to the right of the news desk. I saw a horrifying sight, the same ludicrous image the viewers saw: both Crys and I were sitting on the set, looking at the monitor, with me holding the little lapel mic in front of her face. We tried to keep our composure, but instead, we erupted in uncontrollable laughter. I couldn't even spit out the names of the *Tonight Show* guests. All I could muster was, "That's it. Good night."

Once we were off the air, I buried my head in my hands, leaned forward, and rested my head on the anchor desk. It was the ultimate irony; I was laughing incredibly hard, but at the same time, I felt like crying. Sure, it was funny, but this was supposed to be a professional newscast, not a comedy of errors. As we walked from the studio into our tiny newsroom, the phone started ringing. I sat down at my desk and answered it. The caller, who very well may have been our only viewer, made a simple comment that underscored the newscast and much of my time at WCWB: "Y'all are funnier than *Saturday Night Live*!"

After two years at WCWB, I wanted out, so I sent 359 resumes to television stations across the country. Back then, news directors interested in hiring you requested videotapes, so I ended up sending out more than one hundred tapes, making me a familiar face at the local post office. I didn't think anyone besides our lone caller after the microphone fiasco watched our newscasts, but one postal employee who worked behind the counter actually recognized me. He glanced down at the label on the large envelope I was mailing, with WCWB's return address and an NBC logo. He looked down at the envelope and then at me. He repeated this action several times. Finally, he said in an excited voice, "Hey, I know you. You're that 41 newsman, aren't you?"

"Yes, sir, I am," I replied.

He then uttered eleven words that affirmed just how bad this television station really was: "When are y'all going to get your shit together out there?"

I smiled but didn't respond. He had a valid point.

Channel 41 may have been a terrible television station, but it gave all of us an extremely valuable gift: experience. We desperately needed that experience if we wanted to move on to bigger and better television stations. We were much more than a six-person team struggling to put a watchable product on the air. We were friends, a small, tight-knit family that shared the same aspirations and frustrations, and all of us did eventually leave WCWB to pursue our dream to work at what we considered real television stations.

II.

The Road to Dallas

Those 359 resumes and one hundred videotapes I sent out while at WCWB led to three job offers. Two of them came from television stations in Georgia. The other came from a television station in a place I had never even heard of: Kearney, Nebraska. All three stations offered me positions sight unseen, without face-to-face interviews. I guess they liked my audition tapes.

Having been raised in South Florida, I had never experienced the lifestyle and culture of a farming community. I wasn't sure what to expect or if I was going to like it, but I chose Kearney anyway. I gave WCWB two weeks' notice and headed to the vast fields of the cornhusker state.

The Nebraska Television Network (NTV) comprised four stations across the state that all broadcast the same signal. If market size was based on geography, the Lincoln–Kearney–Hastings–Grand Island television market would have been one of the largest in the country—but geography means nothing when ratings are counted. Ratings are based on television sets and viewers, not sprawling pastures of steers and heifers. Cattle outnumbered humans in the Kearney viewing area.

Agriculture influenced just about everything in Kearney. Restaurants featured "corn-fed Nebraska beef." Every morning, NTV presented an hour-long show called *Ag Mart A.M.* The hosts discussed yields, weather conditions, and market prices for a myriad of crops and livestock. Until living in Kearney, I never even heard of barrows and gilts or milo. Every commercial on our ten p.m. newscast touted some agriculture-related product. Before each weather segment, an announcer's voice would tell viewers, "Bob's weather is brought to you by Acco Paymaster seeds."

My favorite ad ran almost every night. It featured a terrifying creature that resembled a giant caterpillar. The fuzzy monster inched its way across a farm field, amidst a surreal purple-tinted electrical storm. Suddenly, a powerful bolt of lightning exploded across the screen, striking the creature and causing it to explode. The deep, authoritative voice of the announcer proclaimed, "Zap rootworm with Dow Guard!"

I started working at NTV in the heart of winter, and I quickly learned how the tiny farming community could be transformed into the North Pole. When I left for work one morning, knowing a huge winter storm was inching closer to us, I took a sleeping bag with me in my car in case we got snowed in at the station and couldn't make it back to town. The blizzard blew in that night with a fury. The darkness, combined with high winds and heavy snow, made the twelve-mile drive home on the two-lane road cutting through massive cornfields and pastures a treacherous proposition, so I decided to spend the night at the station. After the ten p.m. news ended, Kevin Cochran, one of the news anchors, asked if I would accompany him on the dangerous drive home. He didn't want to attempt it alone. I really didn't want to go, but when Kevin said he wanted to ride out the blizzard at home with his wife and baby, I couldn't say no. He offered to pick me up from my apartment the next day and take me to work.

As we drove toward town, the raging wind blew the heavy snow horizontally. Snow covered the road, and we couldn't see the center line. We could hardly see anything around us other than falling snow. The road's narrow shoulders ended in steep embankments. Drainage ditches lined both sides of the highway. One bad move, and we would slide into the ditch. Kevin drove very slowly, but the stress was killing me. Remember, I grew up in Florida. I had never experienced anything like this before. I feared for my life. This was the most anxiety I had ever felt in a car. If we ran off the road, would anyone find us? They likely wouldn't see us in this whiteout, and this was before cell phones.

We were the only car on the road. We were the only people either brave enough or stupid enough to endure the horrendous weather. We had no business driving in this situation. The twelve-mile drive back into Kearney, which usually took about fifteen minutes, took almost three hours on this frigid and blustery night. I was so nervous that it seemed like we were in that car for ten hours. When we finally reached my apartment complex, I felt relieved and extremely fortunate to be alive. That was one harrowing drive.

The next morning when Kevin picked me up for work, I saw several of my neighbors trying unsuccessfully to start their cars. The wind chill was seventy-five degrees below zero. I admit, I was a winter wimp—for this South Floridian, winter usually meant any temperature under sixty degrees, but seventy-five below? I didn't think it got that cold in Antarctica.

As we made the trek back to the station on the same road that had caused us major heartburn the night before, the conditions were much better. The road was still covered with snow, but at least we could see where we were going.

When we pulled into the NTV parking lot, I couldn't find my car where I had left it—at least it didn't appear to be. Finally, I saw a portion of the fender sticking out from a massive snowdrift. When I left work that day, I literally had to dig my car out of the snow, something I could never have imagined doing while living in Florida.

I quickly came to the realization that Kearney's frozen tundra was no place for me. Four bone-chilling months after arriving in Kearney, I received a phone call from the news director at WLOS, the ABC affiliate in Asheville, North Carolina. Asheville, combined with Greenville and Spartanburg, South Carolina, is the thirty-seventh largest television market in the country. The WLOS news director still had the resume and videotape I had sent him from Georgia, and he offered me, without a face-to-face interview, a job anchoring weekend newscasts and reporting three days a week. The Deep South was calling me back.

Ashville is known as the Land of the Sky, the LOS in WLOS. Its majestic mountains, scenic vistas, soothing waterfalls, and amazing fall colors easily made it the most beautiful place I've ever lived. From the station parking lot, we could see Mount Pisgah and several layers of the Blue Ridge Mountains along the horizon. The station, located on Sunset Mountain, overlooked the Grove Park Golf Course, and the historic Grove Park Inn Resort shared the mountainside location with WLOS. The Blue Ridge Parkway and Appalachian Trail ran through Asheville, making it an outdoorsman's paradise. I loved Asheville for its natural beauty and especially its people, who were salt-of-the-earth friendly.

My most memorable story at WLOS involved some hilarious outtakes that landed me in hot water with my boss. I came up with what I thought was a great idea for a weekend newscast that fell on April Fool's Day. A videotape known as the outtakes reel contained a plethora of hilarious bloopers committed by the station's reporters and anchors. In one of them, our investigative reporter, Sherrill Barber, lost his balance while shooting a standup. It appeared on the reel in both real time and in slow motion. The look on Sherrill's face in the slow-motion version was priceless. His eyes began to open very wide as he started to fall backward. In another humorous outtake, reporter Debra Furr produced a story about members of a new religious group who practiced transcendental meditation. She fronted, or read her story from the news set, while sitting beside the anchors as she introduced the taped portion of her story. She lost her composure and cracked up while delivering her intro in a serious story about religion. To this day, I'm still not sure what made Debra laugh so hard.

I thought sharing a few of these outtakes with our viewers would be a fun way to celebrate April Fool's Day, endearing us to them by showing them we had no problem laughing at ourselves. The segment received an overwhelming response; our phones lit up after our six p.m. newscast. "Are you going to run it again at eleven?" viewers kept asking, so we decided to air it again on our late newscast. And why not? It was good-natured fun that evoked laughter.

Unfortunately, Karl Zedell, the news director, didn't see it that way. On Monday morning, he called me into his office. I could tell by the expression on his face that he wasn't happy. He shut the door behind me. "I can't believe you used such poor judgment by airing those outtakes," he said, scolding me with a prolonged, piercing stare. "You aired Debra's outtakes. Did you know I reprimanded her for that?"

I had no idea.

"And then you aired it again a second time at eleven," Karl said. I explained my intent, but it fell on deaf ears. He placed a written letter of reprimand in my personnel file for using "bad judgment." The viewers never knew that the same outtakes they had clamored for got me into hot water.

My relationship with Karl worsened after the April Fool's incident. One day, he asked me to come into his office and said, "Steve, I'm taking you off the weekend shows." I asked him why, because our ratings had steadily increased since I started anchoring. "Debra says she wants to anchor, and if she doesn't get anchoring experience, she'll leave the station."

I was very upset. I asked him, "What about me? What if I told you I'm going to leave if you take my anchor experience away from me?" He told me he hoped I would maintain a positive attitude. I didn't think the situation was fair, so I did something I would later consider a mistake. I went to talk with the general manager about it.

The GM essentially gave me a pep talk. He said, "Steve, why don't you show Karl you're a better reporter, and maybe he will put you back on the weekend news?" I saw that my attempt to stay on the weekend news wasn't going anywhere, so I stayed positive. I told the GM I would accept the change, and I asked him to keep our conversation confidential.

The next day, however, I ran into Karl at the water fountain, just outside the newsroom. He got very close to me, stared me down, and said, "I understand you went up to the GM's office to talk about the situation with Debra. He said you were very positive with him, and I appreciate that." But I could tell by the look on his face that he was not happy. Without question, he was upset that I had gone over his head to talk with his boss. I regretted my decision, because it affected my relationship with Karl.

A few months later, Karl called me into his office again. He said, "You know what, Steve, I thought about putting you on probation, but I decided I can't do that. I've decided to let you go."

What? He was firing me? For what? I wasn't quite sure what I had done that merited being "let go." I was devastated. I had never been fired from any job in my entire life. Again, however, I tried to look ahead and not back. Perhaps this would lead to an exciting new opportunity. I was back to sending out resumes and videotapes.

Not long after, a news director in El Paso called me and said he had a reporter position open. I liked El Paso; I had been there twice to visit my aunts, uncles, and cousins. El Paso had split personalities. The first was always affected by what happened just across the border in Juarez, Mexico's fifth largest city. El Paso's other personality came from Fort Bliss, a US Army base. Thousands of military retirees fell in love with the city while stationed at the base and stayed put once they finished serving.

I worked at KDBC during a very tense time along the United States–Mexico border. A drug cartel had kidnapped an undercover US Drug Enforcement Administration agent on assignment in Mexico. The US Customs Service beefed up vehicle searches and questioning at all border crossings. The result was long delays from extremely long lines at border crossings. It usually took us a few minutes to cross an international bridge to or from Juarez, but after the searches began, it could take up to six hours. Can you imagine sitting in your car for six hours, waiting to cross a bridge? You could drive halfway across Texas in that time. People who lived in El Paso stopped driving to Juarez, and vice versa. I did stories on both sides of the border about the devastating economic impact in both cities. Finally, the crisis ended when US agents found the body of the DEA agent in Mexico.

After one year in El Paso, I learned of my next opportunity in the TV news business. I received a call from Steve Hammel, Assistant News Director at KDFW, the CBS television station in Dallas. KDFW was one of 100 stations I had sent resumes to while still in Macon. Hammel said he wanted to fly me into Dallas to interview for a reporter opening. Right from the start after I graduated college, I had set a personal goal to work in a top-ten market—Dallas–Fort Worth was the eighth largest TV market in the country—but I had honestly never thought it would happen this early in my career. I was twenty-eight, only six years out of college.

I went to Dallas with low expectations. I considered myself a long shot at best. Though KDFW had contacted me about the position, I still didn't think a major-market TV station would hire someone from a small market like El Paso, but I went in with a positive attitude, thinking the interview would provide great experience. I felt very comfortable during the interview because I didn't think I had any chance of getting the job.

At the end of the interview, Hammel said something I had never expected to hear: "Steve, we would like to offer you the reporter position." I couldn't believe it. I didn't hesitate to accept. I was ecstatic. After only six years in the TV news business, I would be working at a major-market television station.

I would spend the next twenty-eight years working at KDFW and WFAA in Dallas. It was in Texas where I matured as a journalist and person. My journey toward growth began with a major story that captured the attention of the entire world and left me in awe.

WFAA promotional photo.

III.

Fifty-Eight Hours in a Hole

When I arrived at work on October 14, 1987, the KDFW assignment manager said, "I hope you're ready to go to Midland. An adorable little girl fell into a very narrow well, and she's stuck." Little eighteen-month-old Jessica McClure had been playing with four other toddlers in the backyard of her aunt's home daycare when she had somehow slipped through an eight-inch-wide opening and fallen down the shaft of an abandoned well.

Smart reporters and photographers at KDFW stored go bags—small suitcases or bags packed with clothing and toiletries for several days—in their cars in the event of big breaking news. Unfortunately, that group did not include me. As I left for Midland, I didn't have a go bag or time to go home and pack. I drove my car—without a go bag—to Dallas Love Field and took the first Southwest Airlines flight to Midland, where I would meet up with veteran KDFW photographer Don Chappell, who had taken an earlier flight.

I arrived at the scene six hours after Jessica fell into the well. By then, news media from across the country had begun crowding into the family's backyard. Police restricted access, keeping reporters and photographers outside the perimeter of the yard. Don managed to find a tall aluminum ladder, and he sat on the top platform with his camera on his shoulder, looking down at the well and the surrounding chaos. He would be in a perfect position to capture the money shot when rescuers brought Jessica out of the well to safety.

Rescue workers removed a wooden fence surrounding the backyard to clear a path for heavy equipment. I climbed up the ladder to a height just below Don so I could also have a bird's-eye view of the well. Throughout the ordeal, that uncomfortable ladder would be our base. We would stay on it for hours at a time, watching the extremely complicated rescue operation unfold. We would occasionally climb down to stretch our legs, but only for a few minutes. We didn't want to miss anything.

As we looked around from the ladder, we saw that everyone around the area of the tiny well opening seemed to be wearing the same solemn facial expression, from police officers, firefighters, and paramedics to family members and neighbors. Don and I clung to that tall ladder as the world watched drama unfold on television. Everyone in that backyard felt a deep emotional connection to Baby Jessica. She was fighting for her life, and time was not on her side. I was deeply moved by the awe-inspiring sight of all these people working together as one. Their determination, fortitude, and courage left me in awe and, at times, in tears, before they ever got close to rescuing Jessica. Crews dug a thirty-inch-wide hole parallel to the well. Once they reached Jessica's depth at thirty feet below the surface, they bored a horizontal tunnel to reach her.

The anxiety in the air in that backyard was intense and overwhelming. You could even see it on the faces of the news media. At times, we could hear Jessica crying or whimpering, but at one point, the well fell terrifyingly silent. Jessica had stopped responding to rescuers' calls. The scene quickly changed from a constant buzz of people talking and shouting orders to deafening silence. I felt sick to my stomach as I feared the worst. The rescuers kept calling to her: "Jessica, Jessica, Jessica." But she wasn't responding. Everyone held their collective breath. Jessica's mother, Cissy McClure, then walked up to the side of the well. She leaned over and began singing Jessica's favorite song, "Winnie the Pooh." An agonizing pause followed, lasting several minutes, but it seemed like hours. Finally, we heard a sound coming from the well. It was Jessica's sweet voice. She was singing the same song her mother had sung. Thank God, she was still alive! My eyes became very watery.

More than two days after Jessica had fallen into the well, the anxiety-filled waiting and roller coaster of emotions were taking their toll. It was excruciating. But then everything changed. Suddenly, we could feel optimism in the air. We could hear it in the rescuers' voices and see it on their faces. For the first time in two days, we saw smiles and heard laughter. After waiting so many long hours for new information, we sensed a renewed, upbeat atmosphere. It didn't take long for the fabulous news to spread among the media: The rescue workers had finally broken through to the well, just below Jessica. We were told that a paramedic had been lowered into the trench and had crawled through the horizontal tunnel to get to Jessica. He had desperately tried to pull her down but she was lodged in tightly in the tiny eight-inch-wide hole. The paramedic then had used Vaseline to coat the sides of the well. Finally, Jessica had begun to move, slowly sliding down toward him.

Don and I couldn't see any of this unfold from our perch atop the ladder, but we could feel the excitement building. The anticipation and anxiety reached a climax. An incredibly momentous event was about to happen. Don pointed his camera toward the well, as did scores of other photographers. I noticed a few people at the top of the well smiling and patting each other on the back, and I saw a few of the workers giving thumbs-up signs to each other. Finally, after Jessica had been in the narrow well for fifty-eight grueling hours, we watched as a pulley slowly lifted the rope out of the hole. I held my breath. Loud cheers and applause erupted as the paramedic emerged with baby Jessica in his arms.

Everywhere I looked, I saw grown men in tears. I was no different. The paramedic handed her off, with her tiny head heavily bandaged, into the awaiting arms of another paramedic, who rushed her to an ambulance that would take her to the hospital. These final moments of Jessica's rescue were broadcast live across the world. All the collective prayers had been answered. The atmosphere turned into complete jubilation. In the ensuing hours, we heard the constant blare of car horns honking and firecrackers exploding across Midland. People celebrated like it was Independence Day or as if their home team had just won the Super Bowl, but this victory was different because it was celebrating the best qualities in human beings: cooperation, compassion, kindness, and love. For fifty-eight hours, these people had come together with one simple goal: saving the life of a little girl.

I stayed in Midland doing follow-up stories on the amazing rescue—but you might recall I hadn't brought a go bag. I didn't have a toothbrush, a razor, or underwear. The only clothes I had brought to Midland were the ones I had been wearing for more than fifty-eight hours. After baby Jessica's rescue, I went to a mall and bought enough clothes and toiletries to last a week.

Over the next few days, I interviewed the true stars of the drama, the rescue workers. I was impressed with these men. I admired their strength, courage, determination, and simplicity. Many of them were rugged oil field roughnecks who perform some of the toughest, most physical work possible, but when they talked about saving Jessica, they appeared vulnerable, sensitive and emotional, not what you would expect from these resilient men. I also did a story with a Midland man who wrote a beautiful song about the rescue. He called it "Fifty-Eight Hours for Jessica." The lyrics paid a heartwarming tribute to the rescuers. In my final story from Midland, I covered Vice President George H. W. Bush meeting with the rescuers. Bush did more listening than talking as the men shared their stories with him. He shook their hands, patted them on the back, and thanked them for their selfless efforts in saving baby Jessica.

Almost three decades later, when I watch the money shot of Jessica emerging from the well, it still evokes the same deep emotions I felt on that ladder in October of 1987. I get a lump in my throat and a tear in my eye. Jessica had an amazing impact on the planet: For fifty-eight hours, people across the world seemed a little closer together, all because of a little girl who became known as everybody's baby and because of the men and women who made it their personal mission to save her life.

IV.

Horror in a Boxcar

Jessica McClure was one lucky little girl to have so many rescuers. Sadly, in the next big story I covered, the rescuers arrived too late. In July 1987, I went to the tiny West Texas town of Saragosa to do follow-up stories on a devastating tornado that had ravaged the area six months earlier. The twister had cut a half-mile-wide path through the town, killing thirty-one people.

My photographer and I had just finished shooting a few interviews when the executive producer called and told me, "We're moving you. Nineteen illegal aliens suffocated in a boxcar in Sierra Blanca, Texas, not far from you. You need to head to Pecos. We're going to fly you there."

The station arranged for us to fly in a single-engine airplane from the small airport in Pecos to an even smaller airport in Van Horn. (Calling them airports may be an overstatement.) I had never flown in a small airplane before, and I became a bit concerned when the pilot asked, "Did you guys see a highway back there?"

I said, "Yes, about ten minutes ago." He turned the plane around and found the highway, which led us to Van Horn. From there, my photographer and I drove a rental car to Sierra Blanca. When we arrived, bodies were still being pulled out of the boxcar. The Hudspeth County Sheriff did an interview with us, telling us this was the result of a human-smuggling effort. A coyote, or smuggler, had led the nineteen people across the border into El Paso, where he had loaded them into the boxcar. The freight train was bound for Dallas, where the immigrants had hoped to find work. The coyote had ridden in a different boxcar, planning on unlocking the door when the train came to a stop, but somehow, the boxcar carrying the immigrants had separated from the rest of the train. It had sat isolated, parked on a single railroad track in the middle of the scorching West Texas desert. Temperatures inside the boxcar reached 120 degrees. Hours after the boxcar detached, sheriff's deputies had discovered the boxcar. Miraculously, they had found a single survivor of the calamity, a twenty-one-year-old man.

Though weak and dehydrated, the survivor, Miguel Tostada Rodriguez, was still at the scene when we arrived. He told us his heartbreaking story through an interpreter. Tostada described the horror and panic inside the boxcar. As the others had started to suffocate, he had found a spike on the floor of the boxcar. He had used the spike to pick and pick at the wooden floor until he had enlarged a small hole. He told us that he had put his face down on the hole he created so he could breathe as the eighteen other people had begun dying around him. Tostada's eyes filled with tears as he described how the others had started fighting with each other out of desperation to breathe. His agonizing expression told his story as powerfully as his words. Seeing the pain on Miguel's face, I could only imagine the bloodcurdling events that had occurred inside that boxcar. He had witnessed something beyond horrible.

Miguel had wanted desperately to help the others, but there had been nothing he could do, so he had saved himself. His quick thinking spared his life. I deeply empathized with Miguel. I tried putting myself in his shoes and imagining what he had endured. What would I have done if faced with the same predicament, with everyone dying around me and I was the only person who could breathe? The reality of what happened inside that boxcar gave me nightmares. Two days later, a photographer and I found ourselves in the heart of Mexico. We had been sent there to cover some of the funerals and to learn more about the people who had died in the boxcar. Once we landed in Aguascalientes, we hired a bilingual taxi driver. We paid him a hefty sum to serve as our guide and translator. He drove us to Pabellon de Arteaga, a small town where most of the boxcar victims had lived. We wanted to meet their families to gain perspective on why they had left. Our driver stopped the car, and got out to ask the locals a few questions.

Everyone seemed to know each other in Pabellon. The locals gave us directions to a house where one of the victims had lived. As we drove into the neighborhood of small one-story houses, we saw dozens of people congregating in front of one of them. We got out of the car and walked up to the group with our guide. The doors of the house were open. We could see a young man lying in an open casket inside.

The victim's father came out of the house and talked with us. Through our translator, we learned that the man's son, like the others who had died on the boxcar, had planned to find a restaurant job once he had made it to Dallas. Pabellon didn't offer many opportunities to make a living, so the young victims had left their families behind in Mexico to provide financial support for them from across the border. Their plans were to wire most of the money they earned in Dallas to their wives and children back in Mexico. Hearing this, I could clearly understand why they would want to come into the United States illegally; they were making a tremendous sacrifice to improve the lives of their families.

This experience changed my perspective on illegal immigration. Being in Mexico, seeing how these men had lived, and learning about their desire to make life better had a powerful impact on me. For the first time, I could relate with illegal immigrants because they shared the same values Americans hold precious. I suddenly understood why immigrants leave their homeland and cross the border into the United States. I would have done the same thing in their shoes. They loved their wives. They loved their children. Their desire was simply to provide for those they loved. Sadly, however, that noble mission had ended up costing them their lives. I had an entirely new understanding of the phrase "land of opportunity." These immigrants had been searching for a better life, just like my grandparents had when they had come to America from Eastern Europe. No longer would I ever look at these people as just "illegal aliens," but as human beings who were desperately trying to improve the lives of the people they loved the most, their families.

Pabellon de Arteaga mourned in unity as a community. The victims had been their *familia* (family), *amigos* (friends), and *vecinos* (neighbors). Hundreds of people converged on the plaza in the center of town to grieve. The air was blisteringly hot and sticky-humid, and it was impossible to stay dry. Nurses in white uniforms were scattered around the plaza, carrying intravenous bags filled with saline solution, ready to help anyone overcome by grief or the heat. Several women fainted.

The crowd waited patiently in utter silence for more than an hour until hearses carrying the victims arrived. I could hear several mournful wails of grief-stricken relatives as the hearses slowly drove the perimeter of the square. Then it turned silent again.

Suddenly, a man in the crowd shouted, "Viva Mexico!"

Those two words moved the throngs of mourners. They began chanting together, "Viva Mexico! Viva Mexico! Viva Mexico!" It gave me chills up and down my spine. It felt like a scene from an epic movie, but this was no movie. This was life in Central Mexico.

V.

The Subterranean Little Troll

On September 4, 1993, the sounds of playing children and cheering soccer moms and dads filled Carpenter Park, a sprawling athletic complex in Plano, Texas. A seven-year-old girl named Ashley Estell disappeared from a playground at the popular park as her brother played in the Labor Day soccer tournament. A massive search followed. The next day, police discovered Ashley's strangled body along a gravel road a few miles from the park. Three days after that, police picked up Michael Blair, a twenty-two-year-old carpet cleaner and convicted child molester, who was hanging around the crime scene. Detectives questioned Blair for ten grueling hours before arresting him and charging him with capital murder for Ashley's death.

Because of the sensational nature of Ashley's murder and a barrage of local and nationwide publicity, the judge moved the trial to Midland. I sat in a packed courtroom as prosecutors showed the jury video of the marathon police interrogation. The hours and hours of tedious questioning were hard to watch; I noticed a few jurors having a hard time keeping their eyes open too. But suddenly, the questioning turned very interesting when one of the detectives doing the interrogation said to Blair, "We know you were there, Michael. We know you were there."

Blair became angry. He raised his voice in frustration and said, "I don't know. Maybe I was there or maybe I wasn't. I just don't remember."

He seemed like he was on the verge of confessing to Ashley's murder. Why would he ever say he didn't remember if he had been at Carpenter Park if he hadn't been there? As the detectives continued their marathon questioning, however, Blair changed his tone again and once again maintained his innocence. "I didn't kill that little girl," he said.

During closing arguments, prosecutor Bryan Clayton belittled Blair. He looked straight into Blair's eyes while addressing the jury, describing Blair as a "subterranean little troll" who killed Ashley.

I had covered Ashley's disappearance, the search to find her, and Michael Blair's arrest, along with the three-week trial in Midland. I was hoping the verdict and sentence would provide a sense of relief and closure for Ashley's family. The jury deliberated for only twenty-seven minutes before finding Blair guilty of capital murder. They sentenced him to death by lethal injection. Unfortunately, the Michael Blair story was far from over.

Once Blair was on death row, I called the Texas Department of Corrections Public Information Office to request an interview with him. I didn't think he would agree to an interview, but to my surprise, he decided to talk with me. I went into the interview with mixed emotions, partly because I didn't want to give Blair a public forum in which to proclaim his innocence. Critics often blast the news media for glamorizing criminals like Blair by giving them air time. Like it or not, interviews with high-profile murderers are standard in the news business. Blair was the latest in a who's-who list of murderers who had committed sensational crimes: Charles Manson, Timothy McVeigh, John Wayne Gacy, Jeffrey Dahmer, David Berkowitz (Son of Sam), Ted Bundy, Richard Ramirez (Night Stalker), Richard Speck, and Ted Kaczynski (Unabomber).

The Livingston Unit, located a few miles from Huntsville, Texas, housed death row. Prison guards and a public information officer led us through several secured gates into the prison, down a long hall, and into a cramped interview room. A sheet of fortified glass divided the room, with a chair on each side. My photographer set up his camera on a tripod in the tight space behind me. Two guards escorted

Blair into the interview room, and Blair clipped on the microphone. As with all death row interviews, we communicated by telephone.

I introduced myself. Blair nodded. He seemed calm as he answered my list of prepared questions, all along maintaining his innocence. His answers didn't produce any surprises, but then the interview took a bizarre turn when I asked Blair why he had participated in the search for Ashley Estell. His calm turned into anger and defiance. He screamed, "I just wanted to help!"

"But Michael, you're a convicted child molester," I reminded him.

He became even more agitated, raising his voice again. "What if you had a heart attack right now," he said. "Would you want me to help you, or should I let you sit there and die? I told you, I was there to help them search for her."

I just looked at him. I didn't know what to say.

"Why don't you find the evidence to prove I'm not guilty?" he asked.

"Why, Michael?" I repeated. "Because I don't think you're innocent." I had never doubted Blair's guilt. The videotaped interrogation, more than any other evidence, had convinced me that he had killed Ashley.

By the expression on his face, I could plainly see he didn't like me.

Blair's attorneys filed an appeal after his capital murder conviction, insisting that the jury had convicted the wrong man. They sought DNA testing on hair and fingernail scrapings used as evidence in the trial. Eight years after Blair was sent to death row, the judge allowed testing to begin. The tests began in 2002 and continued through 2008, when they revealed that the hairs and fingernail scrapings did not belong to either Blair or Ashley.

With this new development in the case, I put in another request to interview Blair. My first interview with him must have made an impression, because once again, he agreed. As the guards escorted him into the interview room, he looked at me in disgust and immediately picked up the phone. "Oh, it's you again," he said, still with that disgusted look on his face. "I told you I didn't kill Ashley, but you didn't believe me."

I started to ask him a question, but he put the phone down and held up his hand, asking me to wait. He opened a briefcase that he had brought in with him, pulling out a gallon freezer bag filled with wallet-sized photos. He took out the photos and began laying them out on the narrow table under the glass. I had no clue what he was doing. Once he had finished laying out all the photos, he picked up the phone. "Do you see these kids?" he asked, pointing to the photos. "I molested all of them. I am a child molester, but I'm not a child killer. I didn't kill that girl."

His confession left me stunned and confused. My mind raced with questions. Why was Blair so willing to admit that he had molested these kids? Who were these children? Why was Blair allowed to have photos of his alleged victims? Were any of these cases ever investigated?

Blair acted annoyed and belligerent throughout our interview. He answered several of my questions with one-word answers. I knew he didn't like me because I refused to buy into his assertion that he hadn't killed Ashley, but the feeling was mutual. I didn't like him, either. I was looking into the eyes of a man whom I believed was not only a child molester but also a child killer. I didn't have any doubts about it, and I still don't today.

For days, I couldn't stop thinking about my interview with Blair and those unsettling photos of children. Knowing he had the photos really bothered me. I wanted to do something about it, but I wasn't sure what to do. Then, one week after the interview, I ran into two of my friends, Assistant District Attorneys Curtis Howard and Michelle Voirin, at the Collin County Courthouse. They prosecuted sex crimes involving child victims, so I told them about my interview with Blair and the photos he had shown me. I asked them, "If Blair is so adamant about confessing to these crimes to show he's a child molester and not a child murderer, why hasn't anyone investigated all these cases?" Michelle and Curtis looked at each other but didn't say a word. I had a feeling they knew something they weren't telling me.

Weeks later, I learned from another courthouse source that Blair had made the same confession in a letter he had sent to the Collin County District Attorney before my interview with him. In 2003, the Dallas County District Attorney's Office used that same letter as evidence when they charged Blair with four counts of aggravated sexual assault of a child. Blair pleaded guilty the following year and received three consecutive life sentences. His confession ensured that he would stay in prison for the rest of his life.

In June of 2008, the Texas Court of Criminal Appeals overturned Blair's capital murder conviction in Ashley Estell's death based on the DNA tests of the hair and scrapings. The Collin County District Attorney's office quickly admitted that it no longer had enough evidence to prove Blair's guilt, and three months later, a Collin County court dismissed the capital murder case against Blair. He was moved off death row and into a regular prison cell.

To this date, Blair has not been retried for Ashley's murder. He avoided a lethal injection, but his willingness to confess to sexually abusing children had given prosecutors the evidence they needed to ensure that he would never walk out of prison a free man.

When Blair's conviction was overturned, I pitched a story idea. I wanted to return to Midland, fourteen years after the capital murder trial, to talk with the same jurors who had found him guilty and sentenced him to die. I was curious to see how important the discounted hair and nail-scraping evidence had been in their decision to find him guilty. I wanted to know if they looked at the case any differently after knowing that DNA tests had proved the hair found in Blair's car wasn't his or Ashley's.

I managed to contact six of the jurors. "No, I'm sorry, I don't want to get back into that. It happened a long time ago, and I'd rather not revisit it," said one juror.

Others seemed very interested in doing the interview. "Of course I'll talk with you. I still think he did it," said another juror.

Of the six former jurors I found, three of them agreed to meet me in the same courtroom where they had sentenced Blair to death. I interviewed them together, asking about the new DNA evidence that appeared to exonerate Blair. "It wasn't the hair that led me to believe he killed that girl," said one juror.

"Then what was it?" I asked.

"It was the interrogation," said the juror. "He almost admitted he was there at the park, where Ashley was abducted. Why would he ever say he didn't know if he was there, if he wasn't?"

The other two jurors agreed. For them, there was nothing stronger than the video of the interrogation. "He looked and sounded guilty, and all the evidence seemed to coincide with his guilt. The hair wasn't important," said another juror. It was very interesting that they were echoing my own sentiments. I shared their belief that Blair was Ashley's killer.

I asked the three former jurors one last question: "Given what you know today, would you still have found Michael Blair guilty and sentenced him to death by lethal injection?"

Without hesitation, all three of them answered the same way at the same time: "Yes."

There are still those people in the Dallas–Fort Worth area who believe someone else killed Ashley Estell. I am not among them. Plano police investigated several other possible suspects, but those leads did not produce any arrests or new charges. I believe Michael Blair is the subterranean little troll who strangled Ashley. I find it comforting that his bizarre strategy to paint himself as a child molester but not a child killer backfired on him. I'm sure in his mind, confessing would ultimately lead to his release from prison. Instead, he sealed his own fate, a life behind bars in a Texas prison, a place where the deranged misfit fits in perfectly.

VI.

The Amazing Jimmy D and Katy

Television news reporting exposed me to the best and worst of humanity. Michael Blair, without a doubt, was one of the worst people I ever met. In contrast, an amazing man I knew as Jimmy D was by far one of the best. I always said if I made a top-ten list of my favorite human beings on the planet, Jim Dunlap would top the list. Jim's three loves in life were children, animals, and family. When I first met Jim at the Plano Balloon Festival in the early nineties, it felt like we had known each other for years. He knew who I was from watching me on the news, and I recognized him from his appearances on television too.

Jim was a local celebrity. His menagerie of animals at the Plano School District's Outdoor Learning Center always attracted attention. He did guest appearances on several local television stations and hosted his own show, *Animals, Animals,* which aired on a local cable channel. Jim was one of those rare people who instantly made you feel like he was your best friend for life after you'd spent only a few minutes with him. As a teacher, Jim had a tremendous impact on generations of children. This man was truly special. It didn't take long for us to become close friends.

The first time I met Jim, I told him to let me know if he had any good story ideas at the learning center. "I'm always looking for good ideas," I told him.

"Well, I've got a million of them. Every animal I have has an interesting story," he said, as he opened a large metal crate. I had no idea what was inside it, but as he opened it, I suddenly jumped back five feet out of fear. Inside was a gigantic Burmese python he lovingly called Katy. I was deathly afraid of her. She was the biggest snake I had ever seen. Katy weighed almost 200 pounds and was more than eighteen feet long. She was about ten inches thick, and her head was huge, about the size of a small football. I could not believe the enormous size of this creature. She weighed more than me.

"Do you want to touch her?" Jim asked.

I sheepishly said, "I guess so," attempting to hide my fear. I gently put my hand on her skin, petting her as if she were a dog. She felt cold, but soft. Jim picked Katy up and put a section of her body around his neck. He had no fear. In fact, I could tell he loved this big snake very much. I could see the pride and affection on his face and in the way he gently handled her.

A wonderful friendship was born on that day. Jim and I talked with each other regularly. I would always call him and ask, "Jim, whatcha got cookin' today?" He didn't always have a story idea for me, but when he did, it was always compelling, interesting, and very visual, the three key ingredients for a great television news story. Through the years, I did dozens of stories with Jim. He became my go-to expert on all things related to wildlife. We interviewed him about coyotes and bobcat sightings in neighborhoods, neglected lions, monkeys, apes, spiders, armadillos, alligators at a local lake, and, of course, his specialty, snakes, but through the years, the stories that made the biggest impact involved Katy. Katy became a local celebrity just like Jim.

Katy became Jim's best teaching tool. He would lug her big crate to classes at Plano schools. In three decades, every student who attended public schools in Plano had an up-close-and-personal experience with the gargantuan python. The kids were enamored with her. Who wouldn't be? No matter how badly the kids were acting in class, Jim pulling out Katy had an instantaneous calming effect. Katy was way cool, and so was Jim.

I called on Jim once when I did a story during snake mating season. Rat snakes were showing up in Plano neighborhoods in droves.

I thought it would make a cool live shot to hold a snake, so I called Jim and asked him if I could do something live at the learning center while holding Katy in my arms. What a great visual that would be. Jim's reply was usually the same, no matter what I asked him for. "Of course," he said, "come on down." I was still a little apprehensive, but Jim had a calming effect that emphasized that all would be OK and I shouldn't worry about becoming a food source for Katy.

I wasn't capable of holding all 200 pounds of Katy in my arms and around my neck, so Jim lifted the first five feet of her and carefully placed her in my arms. Two-thirds of her body still sat on the ground. I embraced her about two feet below her head. As I held Katy, her head slowly moved back and forth and her long, skinny tongue kept popping out. Of course, it freaked me out a little bit, but I was OK. Jim loved Katy and assured me she was gentle and harmless, and I believed him.

"Stand by," the associate producer said in my earpiece. Then, I heard my cue: "Go. You're live."

I looked at the camera, and said (or thought I said), "This is Katy. Katy is a giant Burmese python. She weighs 180 pounds and is eighteen feet long. The snakes slithering into Plano neighborhoods aren't quite as big as this one, but they're still causing concern among homeowners." That was the cue for the director to start the taped portion of my story.

As soon as I was off the air and the tape started playing back at the station, Jim gave me one of his infamous looks. His eyebrows were raised, his head tilted down. He looked like he had just heard the most ridiculous words ever spoken. Finally, after a long pause, he said, "Steve, do you have any idea what you just said?"

"Of course I do, Jim. I said Katy is 180 pounds and eighteen feet long."

"No you didn't," he told me. "I wished you would have said that."

Frightened, I asked him, "Oh no, what the hell did I say?"

He replied, "You said she was 180 pounds and eighteen inches long! That's a really fat snake!" Once again, I felt like a total schmuck. I had just told hundreds of thousands of Dallas–Fort Worth television viewers that the largest snake they had likely ever seen was only eighteen inches long.

Jim never let me live that live shot down. Throughout our decades-long friendship, he would bring it up, and it always made for some great laughs.

Katy became the focus of another one of my stories a few years later. Jim called me up, sounding like a worried-sick dad. "Steve, I'm really worried about Katy. She hasn't eaten in months. We don't know what's wrong with her. We're taking her to the small animal clinic at Texas A&M University Veterinary School in College Station. A veterinarian is going to perform surgery on her."

I was hoping he would ask me to come with him so we could do a story on it. I mean, how often do you see surgery performed on a giant snake? I thought it would be an amazing story. "Jimmy D, how would you feel about us tagging along?" I asked.

"I was hoping you would ask," he replied.

Once inside the clinic, my photographer and I were led into an operating room, which looked just like an operating room designed for humans, and the medical staff prepped the colossal patient for surgery. And then they brought in the patient.

This was a sight to behold, creating a spectacular shot for my photographer. Six people carried Katy, who was stretched out straight, all eighteen feet of her. Every three feet, a person held a segment of her. As the procession came to a halt, they lowered her onto the operating table ever so gently. Then it was time for Katy to be put under with general anesthesia. The surgeon placed a small mask over her head. Unbelievably, she stayed calm and started breathing in the gas. It didn't take long before she was out cold. The veterinarian, who was wearing latex surgical gloves that went all the way up to his shoulders, said, "Before we cut her open, I want to try something.".

He stuck his right hand up Katy's anus. Was I actually seeing what I thought I was seeing? What a visual! The doctor's arm disappeared inside Katy all the way up to his shoulder. I had no idea what he was doing, but it didn't look like fun for him or Katy.

The surgeon carefully pulled his arm, and finally his hand, out of the snake's anus. In his gloved hand was a rock-hard chunk of feces. "I think I found the problem," he said. "Katy has an impacted bowel." *Snakes have bowels?* I hadn't known that. Boy, was this educational! The doctor explained that the feces had been in Katy for so long, it had calcified and she couldn't pass it. That's why she hadn't been eating.

He stuck his arm in again and again and again, pulling out even more chunks of feces the size of baseballs. Describing the sight as "totally disgusting and grotesque" is inadequate. Most of the video my photographer shot was unusable. Can you imagine seeing this scene play out on your local news? I can almost hear the anchors teasing the story: "Still to come, snake shit almost shut down a local celebrity. We'll show you how, next."

Jim was relieved that Katy didn't need surgery. And he kept those chunks of feces in a container on his desk at the Outdoor Learning Center. That's what I call love. One week later, Jim called me again. "I've got a good follow-up story for you. We're going to try feeding Katy today."

I simply replied, "I'll be there."

The feeding was intense. Katy hadn't eaten in months, and this would be the first time since her fecal evacuation at Texas A&M. Jim attached a dead rabbit to a special feeding device that looked like a long stick. As he tried to force the rabbit into Katy's mouth, he talked to her like a daughter, encouraging his "big girl" to take the food. "Come on, Katy. You can do it," he said. His staff also encouraged her to take the food, but Katy didn't seem interested.

It took about forty-five minutes of maneuvering and pushing before Jim was finally able to get the rabbit deep into Katy's throat and release it from the device. We watched as the big bulge in Katy's skin moved further and further along her body. Jim was ecstatic, crying, "She's doing it! She's doing it! Katy is eating again!"

Snakes, like people, don't live forever. In 2007, I got a call from Tammy Welch, the Learning Center office manager, giving me the bad news. "Katy died," she said. "I'm really worried about Jim. He's devastated." It was easy to understand why. Katy and Jim had worked together as a team for more than three decades. Jim estimated that Katy's age was probably thirty-four when she died.

I felt very sad when Katy died because I knew how much Jim loved her. She had been so much more than just a giant snake to him; she had been his teaching companion and faithful friend, and when she was cremated, Jim kept her remains close to him, on his desk at the center.

When Katy passed away, I did a story on her, using some of the wonderful video we had shot through the years. Jim and I did the math on how many students had come into contact with Katy during her life. The number was astronomical. More than 100,000 children knew Katy. She had served as a symbol of outdoor learning, teaching kids to respect and appreciate nature's treasures.

Jim and Katy taught all of us important lessons about the value of coexistence between humans and wildlife. Through Katy, Jim also helped me get past my fear of snakes. I, too, no longer looked at Katy as just a snake; she was something special that transcended other reptiles and wildlife at the Outdoor Learning Center. Katy was the ultimate teaching tool and, to the students, a beautiful but mysterious symbol of the coolest things on the planet.

In 2008, just a year after Katy died, Jim underwent surgery to put stents in his arteries. He had been struggling with heart disease in 1979, though I had never known because he never talked about it with me. One year after the surgery, he called me with an unexpected and unsettling question that really threw me for a loop: "Steve, can I ask you something personal?"

"Of course, Jimmy," I replied.

His voice became grave. "This is going to sound really strange, but will you speak at my funeral?" This was incredibly out of character for

Jim, who was always upbeat, funny, positive, and full of life. My inclination was to respond with a joke or to say something sarcastic—we had that kind of friendship—but this time, he sounded very serious.

I knew he wasn't kidding, so I said, "Of course I will, Jimmy. But that's not going to be for a very long time. I have a feeling you're going to be with us for a while." He thanked me, and I hung up the phone, wondering why he had chosen to ask me that question then.

Jim's battle with heart disease got worse, and he retired from his beloved job in December of 2010. Three years later, his dear wife, Peggy, died of cancer. Jim never seemed the same after. He seemed lost without her. He volunteered at the Dallas Zoo and the Outdoor Learning Center, but when I saw him and talked with him, I always sensed an underlying sadness.

Jim's heart condition had landed him in the hospital numerous times since 1979, but the frequency of those hospital visits increased after Peggy died. Her death and his declining health took a toll on his psyche, and in April of 2015, he was in the hospital again. I checked up on him via a Facebook message. He replied, "Feeling better and should be back home soon."

Two days later, Tammy called me, and delivered another dose of heartbreaking news. "Jim passed away last night," she said. It was two years and two months after Peggy had died. Tammy was devastated. I was devastated. Anyone who had ever known Jim was devastated.

I hung up and cried. Our community had lost one of its best teachers, an icon who had touched thousands of lives, and I had lost a wonderful friend who had given me much more in life than great story ideas. Jim Dunlap always warmed my heart with humor, kindness, and compassion. I couldn't help but think of all the students across several generations who had loved him and learned from Plano's Dr. Doolittle. His dry humor, hysterical facial expressions, and kind, generous heart made him larger than life.

Hundreds of people came to a memorial service for Jim at Plano Senior High, a fitting location because it was the first place he had taught in Plano before starting the Outdoor Learning Center. I made good on my promise to Jim to speak at the service, as did many others who wanted to publicly pay tribute to this special man. It was truly a celebration of his life. Most of the stories people told about Jim were met with big laughs, including my tale about 18-inch-long Katy, the live shot Jim would never let me forget. The service produced many more laughs than tears, which speaks volumes about how the amazing Jimmy D lived his life. I miss him very much, along with his beloved sidekick, Katy.

VII.

Big Rockin' Daddy Meets the King

In thirty-four years in television news, I reported about 8,500 stories. People always ask if I have a favorite story among that body of work, and I do. It all began with a phone call from Ceil Blakey, a woman from Richardson, Texas, whom I had never met. She said her son Gary was dying of cancer and didn't have much time left. Gary, a rhythm and blues singer known as Big Rockin' Daddy, performed at Dallas nightclubs and had one last wish before he died. He wanted to meet his idol, the legendary King of the Blues, B.B. King. Ceil explained to me how she had tried to make Gary's dream come true. She had spoken with King's manager and had arranged for Gary to meet King before his induction into the Rock and Roll Hall of Fame. Gary and his wife had flown to Cleveland, but when they'd gotten to the hall of fame, security guards had said they didn't know anything about the meeting and had refused to allow them backstage. The guards hadn't seemed interested in making an effort to confirm the couple's claim. The Blakeys, extremely disappointed, had walked away, climbed into a cab back to the airport, and returned home to Dallas, without meeting B.B. King.

I didn't know Ceil Blakey, and I wasn't sure why she had decided to call me, of all people, but I was sincerely moved by her predicament. This desperate mother only wanted to see her son get his last wish. "Steve, is there anything you can do?" she pleaded. I wasn't sure what to say or where to start. I asked her for a phone number for King's manager and told her I would make a few phone calls and try my best to help. If there was any way I could play a role in making Gary's wish come true, I would happily do so.

I called King's manager. He had a thick New York accent and used the word "baby" in every other sentence. I introduced myself as a local television news reporter from Dallas. I told him, "I'm not interested in discussing what went wrong in Cleveland. I just want to know if there's any way Gary could meet B.B. King somewhere else."

"I'll tell you what, baby," he said. "B.B. is going to perform at the New Orleans Jazz Festival next week. It's too crazy there, but if you can get Gary to the Grand Casino Resort in Gulfport, Mississippi, the following week, we will make it happen."

When I asked him if I had his word on that, he said, "Absolutely, baby."

I called the Southwest Airlines Public Relations Department and explained the situation. They agreed to give Gary and his wife two free roundtrip tickets to New Orleans, about an hour away from Gulfport. A photographer and I would accompany them on the trip. Our plan was to rent a van in New Orleans and drive Gary and his wife to Mississippi.

Everything was coming together. The only missing element was the Grand, so I called the resort and talked with Jean Wiesenberg, the Grand's PR director. I explained Gary's situation and his last wish. Jean fell in love with the idea and vowed to do everything she could to make it a very special weekend for Gary and his wife. The Grand comped the Blakeys' hotel room and meals and gave them front-row seats for the concert.

It looked like we were actually going to fulfill Gary's wish. If I could pull this off, I'd have a very compelling story for the news—but even better, I could play a role in making this dying man's last wish come true.

Everything went exactly as planned. Jean greeted us as we arrived at the Grand that afternoon. She couldn't hide her excitement. She kept saying how "wonderful" it was to have Gary and his wife at the Grand. She asked all of us to meet her back in the lobby an hour before King's performance.

When we returned that evening, she escorted us into to the greenroom. Two big reclining chairs sat in the middle of the room, facing each other. My photographer set up his camera on a tripod and clipped a lavalier microphone on Gary, who sat down in one of the chairs. The greenroom door opened, and in walked B.B. King. The blues legend sported a big warm smile as he shook Gary's hand and sat down in the empty chair.

Gary professed his love for King's music. "I perform several of your songs," he said proudly.

Gary then asked B.B. why he had named his famous black Gibson guitar Lucille. I'm sure King had told the same story hundreds of times, but he seemed to enjoy telling it one more time to Gary. It was a great story. King said he had been playing at a little dance hall in Arkansas that had used a barrel of kerosene to heat the place. Two men had started fighting, knocking over the kerosene. Both died in the fire, and King went back into the burning building to retrieve his beloved guitar. The next day, he learned the two men had been fighting over a woman named Lucille, so he named that guitar Lucille, as well as all the other guitars he owned.

In the middle of their conversation about Lucille, Gary suddenly turned around, looked right at me, and said, "I can't believe this, Steve. I'm sitting here in a room, talking with B.B. King, just like he's my neighbor."

B.B. laughed. It was a beautiful and touching moment. I was overwhelmed with joy for Gary.

Finally, King asked Gary, "Is there anything you'd like to hear tonight?" Gary told King that his band played "The Thrill Is Gone" as part of their set when they performed and that it had always been his favorite.

"Hmmm," King said, "let me see what I can do," but we knew he would play it; it was his signature song.

As the conversation ended, King embraced Gary and left.

As we left the greenroom, we focused the camera on Gary. I asked him to share his thoughts and feelings about meeting his idol. Gary held back tears. His voice cracked as he said, "He's a wonderful man. He was so gracious. And I am so blessed to have met him." Mission accomplished.

Next, Jean led Gary and his wife into the concert hall to a table right up against the stage and gave them a stack of coupons for free drinks.

Halfway through the concert, the music stopped. B.B. sat down on a stool and started talking to the standing-room-only crowd. "Ladies and gentlemen, we have a very special guest with us tonight," he said. "His name is Gary, and he's from Dallas. Gary is sick." He turned his attention toward the table where Gary was sitting. As he looked into Gary's eyes, he pointed at him. "I've always said ain't nothin' over til it's over," King said, "and don't you forget that." The audience applauded.

With those powerful words of wisdom, King began playing the familiar licks of his biggest hit, "The Thrill Is Gone."

Three weeks later, Ceil Blakey called to tell me Gary had passed away. Although the news made me very sad, it left me with a feeling of happiness and satisfaction, knowing that Big Rockin' Daddy had gotten his wish to meet the King of the Blues.

VIII.

I've Got What?

Irony is a recurring theme in my professional and personal life. In March of 1997, a few weeks after Gary "Big Rockin' Daddy" Blakey died of cancer, my life changed in an ironic heartbeat. Life was good. My wife, Susan, was eight months pregnant with our second child. Our firstborn son, Jordan, was about to turn three. We had just moved into our first house.

The initial sign of something amiss had come to me three and a half months earlier, in early December, while I was taking a shower. I was soaping up my left armpit when I felt something deep under my skin. It felt like a golf ball. I didn't give it much thought, however, because of what had happened a year earlier, right before I had left for Super Bowl XXX in Tempe, Arizona, when the Dallas Cowboys were in the big game for the third time in four years.

KDFW was sending a team of sports and news people to cover the game and all the hype leading up to it. The day before we left for Phoenix, I went to see my doctor, Phillip Aronoff. I showed him a lump in my left breast. He sent me to Dr. James Davidson, who specializes in breast diseases. Dr. Davidson used a magic marker to draw a line across the side of my breast. "I want to cut along that line and take that lump out so we can see what it is," he said.

I told him I was leaving for Phoenix to cover the Super Bowl in the morning and asked if it could wait a week.

"Sure, you can wait, Steve, but waiting is like sitting on a ticking time bomb," he warned. Dr. Davidson told me that one out of every one hundred breast cancer cases involve men. That scared me; with my luck, I would be the one in one hundred. I asked him if I could still go to Phoenix if he removed the lump right then and there. He assured me I could still go, though I would be "a little sore," so I agreed. He numbed the area and removed the lump, then sent the tissue off to a lab for biopsy.

Two days later, while I was in Phoenix, Dr. Davidson called me with great news. The results had come back negative. The lump was a fat necrosis, dead or damaged fatty breast tissue. He explained how fat necrosis could be caused from simple trauma, like a pet jumping on your chest. I told him I had a Chihuahua who often jumped on me. What a relief.

One year later, when I felt the golf ball in my armpit, I assumed it was another fat necrosis, so I blew it off. I felt fine and didn't have any symptoms that would make me think I had any health problems.

Three and a half months after that, I got a nasty sinus infection. I went to Dr. Aronoff's office on Wednesday, March 12, 1997, hoping he would give me some good meds to clear out my sinuses and get me well. While I was sitting in his exam room, I had conflicting thoughts about showing him the golf-ball-sized lump in my armpit, but finally, I said, "Doc, I want to show you something. Feel this."

As he felt my armpit, his entire personality changed. He became very serious, grave and focused. "Steve, I want to send you back to Dr. Davidson right now and see what that is," he said. "I want X-rays and a sonogram."

I asked him what he thought it could be.

"I could show you medical textbooks where it could be thirty different things. The worst case scenario: lymphoma," he said.

"Lymphoma? Isn't that cancer?"

"Yes, Steve," he said, "but let's take it out first and see what it is before jumping to any conclusions."

I went straight from Dr. Aronoff's office to see Dr. Davidson, who had removed the fat necrosis from my breast a little more than a year earlier. Dr. Davidson examined my armpit and said, "Steve, I want to take your lymph nodes out tomorrow. It is very close to your vascular system, so we're going to have to put you under."

I was scared and overwhelmed. I had a bad gut feeling. I just knew in my heart of hearts that I had cancer. I couldn't stop thinking about Dr. Aronoff's reaction when he had first felt my lump. I wanted to be optimistic, but I feared I had the worst-case scenario. I didn't sleep that night, wondering if I was about to become a cancer patient.

The next morning, Susan and I went to the surgery center. She stayed in the waiting area while I was prepped for surgery. All I remembered was getting an IV and then waking up in a recovery room.

On Friday morning, the day after the surgery, while recovering at home, I called Dr. Davidson's office to see if the biopsy results were in. His office manager answered the phone. She told me they had sent my specimen to another lab. "That's usually a good sign," she told me. "If it's cancer, they usually know immediately." I hung up, feeling a tremendous sense of relief—but that relief was short-lived.

Dr. Aronoff called me five minutes later and said he had the results of the biopsy. "I just talked with Dr. Pascoe, the chief pathologist at Presbyterian Hospital," he said. You have Hodgkin's lymphoma."

I've got what? My gut feeling had been right: It was the worst-case scenario. I had just heard three of the most dreaded words anyone could ever hear: *You've got cancer*. I didn't know how to react. I felt like crying, wondering, *Am I going to die? If I am, how long do I have left? Will I live to see my son being born? Is my wife going to be a widow? Am I going to suffer?* And the most pressing question: *How am I going to tell my family?*

"Steve, I know this is going to sound crazy," said Dr. Aronoff, "but if there's one good cancer to get, it's Hodgkin's. It's not only treatable, it's curable."

Curable? I didn't know any type of cancer was curable. My head was still reeling from those three terrible words.

"With chemotherapy and radiation, you have a really good chance of being cured," Dr. Aronoff said reassuringly. Dr. Aronoff said my first step would be choosing an oncologist, and he promised to call me back with a few recommendations. I should have focused on the word "cured," but all I could hear was "chemotherapy and radiation." I had heard all the horror stories of how sick cancer patients can get from both treatments.

I hung up the phone and sat on my bed in a daze. I cried for about five minutes. Once the tears stopped flowing, I thought about the reality of having cancer. I knew I hadn't done anything to bring this disease on. I ate healthy and exercised regularly. No one in my family had ever had Hodgkin's lymphoma, so I knew it wasn't hereditary. My shock, sadness, and fear quickly turned into a feeling of resolve. I wasn't ready to die. It wasn't my time yet. The doctor had said Hodgkin's was curable, so I vowed to fight it with everything I had. I would not surrender. *I will survive, and I will beat this.* I didn't want to waste any time. If I could start chemo that day, I would. With that decision, I felt an overwhelming sense of inner peace, confidence, and strength.

Susan works at J. C. Penney's corporate headquarters in Plano. When she had left for work that morning, she had told me to call her if I heard anything about the results. I was very nervous and apprehensive about calling her with the diagnosis, so I prayed, and then I called her.

I took a deep breath and dialed her number. When she answered, I said, "Susie, it's Hodgkin's lymphoma, cancer of the lymph system."

She immediately started crying hysterically and said, "Oh, my God. Oh, my God." I tried to calm her down, reassuring her that everything was going to be all right, but she wasn't convinced. My revelation left her emotionally devastated.

"I'll be right home," she said.

A coworker drove Susan to our house. She came in the front door, ran to me, and embraced me. She cried, but I felt strong. "Don't worry," I told her. "I'm going to fight this. I'm going to be fine. You have to believe that. I am going to be fine."

She eventually calmed down. I believed my strength made her feel better about our predicament; if I could handle this, she could too. We had other things to worry about; in a few weeks, we would have another son.

Later that day, I called my brother and sister in South Florida to tell them the news. Both of them reacted in disbelief, offering their support. They both asked the same question, "How are you going to tell Mom?" Mom had recently lost her own mother and my dad, so we knew she would have an extremely difficult time accepting that her youngest son had cancer.

My siblings and I came up with a plan. My mother also lives in South Florida. My brother and sister would drive to her house on Sunday so they could be there to comfort her when I called from Texas to tell her the news.

It went about as well as expected. When I told her I had Hodgkin's lymphoma, Mom asked my brother, "Raymond, what is Hodgkin's lymphoma?"

"Mom, Ray's not a doctor," I told her. "I'm the patient. I can tell you what Hodgkin's is. It's cancer of the lymph system."

She seemed disoriented, as I had expected. I tried telling her what Dr. Aronoff had told me, that Hodgkin's disease is not only treatable but curable. I don't think she heard me. She was too upset. But having my brother and sister there helped tremendously.

On the same day he had diagnosed me with cancer, Dr. Aronoff had called me back and recommended I see Dallas oncologist Sherron Helms. "She's an excellent doctor and has a great bedside manner," he told me. As soon as I hung up the phone with Dr. Aronoff, I called Dr. Helms's office and made an appointment to see her the next day.

I knew it was very important for me to feel good about my oncologist because he or she would be the most important person to help me survive cancer. I wanted a doctor who would have my full trust and confidence. I liked Dr. Helms very much. She had a kind disposition and a very sweet, sincere, gentle personality. She truly cared about her patients, including me. Dr. Helms's personality was calming and reassuring as she explained the staging process, a series of tests that would determine what stage of the disease I had—was it isolated to the lymph nodes in my armpit or had it spread to other lymph nodes and my internal organs?

Dr. Helms feared I was stage three. She could feel my spleen when she pressed her fingers on my lower abdomen. She said that her being able to feel the spleen could mean it was enlarged, a common sign of more advanced lymphoma. Stage three would require at least a dozen chemotherapy treatments. She asked me to come back to her office later in the week for a bone marrow test, but I didn't want to come back. I wanted to do it right then, to get the fight started immediately, so Dr. Helms brought in a nurse, who numbed my hip area. The nurse held my hand as Dr. Helms inserted a needle through my hip bone and into the marrow. The pain was intense. I held the nurse's hand so tightly, I thought I was going to break it.

Over the next few days, I had several more tests, including a CT scan and a gallium scan, which shows swelling, infection, or cancer in the body with the use of radioactive gallium injected in the veins. The technician administering the test asked me if I had a sinus infection. I was amazed and asked her how she knew. She said, "I can see it."

Once I finished all the tests, Dr. Helms gave me some encouraging news: I had stage 1A Hodgkin's. The "1" meant it hadn't spread beyond my armpit, and the "A" meant I was asymptomatic—I didn't have classic symptoms associated with the disease, like night sweats, fever and chills, persistent fatigue, unexplained weight loss, or loss of appetite. Dr. Helms said that with stage 1A, I would have six to eight weeks of chemotherapy followed by one month of radiation, and thankfully, my spleen looked normal. "Susan and you should go out and celebrate," Dr. Helms told me.

It was good news, indeed. Because I had waited three and a half months before showing the lump to my doctor, the cancer could easily have spread to my organs and throughout my body. Thank God it was stage 1A. It meant my cancer would be easier to treat. But I wasn't in any mood to celebrate. I had a long road ahead. My cancer battle was only beginning. The time to celebrate would be when I was free of cancer, not now.

IX.

The Cancer Chronicles

Sharing my cancer battle with our television viewers was the last thing on my mind; all I really cared about was getting healthy. But on the day after Dr. Davidson surgically removed my lymph nodes, an idea popped into my head that had me thinking like a journalist instead of a patient. If it was cancer, we would have a rare opportunity to tell the story of cancer through the eyes of a patient from the day of diagnosis, through treatment and to the final outcome, whatever that may be.

When I bounced the idea off our medical reporter, John Hammarley, he replied, "I was hoping you would say that."

When I learned I had cancer, I could only wonder how many other people were exactly like I had been, blowing off a lump and rationalizing it, saying, "It can't be anything serious." By allowing John to follow my cancer journey, I had one simple goal: to touch one person's life. If any of the stories persuaded a single person with a lump to get checked, we would accomplish something very meaningful. Think about it: If that person's lump turned out to be benign, we could give that person peace of mind knowing he or she was cancer-free, but more importantly, if the stories persuaded one person to see a doctor and the lump turned out to be cancer, we might have played a role in catching the disease early enough to save that person's life. Just one person, that's all it would take to be successful.

John bounced the idea off our news director, who liked the idea but wanted to make sure I was committed to sharing my story no matter how my treatment turned out. "Once we do this, we have to stick with it," he said.

I told him two simple words: "I'm in."

John came up with a cool name for the series. He called it "The Cancer Chronicles."

John's first installment of "The Cancer Chronicles" focused on my Hodgkin's diagnosis, the impact on my family, and my first chemo treatment. He interviewed my very pregnant wife and my doctors, and he explained to viewers what causes lymphoma, showing a graphic of the lymph system and then video of a typewriter. "Lymph nodes are small bean-shaped glands that fight infection," he reported. "Each time a cell divides, a biological manuscript three billion characters long must be duplicated. Think of the mistakes a skilled typist could make in a document that complex. When cells make a mistake, a cancerous tumor takes shape."

Before my first treatment, a nurse named Myrna Stoler (no relation) escorted me into a separate room for a chemo briefing. She described the four chemotherapy drugs I would receive—Adriamycin, bleomycin, vinblastine, and dacarbazine, a combination commonly known in cancer treatment as ABVD—and discussed the potential side effects of each one. It was a hard dose of reality to swallow. Adriamycin was the most potentially harmful chemo drug I would get, for which the nurse recited a long list of possible side effects. If Adriamycin leaks from the vein, it can cause severe tissue, skin, or muscle damage. It may cause severe and possibly life-threatening heart problems, including heart failure. That was just for starters. Adriamycin can also cause another type of cancer, acute myelogenous leukemia (AML), and a blood problem called myelodysplastic syndrome (MDS). And finally, Adriamycin can cause bone marrow suppression that may lead to severe and sometimes deadly health problems, including infections and bleeding. Adriamycin can also cause hair loss, but that was the least of my worries. Nurse Stoler explained that most side effects occur in only a very small percentage of patients, but that didn't make me feel better. These powerful drugs are poison, but

I embraced them. If they did their job, they would kill cancer cells and save my life.

John's second edition of "The Cancer Chronicles" came one month after my first chemo treatment, on April 25, 1997. Susan was nine months pregnant and due any day, with a C-section scheduled for the following week. Her first delivery had been a C-section, so she had decided to have the second baby the same way; her doctor had told her it would be easy to make an incision along the scar from the first delivery.

In the late afternoon, I was at work, writing a story, when Susan called me. "I'm having abdominal pain," she said. "My dad is taking me to the hospital." *Is this it?* I wondered. *Could she be having the baby now?*

Susan called back after my story aired at five p.m. and said, "Guess what? I'm in labor. You need to get down here now." I called the news director to tell him why I couldn't do my six o'clock live shot. I headed to the hospital. John and Paul, my photographer, drove separate cars to meet us there. This would be a compelling part of "The Cancer Chronicles" they didn't want to miss.

When I arrived at the hospital, Susan was in intense pain. Her obstetrician, Dr. Frances Crites, talked to us and then directed her attention to Paul, laying down the ground rules regarding his videotaping of the C-section. "No lenses over my field of surgery," she demanded before she shared a disturbing story of how an overanxious father had dropped a lens cap into her surgical area, causing a delay as hospital staff had to re-sterilize everything.

The C-section went perfectly. A sheet separated Susan's head from the surgical area, so we couldn't see anything graphic. Paul shot the surgery very tastefully. As Dr. Crites lifted Jacob Joseph Stoler above the sheet, Susan saw him for the first time and cried tears of joy. Not-so-little Jake weighed nine pounds and thirteen ounces. The nurses said of all the babies born at the hospital that day, he was the biggest.

Once things had settled down, nurses brought Jake into Susan's hospital room. John gave us time to collect ourselves and then interviewed me on camera. His first question: "Well, Steve, what are you feeling right now?"

I smiled as I shared my thoughts. "Having a new addition to our family as I'm going through chemo is a true blessing. Who can think about cancer when you have this adorable little baby looking at you, knowing it's your child? Having a new member of our family takes precedence over everything. It brought so much joy into our lives at a time when we could easily have felt despair and fear. It took the focus off my cancer battle and redirected it toward Jake."

Having a baby helped Susan cope. It helped me cope. And it gave us both inner strength. When I was diagnosed with cancer, I had wanted desperately to maintain normalcy in my life. My life had still felt fairly normal even after I started chemo, but then Jake came along and changed all that. So much for normalcy.

My wife, Susan, and sons, Jake and Jordan.

At the advice of a KDFW coworker who had survived testicular cancer, I had my hair cut very short. He said it would lessen the emotional blow of losing it. Once I started chemo, I went to Houston's of Dallas to have a hairpiece made. It was a very strange visit, especially when they took hair samples from different parts of my head. They would match that hair with synthetic hair to make a wig. The owner told me to come back once my hair started falling out in clumps so they could shave my head and fit me with my piece. I wasn't looking forward to it.

Every other Friday, I went to Dr. Helms's office for chemo. My hair started to thin out. Every time I would run my hand through my hair, five to ten strands would come out with my hand, but it never came out in clumps. Most of my hair, though shorter, was still intact. Houston's of Dallas kept calling me. "Mr. Stoler, your piece is ready. You can come in and try it on." Their calls left me frustrated and perturbed. I couldn't help but ask them why I would come in for a hair piece fitting if I still had my hair?" I never went back to Houston's because I never lost my hair. To this day, I still wonder what happened to that wig.

After three months and six rounds of chemotherapy, I had another important CT scan. If there were no signs of cancer, I would start phase two of my treatment with radiation. The impending scan stressed me out, but I still felt confident I was cancer-free.

Dr. Helms gave me great news after the scan: No signs of cancer.

X.

The Letter

For the next month, radiation became part of my daily morning routine. John's third installment of "The Cancer Chronicles" focused on this new phase of my treatment. He and Paul came to the clinic to interview my radiation oncologist, Dr. Jeffrey Greenberg, and to shoot some video. They couldn't be in the room during treatment because they would be exposed to radiation, so Paul came in while they were prepping me.

The machine was aligned to tiny tattooed dots on my chest—you really have to look hard to see them, but I still have them today. I was a little self-conscious; this was the first time in my career that I would be on television with my shirt off. I was no body builder; my "six pack" abs looked more like a keg.

In the video, John explained, "Doctors began aiming at Steve's cancer with a completely different weapon, this one loaded with radioactive bullets." As the video showed me lying shirtless on the table, with red lasers shining on my chest, John's narration continued. "Lying alone in a cold treatment room, radioactive X-rays are about to pierce into Steve's body, damaging or killing every cell in its path."

Dr. Greenberg had explained that an important part of his mission as an oncologist is to portray radiation as a positive force that not only helps patients get well but also saves lives. He was very upset by John's descriptions of radiation, feeling that the negative tone of John's words would only enhance the fears of cancer patients.

I wasn't sure what to do about this spat. John was my friend, and I deeply respected his work. I had the same respect for Dr. Greenberg. Like Dr. Helms, he had my trust and confidence. I liked John's story and thought it was well-written. I told Dr. Greenberg that I understood why he was so upset. I suggested he call John to discuss his concerns. I knew John, like most reporters, would be willing to discuss the content of his stories, but I expected John to defend his words, which he did.

John later told me that he and Dr. Greenberg had had a very good conversation explaining how they felt but at the end of their discussion, they had agreed to disagree. I really was the man in the middle. While I understood why Dr. Greenberg had become upset, I could relate with why John had carefully crafted his words to make the story more dramatic. After all, I was a reporter, too.

After part three of "The Cancer Chronicles" hit the air, something very unexpected and amazing happened. The viewers started sending me letters. These letters were not just get-well wishes; they were detailed, heartfelt, and, in many cases, emotional. They moved me in ways I had never imagined. These people, total strangers, empathized with what I was going through. Their letters were kind, compassionate, and sincere. Many of them were written by cancer survivors. Little did these caring people know that they became an important part of my support group.

Their encouragement served as a refreshing change from my many friends and family members who seemed to look at me with what I called tombstone eyes. Even though my prognosis for being cured was very good, I had cancer, and they assumed my life was coming to an end. After all, in most people's minds, there's no cure for cancer.

When I reassured these friends and family members that I would win the battle, I could tell by the look in their eyes that they didn't believe me. They would smile and gently nod as if to say, "Sure, Steve. It's great that you have a positive attitude, but we know what's really happening here. You're going to die." The same people were afraid to utter the word "cancer." They would say, "Steve, we heard about your, uh, your, uh, situation."

I would say, "Oh, you mean cancer." Dr. Helms had told me that of all the patients she had ever treated, I was the most outgoing about having cancer. I wanted to talk about it. I'm not one to keep things inside. I never was. Talking about my cancer helped me. I had no shame, and nothing to hide.

The viewers' heartfelt letters gave me strength and often brought me to tears, especially the ones from cancer survivors. A nineteen-year-old Hodgkin's survivor wrote me a ten-page letter about the impact my story had on her. "You looked pretty grim during the newscast," she wrote. "Believe me, you will look back and smile when you realize how easy it was compared to what could have been." She was only nineteen, but her words showed foresight and wisdom. She could relate with what I was going through because she had survived her own cancer battle; no one truly understands unless they've been through it themselves. Her letter touched my heart, and I wrote her back. In fact, I wrote everyone back. I had to. These kind people had taken precious time out of their busy lives to offer their support for me, so I felt a burning desire to let each and every one of them know how much their letters meant to me.

One of the more interesting letters came from the Powledge Unit in Palestine, Texas. I had no idea what the Powledge Unit was, but as I opened the letter, a tiny piece of paper fell out. It looked just like the paper inside a fortune cookie, but it didn't reveal any fortune. It read, "Inspected by Warden 4372." I suddenly understood that the Powledge Unit was a Texas prison and the letter had come from an inmate.

"I saw the story about you having cancer the other night," he wrote. "I'm not proud of what brought me here. I am now a Christian. I want you to know, every day, during recreation time, nine other inmates and I form a prayer circle. We pray for your health and your family." At first, I laughed. I had this image in my mind of ten men convicted of who knows what holding hands in the middle of a Texas prison, praying for the health of Steve Stoler. Now there would be a sight to behold. But the humor eventually turned into awe. So many people—even prisoners—cared about my health. Their kindness and compassion overwhelmed me.

Most of my KDFW coworkers didn't know I was still having daily radiation treatments. I would pitch story ideas in our morning editorial meetings and then drive to the North Texas Cancer Center in Plano. The treatments were quick. Once the lasers were lined up, I would be radiated for thirty seconds while lying on my back and then another thirty seconds while lying face down. A few minutes later, I would have my shirt back on and be on my way back to the newsroom.

The radiation targeted my armpit area, where Dr. Davidson had removed the cancerous lymph nodes. Dr. Greenberg said it was a great place to have radiation because the radiation wouldn't affect my mouth, throat, or digestive system. After a few treatments, it felt like a mild sunburn. (By the way, I finally lost my hair, but not the hair on my head—the hair on my armpit.)

After twenty radiation treatments, it was time for another CT scan to determine whether the cancer was still gone. If it was, my treatment would be finished and "The Cancer Chronicles" would come to a close. Going in for the scan, I didn't feel nervous; I felt upbeat and optimistic. As crazy as it sounds, I was so confident that Dr. Helms would give me an all-clear, I booked a vacation to the Cayman Islands. Susan and I were ready to celebrate.

Dr. Helms examined the images from the CT scan. She smiled, which could only mean good news. With Paul's camera rolling, she said, "Steve, we think you're cured of your disease, and we expect you to live a long and happy life."

Minutes later, John interviewed me one last time, asking me about my calm reaction. "Steve, you seemed blasé. What were you feeling when Dr. Helms said you were cured?" Truth be told, I had expected this day would come. Throughout the journey, I had strived to put my game face on. I had stayed calm and confident, fighting the battle day by day, one step at a time. I had accomplished a short-term goal and moved on to the next. I had finished one chemo treatment and moved on to the next. I had taken one dose of radiation and moved on to the next. I had tried not to get overemotional. I wasn't surprised when the journey finally ended successfully, because I had done everything I was supposed to do as a good cancer patient, and it had paid off with my survival.

John closed the final chapter of "The Cancer Chronicles" by showing me walk down a long hallway as I left the medical building, cancer-free. Viewers heard my voice under the video. "What I accomplished is, I beat the most feared disease on this planet." I thanked my family and friends for supporting me, as well as the researchers who developed chemotherapy drugs that save lives or at least give cancer patients a chance. I also thanked my doctors who had the knowledge that helped me survive.

John closed the piece by asking me if I feared the cancer would return. "You try not to live every day with fear. But the thought of 'Could it come back?' is always there and it's something you always face," I said.

My cancer experience taught me life lessons. On many levels, I found it enlightening. I learned much about myself and what we as human beings are capable of. I learned that giving up and feeling sorry for yourself are not realistic options. I learned that although people called me brave and courageous, I really wasn't; I just did what I had to do. I believe that most people faced with a similar predicament would take the same approach. I learned that attitude is as powerful a drug in fighting cancer as chemotherapy or radiation. I learned how small acts of kindness can generate great impact.

Perhaps the biggest lesson cancer taught me is that life is a precious gift that should never be taken for granted.

Of the 200 letters I received from viewers, 199 of them were supportive, positive, and empathetic. There was only one exception, a letter from a Dallas man, who wrote me after watching the final chapter of "The Cancer Chronicles." He didn't like my words of gratitude toward cancer researchers and doctors or my nonchalant attitude. He made it clear that he despised my lack of faith. "How dare you be so arrogant by not thanking God for keeping you alive," he wrote.

My blood began to boil as I read his letter. I had to respond. Without hesitation, I called directory assistance for his telephone number, and I called him. Even though this man was a single voice who didn't like what I had said after beating cancer, I couldn't help myself from calling him, because I had to make him see I wasn't this Godless, arrogant, callous person he thought me. I took great pride in my work, and this wasn't the first or the last time I had reached out to a viewer critical of me or my stories. I reached out not because I wanted to change minds and hearts but because it was important to me that people at least had an understanding of why I had written a story the way I had.

When he answered, I said, "This is Steve Stoler from Channel 4 News. I just received your letter, and I felt compelled to call you," I said.

"Well hello, Mr. Stoler," he said. "I never expected you would call me." He sounded surprised, but I continued, telling him how offended I felt by his letter.

"Sir, with all respect, you don't know me. You don't know anything about me," I said. "You don't know anything about my religion, my spirituality, or my relationship with God. Don't you think it took a lot for me and my family to put ourselves out in front of the entire community to share my personal battle against cancer? I chose not to share every personal thought I had. My faith in God is a very important part of my life. I chose to keep certain things private, including my gratitude toward God. You have no idea how thankful I am to him for surviving this."

When I finally stopped my rant, all I heard was silence. I thought for a second he had hung up on me. Then, after a long pause, he said, "Mr. Stoler, you're absolutely right. I owe you a big apology. I can see now exactly how you feel about God and the type of person you are. It was a big mistake to write you that letter."

I believe that by talking with this man and revealing more about my faith and gratitude, I had changed his perspective and made him realize that he had jumped to an inaccurate conclusion.

I told him how much I appreciated his apology. I never heard from him again.

XI.

Excell the Executioner

Robert Excell White killed his victims by shooting them execution style. He deservedly earned the nickname Excell the Executioner. Most Texas inmates sentenced to death spend a little more than ten years on death row before getting executed. White's twenty-five years on death row, longer than that of any other person in the state's history, therefore had historical significance. Only three men in the United States had spent more time under a death sentence. For three Texas families, this was twenty-five agonizing years spent waiting for justice.

White's killing spree started in Waco on May 10, 1974, when he and two other men robbed and stabbed to death local gun collector Robert Perryman. They stole more than two dozen weapons, including a .30-caliber machine gun, before driving north to Collin County. The next day, White and his accomplices took their killing spree to the Hilltop, a tiny rural gas station between McKinney and Princeton that was owned by seventy-three-year-old Preston Broyles. As the men drove up, two eighteen-year-old customers, Gary Coker and Billy St. John, were pumping gas into their car. White approached Coker and St. John with the stolen machine gun, ordering them into the store with Broyles. White then shot all three of them in the back of the head. He and his accomplices left the store with six dollars from the cash register and sixty dollars from the victims' wallets. Three lives brutally snuffed out for sixty-six dollars.

Later that day, police arrested White and the other two men. White confessed to killing Broyles, Coker, and St. John. A jury convicted White of capital murder and sentenced him to death by lethal injection, but only for Preston Broyles's murder, because prosecutors had decided to take only one case to court so if they didn't get the verdict they wanted, they would have three more chances with Perryman, Coker and St. John's murders.

White, then thirty-six, arrived on death row in August 1974. White told his lawyers he opposed their appeals to spare him, but thirteen years later, they unveiled a glitch from his trial: No one had told White that the statements he made to two court-appointed psychiatrists would be used against him. As a result of this glitch, the courts granted him a new trial. A second jury convicted him with the same sentence: death by lethal injection.

I started covering the Robert Excell White story in the early 1990s, years after the murders and both trials. Even though I hadn't covered White's two trials, I was very familiar with the case. It was one of the worst murders in Collin County history. I began covering his story when an assistant district attorney called me with a tip. "Why don't you look into the reasons why it's taking so long to carry out White's death sentence," he suggested. The tipster said his fellow prosecutors and the victims' families felt that "justice was never served" because the death penalty had not been carried out. "For some reason, they won't execute him," he said.

The case intrigued me, so I pursued a story on it. I researched the murders, trials, and victims. I located Gary Coker's grandmother, Billy St. John's brother, and an ambulance driver who had transported one of the victims to the hospital. All three agreed to talk with me. As the years had passed and White stayed on death row, they had become increasingly frustrated and angry about how slow the wheels of justice turned. I could see the frustration in their eyes and hear it in their voices. I felt bad for them. They deserved their day of justice after suffering through this ordeal for two and a half decades.

John R. Roach, the former Texas district judge who had presided over White's second trial, called me. He knew I was very interested in the case because he had seen my stories. "Steve, there's a new development with Excell White I thought you would be interested in. He's finally going to be executed," he told me. I couldn't believe what I was hearing. I had been starting to share the victims' families' pessimism that, after twenty-five years, perhaps White would never be put to death.

Knowing it was finally going to happen, I called the Texas Department of Criminal Justice (TDCJ) to put in a request to witness White's execution. It's not that I had any desire whatsoever to watch someone die, but I felt a responsibility as a journalist to be there for it. I wanted to hear what he had to say and if he would show any remorse. White's death would be the final chapter of a very long, drawn-out story. The victims' family members would finally have justice, and I wanted to be there to share their story.

White turned down my request for an interview, but I was able to witness the execution. On March 30, 1999, a photographer and I drove to Huntsville, a two-and-a-half-hour drive from Dallas. We arrived at the Walls Unit, an old prison near downtown Huntsville, where all Texas executions are carried out. TDCJ communications staff members signed us in and briefed us on the execution process. As a media witness, I didn't know which group of witnesses I would join, the victims' families or White's family, as the eleventh-hour decision is usually based on available space. Before the execution protocol started, I was told I would accompany the victims' loved ones.

The witnesses gathered in waiting areas on different sides of the building, one room for the victims' families, the other for the inmate's family. By design, the two groups never come into contact with each other. Once they were ready to proceed with the execution, prison guards led us into the execution chamber. There was a similar but separate procession with the witnesses from White's family. As we entered the viewing room, I saw that a closed curtain covered the room's large window.

The room was dark and silent. After five minutes, a guard opened the curtains. We could see Excell White lying on a gurney, secured to it with leather straps around his chest and ankles. He had an IV in his arm.

The execution chamber was equipped with a microphone. We could hear what was being said through a speaker mounted on the wall of the witness room. The warden took a few steps toward White and said, "Do you have any last words?"

White didn't hesitate to answer. "Warden, send me to my maker," he said. He offered no words of remorse or apology to the family members of the men he had killed.

The warden gave a nod, and the drugs started to flow through White's veins. All eyes were on White. We could hear him breathing very heavily. That turned into what sounded like snoring. Within a few seconds, the sound stopped. He was no longer breathing. We stood there in deafening silence for five awkward and uncomfortable minutes, until the warden pronounced White dead. Those minutes had felt like hours.

The guards then closed the curtains and we were led back to the waiting area, once again kept separate from the other group of witnesses. The events surrounding White's execution seemed surreal. It was difficult to grasp that we had just watched a man die. Up until White's lethal injection, I had never seen a person die. My reaction was not what I expected. I had thought it would be very traumatic to witness someone being executed. As I had witnessed the sixty-one-year-old killer take his last breaths, I couldn't help but think of his victims: Robert Perryman, Preston Broyles, Gary Coker, and Billy St. John, and how each of them had died. White's death seemed peaceful; he didn't show any signs of pain or suffering. That was a striking contrast to how he had killed his victims. He had shot them in the back of the head in a ruthless and violent manner. White's death seemed almost too peaceful to me.

I surprised myself by feeling this way. I didn't have passionate feelings about the death penalty one way or another, but after getting to know Mrs. Coker and the St. Johns, I empathized with the emotionally painful struggle they had endured for twenty-five years. Like the victims' families, I felt relieved the White saga was finally over. The criminal justice system had finally worked; it had just taken entirely too long.

In August of 2002, three years after White's execution, David Lee, a writer for the *Los Angeles Times*, asked me to moderate a forum called

"Reporting on Executions" at the Asian-American Journalists Association conference in Dallas. Lee had researched execution witness lists in Texas and discovered that I had witnessed two executions.

What I didn't know was that C-SPAN was broadcasting the forum to a live national audience. I started the forum by sharing my personal experience with White's execution: "Robert Excell White was a cold-blooded murderer. White later told a sheriff's investigator that we interviewed for our story that killing those three people was like stepping on a fly. Excell White did not suffer in death like his victims did." I explained to the conference attendees (and the national C-SPAN audience) that I hadn't expressed this sentiment in my story because there had been no place for personal feelings in it and I had wanted to remain objective but that I had been thinking, *That was so easy, painless, quick, and peaceful.* Something didn't seem fair to me: The horrific murders of Robert Perryman, Preston Broyles, Gary Coker, and Billy St. John were anything but peaceful. To me, their killings symbolized the true meaning of cruel and unusual punishment, and after witnessing White's execution, something deep inside me said it had been too easy for him.

Though I rarely shared my personal thoughts and feelings about a story I covered, especially in a public venue, I didn't hold back at the "Reporting on Executions" forum, because the purpose of this event was for conference attendees to hear from people with different perspectives on the death penalty. It called for honest openness.

My comments about White's "easy, painless, and unfair" execution generated a barrage of angry email from C-SPAN viewers around the country. They blasted me, using adjectives like "cruel," "brutal," "inhumane," and my favorite one, "barbaric." I had never experienced this type of criticism before. I had received a few negative phone calls and e-mails along the way, but never anything like this.

I learned an important journalistic lesson from this experience, though: When it comes to the death penalty, abortion, politics, and a plethora of other controversial issues that evoke passionate emotion, keep your damned thoughts to yourself! I expressed them once about Excell White, but I never did it again.

XII.

One Big Lie

This may come as a surprise to some people, but reporters do not do background checks on every person they interview. It's impossible. It would be too time-consuming in a business that thrives on immediacy. Reporters treat most people they interview at face value, but it's difficult to discern who's telling you the truth and who's a pathological liar.

In October 2001, Doug Baum, a sales manager at the Chrysler dealership in Frisco, Texas, called me with a wonderful story idea. Baum said one of his top salespeople, Thomas Larez, a Marine Corps reservist, had been called up for active duty in Afghanistan, and Larez's pregnant wife was due to give birth on the same day he would report for duty. I loved this story. It would be a race against time to see what would happen first, the birth of their baby or his departure to Afghanistan. Baum gave me Larez's contact information, so I called Larez. He and his wife agreed to allow a photographer and me to visit them at their apartment.

Sergeant Larez made a great first impression. He was friendly, polite, soft-spoken and patriotic. I asked him how he felt about the prospect of leaving for Afghanistan either just before or just after his baby was born. He smiled and his eyes lit up as he described his excitement about becoming a father and how much he wanted to see the birth of his first child, but he lost that smile, becoming serious and subdued when he shifted focus to his responsibility to serve our country. He seemed like a great guy. I liked him very much. He appeared to be a loving husband and a proud Marine who was ready and willing to serve.

The Larez baby won the race, but by a nose. Trinity Larez was born on October 18, the day before her father reported for duty. We sent a photographer to the Irving hospital to shoot video of baby, mom, and dad. The next day, Thomas shipped off to Afghanistan.

Two months later, on December 13, one of my competitors at WFAA broke a story about Larez's unexpected return home. Reporter Brett Shipp, a good friend and former KDFW colleague, reported that Larez had found himself on the front lines in a war with the Taliban just four days after Trinity's birth:

> *As a squad leader, he was in charge of escorting Special Operations troops back in from the field. His squad came under fire. Soldiers were wounded. According to an advisory from his commanding officer, Larez was one such casualty. According to the advisory: "His injuries were sustained while saving a friendly soldier, an Army Ranger. Larez took two shots to the upper torso and fragmentations to the upper thigh. He was temporarily blinded following the detonation of a nearby concussion grenade." The advisory goes on to say, "The Sergeant made seven additional kills and was instrumental in the capture of several prisoners." It would be thirty-six more hours before his wife, Pauline, would get word of his fate. Minutes after that, his boss at work got the call. "It shocked me, seriously," said Doug Baum of Bankston Chrysler in Frisco, Larez's employer. "I was really scared for him because his wife called me and she was just crying. She said Thomas was shot three times." The entire staff at Bankston prayed for Larez, never thinking seriously that when he left, he might not return to fill the corner desk office left vacant for him.*
>
> *The desk he sits in right now. Despite all the trauma and close calls, Marine sergeant, faithful employee, and father Thomas Larez is back at work, already trying to live down his hero status. …*
>
> *"I ran out there and was trying to pull [the injured soldier] into a defense perimeter we set up for him," Larez said. "That's what I was trying to do when I got hit." Larez says not only his*

life flashed before his eyes, but his daughter and wife. He says having his daughter back in his arms is an experience worth fighting for. "I think she recognizes me and sleeps on my chest and stuff," he said. "She looks at daddy kinda funny, recognizing my voice and everything." Trinity Larez may now also recognize her daddy's smile, which is hard to forget.

The story left my boss at KDFW, News Director Maria Barrs, very upset and angry because we got beat badly on the story. She called me and said, "You broke the original story about the Marine. Why didn't you know he was back?"

I didn't have a good answer for her. I'd had no reason to believe that Sargeant Larez would be back from Afghanistan so soon. I had thought that if anything had happened to Larez, Baum would call me. I didn't know how else I would have known he was back in town. Barrs told me, "You need to call the guy from the dealership and ask him how Brett found out about Larez's return and why he didn't tell you."

When I called Baum at the dealership, his demeanor surprised me. He sounded upset, sad, and extremely emotional. I asked him, "How's Thomas? Is he OK? I heard he was wounded."

Baum replied, "Steve, I'm very sorry, but I can't talk about it. Chrysler's corporate office asked me not to talk to the media about it." What? Why not? I was very confused. I couldn't understand why Chrysler would ask him not to talk about it. Based on Brett's story, I thought Larez had come back a hero. The situation just didn't make any sense.

I explained to Doug that I cared about Thomas and his wife and that my first concern was his health. That's when Baum got all choked up and said, "My son looked up to Thomas as a role model." I was still confused. I didn't understand the context of his comment and why he was so upset.

After ending our conversation with little information, I called Brett Shipp. "I'm glad you called," said Brett. "We're running a retraction tonight. When I asked why, Brett explained, "I called Thomas's commanding officer at the reserve base in Shreveport today. He told me he didn't write the advisory that Larez showed me yesterday. It was contrived."

I couldn't believe what I was hearing. "You mean Thomas lied about the letter? But if his commanding officer didn't write it, then who did?" I asked.

That's when Brett dropped an even bigger bombshell. "Steve, Thomas was never called to active duty."

All I could say was "Oh my God, oh my God, oh my God." I was flabbergasted. "Are you saying Thomas's entire story was one big lie and he never went to Afghanistan?" I asked in bewilderment.

"Exactly," said Brett.

It got even worse. Brett explained, "Larez's wife received a fake phone call from someone claiming to be with the Red Cross, to let her know her husband had been wounded."

I had so many unsettling questions: How could a man I thought so highly of have been so completely dishonest and deceitful? It seemed like the only truth in this entire story was about his wife having a baby. That would have been a tough one to pull off!

That night, WFAA ran the following retraction:

> *Channel Eight News regrets to report tonight that we must issue a retraction on what many considered a very touching and inspirational story we aired Wednesday night. It was the story of Marine Sergeant Thomas Larez of Dallas who left behind his wife and newborn child to go serve his country, we were told in Afghanistan. We quoted from what appeared to be a Marine advisory, of how the sergeant was injured trying to rescue a fellow soldier. Of how he heroically killed and helped capture enemy soldiers. And finally, we reported of his return to work and to his family. We have now learned from his Marine commander that the story and document was contrived. That Larez, in fact, never left the country and his whereabouts for nearly two months were unknown. Thomas Larez has been dismissed from his job for misleading his*

employer, and his Marine commander says he faces possible disciplinary actions. When contacted for a comment on this story, Larez declined to apologize and would say only that he couldn't believe that it went this far.

I called my boss to update her. When I told Maria about Larez's big lie, she seemed a little more understanding and less upset about missing the story. We also ran a short blurb on our newscast that night, updating our viewers about the bizarre turn of events.

When we went to Larez's apartment to confront him, he cracked the door open about an inch and said, "I'm sorry, I'm not at liberty to talk about it." No one could provide the answers to all the disturbing questions surrounding Sergeant Larez's actions: *Where did he go during his two-month hiatus? Was there another woman? Why would he leave the day after the baby's birth?* All of those questions remain unanswered today.

Thomas Larez lied to a long list of people, including his wife, the United States Marine Corps, his employer, his community, Brett Shipp, and me. All of us fell for his story. It was all too good to be true. Obviously, I misread him more than anyone else I had ever met. At first, I had liked him, respected him, and trusted him. I hadn't seen anything whatsoever that would lead me to believe he wasn't honest, sincere, and a man of integrity. Who would? Who would doubt a proud and patriotic US Marine who was preparing to go fight for our country on foreign soil? I pondered one question over and over again: If I couldn't trust Sergeant Thomas Larez, then who in this world could I trust? His one big lie rocked the foundation of my faith in people.

XIII.

What a Disaster

From the comfort of my living room, I turned the TV on to watch game three of the "Battle of the Bay" World Series, between the San Francisco Giants and the Oakland A's at Candlestick Park. At 5:04 p.m. on October 17, 1989, the stadium began to shake. Al Michaels, sitting in the broadcast booth, knew exactly what was happening. "I'll tell you what, we're having an earthquake," he said as the signal from the stadium flickered off the air.

I couldn't believe what I was watching. The earthquake had lasted only fifteen seconds, yet the Goodyear blimp, which had been flying above Candlestick and had headed toward San Francisco's Marina District after the earthquake, showed the collapse of multi-story homes there. The Marina District was built on a landfill; with no bedrock, the ground had liquefied during the earthquake, causing their buildings' collapse. The terrifying scenes shown live from the blimp got worse, though: A portion of the upper deck of the Bay Bridge came crashing down onto the lower level, killing one person. The upper level of the Nimitz Freeway collapsed onto the lower level, crushing cars and killing forty-two people. When the dust settled, the magnitude-6.9 earthquake had left sixty-seven people dead, 3,000 injured, and more than $5 billion in damage. It was one of the most powerful and destructive earthquakes to ever hit a populated area in the United States.

I stayed glued to my television. I had tuned in to watch a baseball game and instead was seeing fires, demolished buildings, and collapsed bridges. The assignment editor called as I was watching the continuing coverage and said, "We're sending you to San Francisco," he said, inducing that familiar queasy feeling in the pit of my stomach. As I had watched the devastation, the furthest thing from my mind had been the possibility that I would be there, in San Francisco, covering the earthquake.

A photographer and I flew in to San Francisco the next morning. It was my first experience covering an earthquake. As we drove from the airport through downtown San Francisco, I was surprised that everything looked so normal; we didn't see any obvious signs of damage. Then, we arrived at the Marina District. The first thing I saw was several multi-story buildings that looked like the ground floor had disappeared and now the second floor was at ground level. Everywhere we looked, we could see giant cracks permeating buildings. We could also smell the odor from leaking gas lines. We came across some volunteers from the San Francisco Society for the Prevention of Cruelty to Animals, who were going door to door, searching for pets that had survived the earthquake. We interviewed a few of them, along with some homeowners who were forbidden from going back into their damaged homes to retrieve belongings because engineers had deemed the structures unstable and unsafe.

On our first day covering the earthquake, we almost missed our deadline. It was a miracle our stories got on the air. Our station had sent three crews to San Francisco. All three crews couldn't write and edit stories in one satellite truck, so my fellow reporter Stephanie Lucero and I worked out of another station's truck.

Once we finished editing our stories, Stephanie, a photographer, and I took a cab to our live location a few miles away in the Marina District. Our destination: another station's satellite truck, where we would electronically feed our stories back to Dallas. What we didn't anticipate was our cab getting stuck in total gridlock. Our deadline to feed tape was rapidly approaching. We didn't have time to sit in traffic any longer, so the photographer got out of the car, clutching the videotape that had our stories on it. He started running at full speed to the satellite truck.

Doing a live shot for KDFW in San Francisco's Marina District one year after the 1989 Loma Prieta Earthquake. October 1990.

Finally, traffic started to move. By the time Stephanie and I arrived at the satellite truck, our stories had been fed to the station. Less than five minutes later, we were live from San Francisco. When the anchors tossed it to me, I described the heavy damage that viewers were seeing behind me. I then introduced the taped portion of my story. "Here in the Marina District, residents are desperate to retrieve their belongings from their damaged homes, but many of them aren't allowed inside."

The technical director in the Dallas control room punched up the taped portion of my story on the air, but something was terribly wrong. In my earpiece, all I heard was hooting and hollering. I swear I heard someone yell, "Hook 'em, Horns!" I had no idea what was happening, but the portion of my taped story did not air. They came back to me live, and I told viewers we were having technical issues and would have the story for them later in the newscast.

I was furious. Once Stephanie finished her live shot, I asked the associate producer for an explanation about what had happened with the tape. When my photographer had fed the story from the satellite truck, the videotape operator in Dallas had recorded it onto a tape that had raw video from a street party before the annual Texas–Oklahoma game. The associate producer explained that the videotape operator hadn't rewound the tape, so instead of viewers seeing my earthquake story, they had watched fans from the University of Oklahoma and the University of Texas scream at each other. To say I was pissed off would be an understatement.

My photographer asked me what had happened. Although I wasn't live on the air anymore, our signal was still up in the newsroom, so everyone back at the station could still see me and hear every word I said. I think I still had steam coming out of my ears. "They didn't rewind the tape. Can you believe it? They didn't rewind the tape. We've got some really intelligent people back there in Dallas. Thanks, guys. I appreciate your support," I said angrily.

The engineer in the truck came out and said, "Steve, you have a call. Can you come inside?"

The caller was Jim Reed, the station's news operations manager. "Steve, you better be careful what you say when you're off the air," he warned me. "We had you punched up all over the station, and the news director heard what you said."

Still upset, I said, "Good, Jim. I want him to hear me. Maybe he will do something about these stupid mistakes."

When I returned to Dallas a few days later, Jim came up to me and said, "I want to show you something."

He pushed a videotape into a VCR and hit play. It was a recording of my outburst by the bay. The incensed look on my face captured my anger and frustration. We both laughed about it. From that day forward, I kept my emotions in check while in front of the camera, even if I was off the air.

After a crazy, chaotic day, all the photographers and reporters from our station needed rest. We found a hotel room at a Holiday Inn in Belmont, California. The hotel manager had placed a note under the door of every guest room:

> *Thank you for staying at the Holiday Inn of Belmont. I am sure all of you are aware of the natural disaster that took place on Tuesday, October 17th. The earthquake measured 6.9 on the Richter scale and caused considerable damage to the property. Unfortunately, a tragedy such as this can never be predicted and may cause inconveniences to our guests. At times, we may experience water shortages, electrical, plumbing, heating and air conditioning problems and particularly in our case, the lack of complete food and beverage facilities. Please bear with us during these difficult times.*

With all those issues, why would we want to stay there? We had to be on the other side of the bay in Oakland early in the morning, and this would give us a place to sleep for a few hours without wasting time looking for another hotel. Thankfully, the beds were still intact.

My brother Ray had lived in the San Francisco Bay area for many years and had experienced numerous minor earthquakes and tremors. Crazy as it may sound, I wanted to feel an aftershock for myself—just not a big one!

The San Francisco earthquake produced hundreds of aftershocks. One of them came as we were nervously driving across a bridge on our way to the collapsed section of the Nimitz Freeway in Oakland for our morning live shots. As we drove across the San Mateo-Hayward Bridge, high above the bay, we listened to an all-news radio station doing continuous coverage of the earthquake. The anchor suddenly paused. "Do you feel that? We're having an aftershock. It's a big one." I held on to the armrest and dashboard, bracing for the worst, but we didn't feel anything. In the four days we spent in the Bay Area covering the earthquake, we never felt a single aftershock.

I also wouldn't feel the earth move in New Madrid, Missouri, two years later. Climatologist Iben Browning created quite a stir predicting a major earthquake on the New Madrid fault, which stretches from Arkansas through Missouri to Illinois. New Madrid had been the epicenter of one of the most devastating earthquakes ever recorded in North America 179 years earlier, and according to Browning's calculations, the area had a 50-50 chance of being the epicenter of a destructive earthquake within forty-eight hours of December 3, 1990.

Browning's previous predictions based on tidal patters and gravity gave him credibility. He had warned of the San Francisco quake one week before it hit. He had predicted the eruption of Mount St. Helens in 1980. Geologists argued his calculations lacked scientific basis, but that didn't stop people who lived along the New Madrid fault from fleeing the area. Some left a month before the date of his prediction.

I began a series of live reports in Memphis, Tennessee, at the southern end of the fault. My photographer and I then drove north through Arkansas and finally to New Madrid, Missouri. Dozens of satellite trucks converged on a parking lot in the heart of New Madrid. In the business, these large gatherings are known as satellite cities. This was likely the first time in history a satellite city had formed based on a mere prediction of disaster.

Doing a live shot on Beale Street in Memphis on the New Madrid. KDFW, 1990.

Vendors sold souvenir t-shirts. The front of the shirts read, "Should I stay or should I go?" The back said either "I'm staying" or "I'm leaving." I bought an "I'm staying" shirt. I had no choice; I had been sent there to cover the earthquake.

Most locals in New Madrid took Browning's prediction as nothing more than a wild prognostication, welcoming the news media and appearing genuinely happy to have us visiting their town. Not everyone felt so welcoming, however. Some resented all the attention. They shouted, "Go home!" and "Leave us alone!" when they saw us doing interviews or live shots.

The photographer and I stayed overnight in a little motel in Sikeston, Missouri, because there were no rooms available in New Madrid; unlike after real disasters with no warning, the news media had been able to book rooms close to the would-be epicenter weeks in advance. As I got ready to go to bed that night, I looked around my motel room and outside the window at the balcony outside the window. What if Browning was right and we had a major earthquake? No one in their right mind would want to stay on the second floor of this tiny motel when the big one actually happened. It was insane how media people were flocking to the area on the chance there would be an earthquake to report, even though everyone knew it was only a prediction. As for the locals, those who believed it could actually happen had left and those who assumed it could never happen had stayed home.

My coverage of the earthquake that never happened ended abruptly, when I and the photographer were sent to Arkansas to cover the arrest of two men accused of murdering a North Texas girl. Once again, everything changed in a heartbeat, a recurring theme in the news business.

One thing that always bothered me about covering disasters was when we took risks for the sake of enhancing our coverage. We made decisions based on getting a good shot or perspective, without thinking about our own safety. In August 1995, ten years before Hurricane Katrina left much of New Orleans underwater, another hurricane,

Erin, headed directly toward New Orleans as a Category 2 storm with winds up to one hundred miles per hour. Doomsday scenarios predicting what would happen to New Orleans if it took a direct hit were well documented. Almost half of the city, which is built on a delta marsh, sits below sea level. New Orleans is surrounded by the Mississippi River, Lake Pontchartrain, and Lake Borgne. Earthen levees built along the Mississippi were designed to prevent damage caused by seasonal flooding. The fear was that a storm surge caused by a hurricane would cause levees to collapse and flood the city.

Hurricane Katrina would prove that theory in 2005, but Erin would not deliver that devastating blow. The night before Erin's landfall, the giant storm took a turn to the northeast. A photographer, field producer and I flew into New Orleans the next morning, knowing it would slam into the Florida panhandle near Pensacola. We rented a sport utility vehicle and drove east on Interstate 10 toward the hurricane. As we crossed from Louisiana into Alabama, traffic became snarled on the opposite side of I-10. Hordes of coastal residents were evacuating before Erin's wrath came ashore. What's wrong with this picture? We were the only car heading east, toward the powerful hurricane. As we drove through Alabama and into the Florida panhandle, sheets of rain blew sideways across the road.

When Erin made landfall, we were driving directly into her violent winds. Construction barrels and other debris flew through the air. Tall pine trees on both sides of the interstate swayed and bowed. After several large branches snapped off the trees and blew into the roadway, we took cover under an overpass.

"Let's shoot a standup," said the photographer, not wanting to miss a golden opportunity for drama.

We got out of the car, and he stood in front of a thick concrete pylon that protected him from Erin's tenacious winds while I spoke. "I'm standing in the middle of Hurricane Erin," I said as the wind almost blew me down. I moved my feet apart and used my free hand to counterbalance against the wind in a failed attempt to steady myself. "Winds are gusting up to one hundred miles per hour." The wind howled.

Waterlogged and windblown a bit later, we climbed back into the SUV. I called the station on my cell phone to update them on our progress. They asked me to do a live phone report, and I opened the car window so they could hear the sounds of the hurricane. "Listen to the powerful force of Erin's winds," I said. "We can see debris flying by and branches snapping off trees." When I stopped talking, I expected the anchor to ask me a question, but I didn't hear anything. The call had dropped. I tried to call the station back, but I couldn't get through.

We had no business being on that interstate in the middle of a hurricane. It was extremely dangerous. We stayed under the overpass until Erin's violent fury turned into the dead calm of the eye of the storm. It gave us a brief opportunity to move further east, carefully maneuvering around debris on the highway. The eye's placid weather wasn't going to last long, however, so we pulled into a rest stop and took cover inside a concrete building. Within minutes, the violent weather returned with a vengeance. The hurricane wall located behind the eye packs the most powerful punch, with the storm's strongest winds and heaviest rain. As we hunkered down inside the building, we heard the wind howling as it gusted to 150 miles per hour. We rode the storm out anxiously in that small shelter. The building seemed sturdy but didn't steady our nerves. We backed away from the windows, fearing debris could break through the glass. Once again, we were risking our lives for our beloved employer.

Once the worst was over, we hit the road again, heading for Pensacola, which, we heard on the radio, had suffered extensive damage. Once we were there, the devastation became apparent. We shot video of the damage and did a few interviews with storm victims. We then rendezvoused with an engineer in our satellite truck, where we wrote and edited our stories.

After our ten o'clock live shot, the executive producer called and said he wanted us live on the morning newscast, beginning at five a.m. We desperately wanted to find a hotel where we could get a few hours' rest. We drove to several hotels, but none of them had available rooms because locals who lived along the coast had evacuated their homes and taken shelter at inland hotels. One hotel clerk told us the closest hotels with available rooms were in Mobile, Alabama, an hour away. If we drove to Mobile and back to Pensacola, we would only have two hours to sleep. It wasn't worth it, so we decided to stay in Pensacola and sleep in the car. None of us could fall asleep, though. It left us fatigued, grumpy, and ready to go home, a typical consequence of covering disasters.

A huge oil spill in the Gulf of Mexico created another strange set of circumstances and one pressing question: How do you cover an oil spill fifty miles offshore if you don't have a boat or helicopter? On June 8, 1990, an explosion rocked the Norwegian oil tanker *Mega Borg*. The ship burst into flames and began leaking more than four a half million gallons of oil into the Gulf. It took several days for the oil to reach the shore at Galveston Island. There was little for us to shoot in Galveston, where we were sent. We had to rely on video from other television stations that sent their helicopters over the Gulf to the scene of the spill.

Two days after the first explosion, five more blasts rocked the *Mega Borg*, increasing the flow of oil from the tanker into the water. Fortunately, the light crude spilling from the tanker evaporated much more quickly than heavy crude spills like that of the *Exxon Valdez* in Alaska. Light crude is less likely to cause environmental damage to beaches and wildlife. In contrast, however, the *Mega Borg* carried more oil than the *Exxon Valdez;* Environmentalists feared the oil would not evaporate if the slick became too thick.

The Texas Water Commission held several daily press conferences to update the public on the situation. Other than that, there weren't many video opportunities, which was very frustrating. We drove along the beach in Galveston, looking for oil washed up on the shore. We found several large tar balls, but assuming that they had come from the *Mega Borg* would likely be bad. We shot video of the tar but didn't use it. Several other stations shot video of the same tar balls and used it in their stories, even though it wasn't from the supertanker.

The *Mega Borg* fire burned for eight days, making it difficult for firefighters to board the tanker and stop the leak. The oil never reached shore; experts debated whether most of it had evaporated or sunk to the Gulf floor.

Two months later, on July 30, 1990, another oil spill threatened Galveston Bay. A tanker named *Shinoussa* collided with a tug boat pulling three barges toward Houston. Two of the three barges sank in shallow water near the entrance of the Houston Ship Channel. One of the barges, carrying 966,000 gallons of oil, began to leak. Like the *Mega Borg* disaster, the *Shinoussa* spill offered few video opportunities. Once again, the photographer and I didn't have a helicopter or boat to take us to the spewing oil or the slick on the bay. We knew the oil would eventually reach the banks, but we didn't know when. We did our first live report from a pier in Galveston, showing video of cleanup crews loading booms onto boats before heading out to the spill. One of the Houston stations, KTRK, shared its chopper video of the tanker and barges, but it didn't have any shots of oil washing up on shore.

After KDFW's newscast, the five o'clock producer called me. The tone of her voice sounded frustrated and angry. "Why didn't you guys show oil washing up on the beach?" she asked. Honestly, I hadn't heard that oil had washed onto a beach. She said our competitor WFAA had shown video of a bird covered in oil as it lapped up onto the beach. "Why didn't you shoot that?" she asked.

I felt terrible, thinking I had missed a key element that everyone else had in their stories. I walked over to WFAA's satellite truck and asked one of their photographers how they had shot the stirring video of the oiled bird and beach. "We didn't shoot it, KHOU did. They landed their helicopter on Pelican Island in the middle of the bay to shoot it, and then they shared it with us," he said. Armed with this new information, I called the five o'clock producer to explain why WFAA had the money shot but we didn't.

Her reaction wasn't what I'd expected. "I don't know why we sent you down there to cover the oil spill if you can't show us oil," she said.

Out of my own frustration, I responded with some good old-fashioned Steve Stoler sarcasm: "I'll tell you what. If you send us a helicopter, we will fly to Pelican Island to get those same shots. If you send us a barge, we'll float our satellite truck to the island and show you the oil live. But until you do that, I guess we won't have any video of oil or birds."

The spilled oil eventually came ashore that evening and we finally had something to shoot video of, but the whole situation had been a disaster!

XIV.

Mo's Bad Day

On December 17, 1997, I heard five words on the police scanner that sent shivers down my spine: "Hostages at a daycare center." The Rigsbee Development Center was only five minutes from our newsroom. Photographer Tom Quinn and I got there fast and beat our competitors to the scene. As Tom and I arrived, we saw Plano police officers with their guns drawn, taking cover behind their patrol cars. Suddenly, we witnessed an officer running away from the entrance of the daycare. Under each arm, he held a toddler. Their little heads, arms, and legs were flailing as he rushed them out of harm's way. Tom and I didn't know if the kids had escaped or the gunman had released them. Seventy-eight children and five adults were still inside.

We had a front-row seat to this frightening incident, but we had no idea what was happening inside the daycare center. We knew that thirty-three-year-old James Monroe "Mo" Lipscomb had run into the daycare with a gun, but Tom and I didn't know anything about Lipscomb, his mental state, or why he was holding hostages. Like everyone else watching the crisis unfold, we feared the worst.

After talking with some of the parents at the scene, I discovered that Lipscomb's estranged wife worked at the daycare center and their two kids went there. Police eventually released a few minor details and then started negotiating with the hostage taker. As the tense night went on, Lipscomb began releasing the children. By morning, all the children had been freed, except for his own two kids. Finally, after thirty hours, Lipscomb walked out of the building and surrendered to police.

Plano Police kept silent about the intricate details of the standoff to protect their investigation. No surprise there. For nine months, the media and the public could only wonder and speculate how it had all started. It was at Lipscomb's trial when we finally learned the truth. Plano police officer Jeff Rich, the first officer to arrive at Rigsbee, first testified about what had happened before Tom and I had arrived at the scene; until the trial, we hadn't known anything about Rich's close call with the gunman.

Rich testified that he jumped into his car after he had heard an all-points bulletin about a bank robbery, which included a description of the robber's car. As Rich started searching for the car, he heard the dispatcher alert officers about a disturbance at the daycare. The description of the car at the daycare had matched the description of the car involved in the bank robbery. As Rich drove up to Rigsbee, he saw Lipscomb, gun in hand, running toward the front door of the daycare. Rich had yelled, "Stop! Drop the gun!"

Lipscomb had turned toward the officer, raised his gun, and pointed it at Officer Rich. At the same time, Officer Rich had pointed his gun at Lipscomb, yelling again for Lipscomb to stop, but he didn't.

Ironically, Rich had attended a training class a day earlier in which he had undergone high-stress shooting drills. As he held his aim at Lipscomb, he saw a sea of children running toward the front door of the daycare. He had one terrifying thought: What would happen if he missed or the bullet went right through Lipscomb? He knew he couldn't fire his gun and risk hitting a child. He thought Lipscomb was going to kill him, and he was willing to take a bullet or even to die to ensure that no children were hurt. In my book, those are the actions of a true hero.

Rich then made a bold move. He ran straight at Lipscomb, hoping to scare the man or make him miss by closing the distance between them. Lipscomb turned away from Rich and made a run for the entrance. A woman inside frantically tried to lock the door, but Lipscomb pushed her aside and went in. Rich ran after him, but Lipscomb quickly came out the door holding a boy (his stepson) at gunpoint. As Lipscomb held his arm around the child's neck and held a gun to the boy's throat, Rich backed off and took cover behind a tree.

Lipscomb told Rich, "I'll do what I have to do," as Rich pleaded with Lipscomb to let the boy go.

"When he held the kid by the neck with the gun, he was screaming mad," said Rich, who described the horrifying sight for jurors. "I really thought I was going to watch that boy die at Mo's hands. I remember looking down the barrel of my gun, thinking I could take the shot. I needed to move over slightly, but there was a tree that prevented me from moving. If I moved, the tree would block my view, so I was stuck there for the next several hours."

From behind the tree, Rich heard screaming and crying inside the daycare. He used his two-way radio to request more officers. When the dispatcher asked him how many, he replied, "All of them."

As Rich talked with Lipscomb through the door, Lipscomb brought the daycare director, Karen Shannon, into the doorway, holding a pistol to her face. She told Rich, "He doesn't want to hurt anyone. He just wants to see his wife."

Referring to his wife, Lipscomb then told the officer, "Put her out where I can see her," but Rich feared that if he did that, Lipscomb would kill her.

"If you show some give and take, I'll ask my bosses," he told the gunman. Rich convinced Lipscomb to free some of the children. The breathtaking image that Tom and I witnessed of the officer carrying two kids under his arms to safety was part of that first release.

The trial also revealed a possible motive that would help explain Lipscomb's erratic and violent behavior. His estranged wife, Kristen, testified that she and Mo had separated. Kristen had apparently fallen for one of her female coworkers at the daycare and had been contemplating divorcing him to be with her new girlfriend. When Lipscomb had found out about the affair, he had become furious. Kristen had agreed to meet with him at her apartment. Once inside, Lipscomb had pulled out a gun and pointed it at her. He had started crying, accusing her of arranging to have him killed. She had feared for her life. They had talked for a while, and she had convinced him to go with her on a few errands and to pick up the kids from the daycare before continuing their conversation.

Kristin Lipscomb told the jury their first stop was the bank. "Mo" had sat in a chair as she, upset and crying, had talked with a teller. Kristen had jotted down a message to the teller on one of her checks: "He has a gun in the car." As Kristen and Mo left the bank, the teller called 911 and gave the police a description of the car.

Kristen and Mo's next stop was the Rigsbee Child Development Center. On the way there, Lipscomb apologized for pulling a gun on Kristen and made her promise she wouldn't call the police. When Kristen went inside the daycare later, Lipscomb stayed in the car. Kristen told the center's director that she didn't want to put her children in the car with Lipscomb and his gun and asked the director to call the police.

After Kristin Lipscomb's testimony, the judge called a recess and I ran into lead prosecutor Bill Shultz outside the courtroom. He asked about my thoughts on the trial so far. "I'll tell you what, Bill," I said, "Officer Jeff Rich is a freakin' hero. He stood face-to-face with Lipscomb, their guns pointed at each other, and decided not to shoot, fearing his bullets could hit the kids. He was willing to take a bullet and die to protect those kids. He's a hero if I've ever seen one."

Shultz looked at me without showing any reaction and said only one word: "Interesting."

During his closing argument, Shultz told the jury something that sounded very familiar to me. "Officer Jeff Rich is a hero," he said. "He made a conscious decision not to shoot James Monroe Lipscomb, fearing his bullet would harm or kill a child at the daycare. He was willing to take a bullet to protect those kids." I couldn't believe what I was hearing. He had taken my opinion and used it almost verbatim in his closing argument.

When the jury started deliberating, I saw Shultz outside the courtroom again. "Did you hear the part about Officer Rich?" he asked. "I got that from you. Thank you very much."

The jury found Lipscomb guilty and sentenced him to fifty years in prison. The day after the trial, Lipscomb agreed to do an interview with me at the jail. I asked him, "What would you say to the parents of the children you held hostage?"

He looked down at the floor and said, "I would apologize to them. I would tell them I was truly sorry for my actions that caused them great worry and fear. I never intended to harm anyone." When I then asked him why he had bought a gun, he explained how his wife's ex-boyfriend had threatened to kill him. "I bought it to protect myself," he said. We then talked about the encounter with his estranged wife, Kristen, at her apartment. "I showed Kristen my pistol, but I didn't threaten her with it or have any intention of hurting her," Mo told me. In perhaps the biggest understatement of my entire interview with Lipscomb, he described December 17, 1997, as "a bad day that just kept getting worse."

As I left the jail, I couldn't help pondering a plethora of what-if questions about Lipscomb's horrendous decisions that had snowballed out of control that day. Most of those questions centered on his gun: What if he had never bought it? What if he had left it in his car and had never shown it to Kristen? What if she hadn't known it was in the car when he had driven her to the bank? What if he had gotten out of the car at the daycare center without it? What if he had run inside the building without it? Perhaps the situation would not have escalated into a hostage crisis and Lipscomb would not be on his way to prison. Honestly, a part of me actually felt sorry for the guy. Mo's "bad day" cost him at least twenty-four years in prison. His fifty-year sentence will end December 17, 2047. He is eligible for parole in 2022.

After the trial, Officer Rich and I became friends after always running into each other around Plano or at the Collin County Children's Advocacy Center, where he investigated child sexual abuse cases and I did stories. Years after the standoff at Rigsbee, I learned another fascinating fact about it. Rich revealed that he had come much closer to getting shot by Lipscomb than anyone else had ever known. Lipscomb had loaded his inexpensive 9mm Russian pistol with the wrong size of ammo, using .380 bullets instead of 9mm bullets. Rich told me that when Lipscomb got out of the car and pointed his gun at the ground, he had pulled the trigger but the smaller .380 bullet had moved away from the firing pin. Forensic experts who later examined the bullet in the gun's chamber had discovered a strike in the casing and had concluded that when Lipscomb had tried to shoot Rich, the gun's firing pin had missed the primer and hadn't fired.

Looking back on the standoff that almost cost him his life, Officer Rich eloquently told me, "I truly believe God was watching over both Mo and I that day." I couldn't agree with him more.

XV.

Maria and the Mi-T-Fine Massacre

My role in covering a horrific massacre at an Irving, Texas, car wash led to the destruction of the previously good relationship I had with KDFW News Director Maria Barrs.

Twenty-eight-year-old Robert Wayne Harris wanted revenge. His boss at the Mi-T-Fine Car Wash had fired him for exposing himself to two women. Three days after he was let go, Harris showed up at his former workplace with a gun as the car wash opened. He forced the manager, assistant manager, and cashier to lie down in the office and shot each of them in the back of the head. As Harris was about to flee, three other employees arrived for work. He forced them to kneel and shot each of them in the back of the head as well. Only one victim survived.

Harris escaped, prompting an extensive manhunt across North Texas. KDFW wanted me to stay on top of the investigation. "If they're going to arrest Harris, we need to be there," said Maria Barrs. On my way to the police department, I called Officer David Tull, the police spokesperson, again and again, but I kept getting voice mail. With all the local and national media attention on the mass shooting, I doubted I would hear back from him.

When the photographer and I arrived at police headquarters, Officer Tull wasn't in yet. I called the executive producer at KDFW to update him, and he suggested that the photographer and I make a thirty-minute drive to Grand Prairie to talk with William Harris, the shooter's brother. The previous night, William had done an exclusive interview with one of our reporters, claiming he had talked with his brother, Robert Wayne, after the killings, urging him to surrender. The producer of our noon newscast said it would also be a good idea to stop by the car wash, where friends and family of the victims had created a makeshift memorial of flowers, cards, and stuffed animals, so we drove to the car wash and then on to Grand Prairie.

Harris's brother wasn't home.

The noon producer then asked us to do a live shot from the car wash. I was getting very concerned because I wasn't getting any new information and I feared that by not staying at the police department, we were taking a risk. What if the police found Harris? How would we know if we weren't at the police department? We were setting ourselves up for failure. I kept calling Officer Tull but still could not connect with him. I rarely covered Irving, so I didn't have any other sources in the police department who could provide me with new information.

Later that morning, WFAA, one of our competitors, interrupted regular programming with breaking news. Dallas Police had arrested Robert Wayne Harris at a house in northeast Dallas. WFAA was the only station live at the scene as police led a handcuffed Harris into a patrol car. In the extremely competitive Dallas-Fort Worth television market, this was a huge win for WFAA and a big loss for us.

The photographer and I immediately drove to the Irving Police Department, hoping to shoot video of Harris's arrival, but we were too late. I felt absolutely terrible. I hated missing stories. I was usually very good about being where I needed to be to get all the necessary elements for the story. I knew the management team at the station would be looking for answers (and a fall guy), but in this case, I knew I wasn't responsible for missing the arrest. I had followed orders. I had done everything I had been asked to do by the producers.

Soon, one of my fellow reporters called me with a warning: "Maria just called me, and you're next." "She was so pissed off about us missing the arrest, she stomped her feet and cussed out loud in the newsroom when she saw it on Channel 8." I was upset, too. By doing everything management had asked me to do, I had not been in position to get the key element of the story, the arrest of the killer.

When Maria called, she asked, "What happened out there? How did we miss the arrest?" I explained the difficulty I'd had reaching the Irving Police public information officer and how the producers had instructed me and the photographer to visit the car wash and the shooter's brother. "If it were me and I was covering the investigation, I would have kept calling the police constantly until I reached him," she said.

I shouldn't have said anything in response, but her comment made me mad. "Are you pointing fingers, Maria?" I asked. "Because if you are, you should ask yourself another question: Who decided to move us away from the police department? If we would have stayed there, we likely would have known about the arrest."

She fired right back, "Now who's pointing fingers, Steve?"

The call ended right then without any further discussion or resolution. I had a feeling that wouldn't be the end of it.

The next morning, Maria called me into her office. I had a bad feeling. As I walked in, she got up from her desk and shut the door. I could tell by the look on her face she was still angry with me.

She did all the talking and didn't hold back. "When I called you on the phone yesterday, you were downright petulant. Honestly, I didn't want to put you on the story, Steve, because I don't consider you one of our go-to reporters."

Her words were very hurtful. I walked out of her office feeling like she had slapped my face. Later that morning, I was back on the Mi-Ti-Fine story, despite Maria's comments about my reporting ability.

Harris had not only confessed to the car-wash killings but had told police he would lead them to the body of Sandra Gaye Scott of Irving, a woman he claimed he had killed four months earlier. We knew police were going to look for her remains, but we didn't know where. Our helicopter followed Irving police cars to the Trinity River floodplain near Lone Star Park, the horse track in Grand Prairie. The chopper pilot radioed us, saying it looked as if police had discovered a decomposed body next to a ditch. We quickly drove into the Lone Star Park stables area, with a live truck following close behind. To my surprise, a security guard at the entrance let us through.

We set up our live shot on top of the levee overlooking the crime scene. We broke the story twenty-four hours after getting our butts kicked, an excellent example of how life in the news business can turn around. Success can come when you are simply in the right place at the right time. One day earlier, we had been in the wrong place and had gotten caught with our pants down, missing the arrest, but on this day, we were exactly where we needed to be.

Maria's words still hurt, though. After that encounter in her office, I felt awkward and uncomfortable around her. Almost a year later, friend and fellow reporter Jeff Crilley, who knew all about the car-wash debacle and my strained relationship with Maria, told me the station had renewed Maria's contract. Then he gave me some heartfelt advice: "You should go talk with her, Steve. She's not going anywhere. Go in there now and tell her how you feel. It's to your benefit to mend fences. Continuing this bad relationship can only hurt you."

Jeff was entirely right, so I took his advice. I walked straight into Maria's office, asking her if we could talk. I told her that I'd had bad feelings about our relationship since the car-wash shootings. She looked genuinely puzzled. "Refresh my memory," she said. "What happened during the car wash shootings?"

Was she kidding? Did she really have no recollection of the events of that day? I was astounded she didn't remember what had happened, especially because I could not forget. I lived every day knowing that I was working under a supervisor who felt that I was not a good reporter.

I described for Maria all the events that had left our relationship in ruins, including how I had missed the arrest of the Mi-T-Fine killer. I then repeated her exact words: "I don't consider you a go-to reporter." She actually seemed like she had no recollection of the incident. As hard as it was for me to believe, I honestly felt she didn't remember any of it.

"Oh, Steve. If I said that, I didn't mean it. I just told you that to motivate you. I'm fine with you. You do a great job. You see, it worked," she said.

I don't know if I bought her explanation, but I was very happy to put our conflict to rest. Maria hugged me as I walked out of her office. I felt like a tremendous burden had been lifted from my shoulders.

The events surrounding the Mi-Ti-Fine car wash massacre highlight another classic irony provided by the television news business: There we were, covering a terrible tragedy that had left five human beings brutally murdered, and behind the scenes, we seemed to care more about missing a part of the story than about the loss of life. My bruised relationship with Maria was trivial compared to the scope of the killings, but at least I knew what had caused it: the intense competition to cover a big story, and the fragile emotions that accompany it.

XVI.

Presidential Embarrassment

"How would you like to interview, President Bush?" the president of the McKinney Education Foundation Board of Directors asked me. On April 21, 2013, the McKinney Education Foundation was going to be holding its twentieth-anniversary gala in an airplane hangar at the Collin County Regional Airport in McKinney, Texas, and the former president would deliver a keynote speech there, more than three years after his term had ended. His speech would be followed by a sit-down interview, and I would be doing the interview. I thought it would be a great opportunity to have a one-on-one discussion with the former leader of the free world.

The week of the gala, I received a call from Bush's office in Dallas. His communications director said I would receive a list of scripted questions from the office for the interview. She asked that I stick to the scripted questions. Normally, I would have objected. If the interview had been for a news story, I would never have agreed to just ask scripted questions, but in this scenario, I was OK with it because this wasn't journalism. This was for show, and the media wasn't invited to cover the event; the gala was offering the McKinney Education Foundation an opportunity to raise money and giving Bush a chance to promote his new book, *Decision Points*. The questions provided by the Bush team focused on events during his presidency, from the September 11 terrorist attacks to the wars in Iraq and Afghanistan. The list included several questions about the Arab Spring, a series of antigovernment protests, riots, and civil wars in the Arab world.

Emceeing a gala for the Samaritan Inn homeless shelter in McKinney, Texas. After I had served as emcee for eight years, I was put on the board of directors. February 23, 2013 .

With my wife, Susan, and George W. Bush before my presidential embarrassment.

When my wife and I arrived at the hangar for the gala, we were met by an event organizer, who told us President Bush wanted to meet me before the gala started. A Secret Service agent accompanied us to a greenroom set up for Bush in the central part of the hangar. As we walked in, the former president greeted Susan and me with handshakes. He was holding a tablet in his hands and said he was trying to find the score of the Rangers game. He seemed sincere and friendly.

Our conversation turned to the interview, and Bush said he wouldn't answer any questions about President Obama because when he had been president, former president Jimmy Carter had "said some things" that had affected what he had been trying to accomplish in the Middle East.

"I just don't feel a former president should comment on what a sitting president is doing," he said. It wasn't an issue; I didn't have any Obama questions in my prepared list.

The former president asked Susan where she had gone to college. When she replied that she had gone to the University of Texas, he said he would have liked to have gone to UT but had wound up at Yale instead.

Our conversation with Bush lasted twenty minutes. When the event began, we were escorted out of the room. Susan went to one of the tables in the hangar, and I stayed backstage. As Bush was introduced, several Secret Service agents led him out of the greenroom. Just before stepping onto the stage, he turned around and shouted, "Hey Steve! The Rangers are up 4-1."

He started his speech by telling a joke. He discussed life after the presidency, then focused on his new book. He talked about leadership, education, domestic policy, and foreign policy. I glanced down at the first page of my questions. The order of topics: leadership, education, domestic policy, and foreign policy. My questions mirrored the topics in his speech, point after point, issue after issue. It was like he knew the questions I had been given and was answering them, in order, before I was on the stage to ask them. My stress level skyrocketed as I wondered how this could have happened. How could Bush's communications people have given me a list of questions on issues he was going to be discussing throughout his speech? I wasn't sure what to do. I wanted to keep my promise not to go off script.

The former president finished speaking and received a standing ovation. Then I came on stage and we sat next to each other in two large chairs. I started the interview by asking him a few questions about his parents' health and his daughters, Barbara and Jenna. I knew he liked talking about his family; it was safe territory. But then I had to get into the meat of the interview. I skipped some questions and rephrased others, hoping to evoke responses different from the points he had made in his speech.

Whenever he referred to the news media during his presidency, it was in a negative light. Each time, he would pause, look at me, and said, "No offense, Steve." The crowd of 600 people laughed every time.

Finally, the focus of our interview shifted to the Arab Spring, which he had discussed in his speech for about twenty minutes. I asked him a question, and he paused for about three seconds. I could tell by the expression on his face that he was bewildered and searching for a one-liner. Finally, he looked at me and said, "Steve, did you listen to my speech?"

The crowd erupted in exuberant laughter. I felt embarrassed. I wanted to say something that would explain my predicament. "Mr. President, with all respect, your people gave me these questions and asked me not to ask you anything else. I don't understand why they gave me a list of questions that you already answered in your keynote address."

That was my thought, but thank goodness, it's not what I said. McKinney is in Collin County, often described as the most Republican county in the country. The audience revered the former president. If I were to say anything to George W. Bush that could be perceived as rude, disrespectful, or offensive, I would be toast. These people would run me out of the hangar and out of town, so I kept my mouth shut. I swallowed my pride and smiled.

In the next two weeks, that moment came back to haunt me again and again. I kept running into people who had attended the gala. All I kept hearing were "What happened during your interview with Bush?" and "Why did you ask him questions about all the issues he already talked about?" When I told them the story behind the story, they were just as perplexed as I was that his staff would unknowingly allow this to happen.

A few days after my presidential embarrassment, I received a letter from the Office of George W. Bush. Inside was a note.

Dear Steve,

> I enjoyed meeting you and Susan Saturday night. Thank you for sharing the stage with me and your support of the McKinney Education Foundation. Best Wishes to you and your family.

Sincerely, George W. Bush.

These small gestures of appreciation from presidents, former presidents, governors, and many other elected officials serve as an effective PR tool, generating good feelings about politicians, regardless of politics. Recipients can then frame the letters and mount them on the walls of their offices and homes. I'm no different. I framed and mounted my note from Bush. For me, it helped soften the utter embarrassment I had felt the night of the gala. If someone's going to embarrass you in front of a large group of people, it might was well be the former leader of the free world, right?

XVII.

Tales from the Dark Side

"Every day, we met perfect strangers, oftentimes on the worst day of their lives, and we convinced them to do something that most rational people wouldn't ever do: talk to us on camera about that worst moment. That is a skill. We may not be the most educated ones on the block or the smartest guys for the job, but few can match our networking capabilities and the ability to connect with people. That is a skill that you can't teach. You either have it or you don't."

That's how WFAA news reporter Craig Civale eloquently described his skills when interviewing with Baylor Health. After that interview, Civale became the latest addition to a long list of veteran WFAA reporters who had left broadcast journalism for new careers.

These familiar faces from Dallas-Fort Worth television news had seized exceptional opportunities. The Baylor Health System hired Civale as a communications manager. Anchor-reporter Brad Hawkins landed a position as Southwest Airlines spokesman. Anchor-reporter Casey Norton is now director of corporate communications for American Airlines. Reporter Cynthia Vega is a spokeswoman for DFW International Airport. Reporter Chris Hawes is vice president of public relations for Methodist Health System. Anchor-reporter Brad Watson is director of communications for Luminant Energy. Other reporters, such as Mary Ann Razzuk and the late Bert Lozano, left WFAA for global PR firms.

The mass exodus of reporters, all within a two-year period, intrigued me. Around 2014, I asked, why not me? With thirty-four years of experience, perhaps I would find a golden opportunity to take an executive position that paid well.

The television news industry had changed. It wasn't the same business it had been just four years earlier. Similar to businesses in corporate America, television stations have downsized and are finding less-expensive ways to conduct business. When I had come to Dallas in the mid-1980s, television stations had spared no expense. They would send crews anywhere a big story occurred to show local presence. When war broke out in the Persian Gulf or when earthquakes rattled Los Angeles and San Francisco, or when the Berlin Wall came down or a gas explosion devastated Guadalajara, the deep-pocketed stations would send their reporters and photographers, but the economic downturn had forced the industry to cut costs, reevaluate operations, and find new ways to save money. They had become less apt to send their people out of town for big stories. My dear photographer friend Chris Mathis now works for CBS Newspath. Chris and correspondent Don Champion travel across the country to cover the biggest stories. They do live shots for any CBS affiliate that wants the story, allowing local stations to have live presence on big stories without hefty travel expenses. The best part of Newspath is that CBS foots the bill.

The proliferation of social media has also transformed television news. At her first staff meeting as WFAA news director, Carolyn Mungo held up her smartphone and said, "Like it or not, this is how people get their news today. Our challenge is to engage them on this so they'll want to watch our newscasts." Most of us accepted her premise. Social media had created a new world, and we had no choice but to embrace it. Reporters started providing updates on Twitter and Facebook throughout the day. We posted tidbits of information, or "teases," about our stories. It became part of our routine to tweet updates at press conferences, trials, and meetings or as breaking news unfolded. We accepted the change, but many of us didn't like it. We spent more time feeding the social-media beast and less time working on our stories, and that affected the quality of our work.

Social media may help speed up the dissemination of information, but an inherent problem comes with that immediacy: the reporting of

My photographer at WFAA and best friend, Chris Mathis. Chris is now a photojournalist for CBS News. Chris and I always said, "TV news is not rocket science." December 2013.

inaccurate information. Smartphones have created a new genre of citizen journalists who shoot anything they consider newsworthy. They love seeing their videos and pictures on the air, and news departments are eager to use them.

Information travels faster than ever, but with intense competition between media outlets, everyone is in a hurry to be first on the air or web with breaking news. In the mad rush to get the story on the air, facts are not always verified for accuracy. It's reminiscent of what I witnessed during the space shuttle *Columbia* tragedy on February 1, 2003, years before the social-media explosion. The *Columbia* had broken apart above Texas and debris had come crashing down across a wide area. Minutes after the shuttle came down, a raging fire broke out at a Plano apartment complex. Most media outlets made the assumption that a burning piece of debris from *Columbia* had crashed through the roof of an apartment building, staring the fire. Reporters did live shots describing how the debris from the shuttle had likely started the fire.

I had started working at WFAA two months earlier, and the non-compete clause from my KDFW contract prevented me from being on the air. Because I couldn't go on the air, our plan was to show live images from our camera as I relayed information back to the newsroom. I called the news director from the apartment complex.

"Has anyone confirmed that shuttle debris caused the fire?" he asked.

No one had. By then, the Plano fire chief had arrived on the scene but hadn't said anything to reporters.

"We're not putting anything on the air until it's confirmed," said the news director. The other media outlets reported the story based on speculation. WFAA lost the race to get information on the air, the only television station that didn't report the story.

It turned out that we had made the right decision. Thirty minutes after the fire started, the chief came over to brief the reporters. "Our preliminary investigation indicates this fire was the result of an electrical short, and not falling shuttle debris," he said.

Everyone else had made a huge assumption and gotten it wrong, but getting the story right was more important than being first on the air. It wasn't rocket science. It was Journalism 101, where we learned to verify information before reporting it.

Social media only intensified the competition between media outlets to report breaking news first. When big news breaks, social media explodes. Speculation rears its ugly head as news anchors keep telling viewers, "We don't want to speculate." Journalists read Facebook and Twitter posts that reveal new information about the breaking news event; *some* of that information can be accurate, as citizens are often at the scene of a breaking news event before the media arrives. Breaking news creates a desperate rush to get information on the air. Should the media take risks and report information, hoping it's accurate? They do, even though it's a gamble.

That takes me back to the apartment complex fire after the shuttle disaster. WFAA acted responsibly by not reporting information based only on speculation, but in the process of doing so, we likely created the perception that our competitors were a step ahead of us. In the end, we were the only television station without egg on our face, but unfortunately, social media has created an ultracompetitive atmosphere in which getting on the air first often seems more important than getting it right.

The creation of video journalists (VJs), or multimedia journalists (MMJs) have also changed local television news. When I started my career in television news in 1980, reporters in small markets like Macon, Georgia, acted as one-man bands. We shot, wrote, and edited our own stories. That never happened in major markets like Dallas, where, on a typical story, each reporter would go out on assignment with a photographer, who would shoot and edit the story. KDFW and WFAA also had news editors who would assemble the stories electronically. Trained engineers operated all the live trucks.

VJs, however, do everything themselves. Meredith Yeomans is one of six VJs at KXAS. The station supplies her with a camera and laptop. She shoots her own stories, writes them, and then edits them on a laptop. Up until recently, when Meredith went out on a story, she even used her own car and the station would pay for her gas. When the producers want Meredith to do a live shot, she uses a Dejero, which is a transmitter that weighs about fifteen pounds and has straps like a backpack. It uses cellular or Wi-Fi technology to get the signal back to the station. Meredith plugs her camera and microphone into the Dejero, then calls the station to verify that the signal coming in is useable. Meredith then stands in front of her camera, which is mounted on a tripod, to do her live shot.

VJs are usually the youngest reporters on the staff. Many of them have had one other job since graduating college. Don't get me wrong; this doesn't mean they're not good reporters with vast potential. It just means they don't have the same level of experience as veteran reporters who spent years working. Here's an analogy: If you needed surgery to repair a torn ACL, would you prefer a doctor who has been performing the surgery for two years or a veteran surgeon who's been doing it for fifteen years? Veteran reporters have been around the block a few times.

A VJ's quality of work can suffer from his or her overload of responsibilities. Instead of concentrating solely on the content of their stories, VJs have to worry about shooting interviews and video, editing the piece, and then setting up their own live shots. The benefit to the television stations is cost savings. By asking Meredith to use her own car, the station didn't need to buy a new vehicle; by giving her a camera, it eliminated the need for a photographer position; by giving her a laptop, the station has no need for an editor; and by having her do her own live shots with a Dejero, it eliminated the need for an engineer. That's three positions and three salaries the station won't have to pay.

Another cost-cutting move that Dallas television stations had made was to train photographers to run live trucks. Most engineers lost their jobs. The added responsibility left photographers frustrated because running the trucks took their time and focus away from the stories they shot, but they had no choice. In tough economic times, news departments shrank, and so did the quality of the on-air product.

I had to be honest with myself. The explosion of VJs onto the local news landscape left me wondering at what point WFAA would replace a veteran aging reporter like me with a young, less-experienced, and cheaper VJ. I decided that if I was going to leave the business after more than three decades, it would be on my terms, not the station management.

WFAA reporters sign two-year contracts. My contract was set to expire on December 6, 2013. I felt certain WFAA would renew me, and I vowed to stay at WFAA unless I found the perfect opportunity. If not, I would sign another two-year contract.

Still, I was ready for a change. In the next few months, I interviewed for three positions, including one at Atmos Energy and two at local governments.

For years, I had said if I ever left the news business, the one job I would love to get would be doing public relations for the City of Plano. Plano was home, and as the Collin County reporter for two television stations, I had reported more stories from Plano than from any other city. I knew the city leaders well, from the mayor and city council members to the executive team who ran the city and its many departments. Plano City Manager Bruce Glasscock had served as the city's police chief when I had covered Collin County for KDFW and WFAA. Through the years, we had built a strong relationship based on mutual trust and respect. Even when the stories had been controversial or negative, Chief Glasscock would always cooperate with me because he knew I would give him and his department a fair shake. Bruce had moved into city management, and eventually became the top guy.

Bruce called me unexpectedly one day and asked for a favor. Plano had just elected its first African American mayor, Haitian immigrant Harry LaRosiliere. LaRosiliere had been raised in Harlem and had moved to Plano when his wife had gotten a job at Frito-Lay. Bruce told me the mayor could use a quick and informal course on "how to deal with the media," so I invited him to breakfast. We discussed effective ways to craft messages and how to relay those messages to the community by working with the media. The mayor said he had a goal to tell Plano's remarkable story to the entire nation.

His goal stuck with me. Plano did have an incredible story to tell. It had evolved from a small rural farming community of a few thousand people into a hip city of more than 270,000 people, attracting some of the nation's top businesses, such as Toyota, J. C. Penney, Frito-Lay, Liberty Mutual, Hewlett-Packard, FedEx Office, and Dr Pepper Snapple Group.

After my meeting with Mayor LaRosiliere, I called Bruce and asked him to have breakfast with me. We went to Little Gus, a funky little Greek diner in town. Midway through our scrambled eggs and toast, I got down to business. I told Bruce about my meeting with the mayor, who had shared his visionary goal. I told Bruce I knew the perfect person to tell Plano's amazing story to the world: me. He laughed, but he seemed very interested in my suggestion. We met two more times for breakfast at Little Gus. On the third meeting, he offered me a fabulous opportunity. He wanted to create a Media Relations Department and make me its director. I would serve as the city's spokesperson and liaison between the city and the news media. This was it, the perfect opportunity I had been looking for.

When a journalist shifts his or her career to public relations, people in the news business jokingly call it "moving to the dark side." After more than two years on the dark side, I couldn't be happier. I love my job. It involves so much more than working with the news media. I have helped promote a major music festival. I have played a role in developing a water-conservation campaign. I plan press conferences. I write position papers. I have even produced and written a documentary about the development accomplishments of Ross Perot and Ross Perot Jr. I truly believe I have found the perfect job.

News departments at television stations are like extended families, and I miss my friends and former colleagues in the business. Fortunately, I still see many of them when they do stories in Plano, but I don't miss the television news business. After thirty-four years of reporting, anchoring, and producing, I feel like I did it all and left on my own terms. I feel great joy and relief when I think that I won't have to do certain aspects of my former career ever again. At the top of that list is interviewing victims' family members after tragedies. Without exception, this is the worst part of any reporter's job. In any newsroom, reporters have an expectation of talking with people affected by tragedy or personal loss. I get that, but walking up to the front door of a house of someone who has lost a loved one only hours or days before always gave me an uncomfortable, nauseated feeling. I hated doing it each and every time.

Many people think reporters are callous and insensitive, but that's completely untrue. There is a right way and a wrong way to approach people, especially those who have just suffered a loss. Compassion, sensitivity and sincerity go a long way in convincing a person to talk with you about a loss. I once covered a mobile-home fire in rural Collin County. A young mother had lost her child in the fire. She was devastated. The last thing I wanted to do was approach her and ask her if she would talk with me on camera. Surprisingly, however, she walked up to me and started talking with me about her daughter. I put my arm on her shoulder and told her how sorry I was about what had happened, and she opened up to me.

She had no insurance, and she had lost her child and everything she owned. I knew she desperately needed help. I told her that our viewers were very giving and often lent a helping hand to people who needed help. I asked her if she would tell us about her daughter for our story. To my amazement, she said yes. She tearfully and lovingly described her little girl. After the interview, I hugged her.

As I had expected, once the story aired, the newsroom phones lit up with calls from viewers who wanted to know how they could help this woman.

I don't miss covering funerals, either. Some funerals are fair game for coverage. For example, if police officers, firefighters, elected officials, celebrities, or civic leaders die, the public expects media coverage. Family members often invite the media to cover funerals in high-profile deaths. But in other cases, however, families prefer to mourn their loved ones privately and don't want the media there. Those were the funerals I despised covering. Those families deserved privacy when grieving their loss, but all too often, our news managers sent us anyway. We would find an area across from the church or funeral home so we could shoot video, but I felt like a vulture. I wanted to be anywhere else but there. We weren't welcome, but we were there anyway. At one funeral I covered, someone shouted, "Isn't anything private anymore?" It made me cringe.

Covering severe weather always provided an adrenaline rush, and not always in a good way. I can't count the number of times we would chase severe thunderstorms. Some thunderstorms travel fifty to sixty miles per hour. We would find ourselves driving into treacherous conditions with heavy rain, high winds, and hail. One time, my photographer was shooting video while driving on an interstate in the middle of a severe storm as I held onto the steering wheel. It was insanity.

And of course, I don't miss standing on an overpass or beside an interstate during a North Texas ice storm. When winter weather came, we would usually start our morning newscast an hour early. We would have to be in place at four a.m. and do live shots throughout the newscast. We would do the winter-weather live shots from wide-open locations where we could see an assortment of visuals, all while exposed to freezing temperatures, falling ice, and high winds. No matter how many layers I wore, I would freeze my butt off. Every time I would try to warm up inside the van or car, I would hear that familiar voice in my earpiece, saying, "Steve, we need you back in front of the camera. We're coming to you live again." On one live shot, I used a napkin to illustrate how cold it was. The napkin got wet and froze. It was rock-solid.

In my new role as media relations director, I drive to the City of Plano's Emergency Operations Center (EOC) when potentially hazardous winter weather moves in. It's only two miles from my house. I send updates to the media about weather and road conditions or any other information that needs to get out. During the most recent ice storm, I sat in the warmth and comfort of the EOC and watched all those cold TV reporters doing their live shots. The Plano police chief asked me if I missed being out there. "Are you kidding me?" I said. "Hell no. This is wonderful. I'm warm and cozy and I don't have icicles forming on the tip of my nose."

Another facet of the news business I don't miss is the stress and challenge of coming up with story ideas every day. I got pretty good at it. At times, I would pitch several good ideas and the management team would assign a story or two to other reporters, but there were also times when finding fresh ideas seemed impossible. We had to be creative. I would go through my daily ritual of checking e-mail, calling sources, and surfing the web to look for ideas, but I often found myself asking, "What the heck am I going to pitch today?" I always came up with something, even though I always knew when the story was a dud. I would pitch it and hear crickets from the producers and managers in the morning meeting.

I wasn't the best reporter at KDFW or at WFAA. The in-your-face approach that investigative reporters built their reputations on wasn't my style. I confronted people when necessary, but my forte was communication. I tried to treat people fairly, no matter what side of a story they were on. I built relationships based on honesty, sincerity, and ethics, and my style worked for me throughout my career. I knew that if I held true to my personal standards, I could persuade almost anyone to talk with me, regardless of the situation. If they trusted me and felt at ease, they would be more apt to open up with me in an interview. I built a reputation in the community based on trust, respect, objectivity, and fairness. My sources knew me as a person first and journalist second. I made many friends along the way. They would talk openly with me, and pass on tips for possible stories. They knew I wouldn't burn them. Challenges did accompany my style of reporting, however. News managers often perceived me more as a nice guy than as a hard-nosed journalist. They saw the end product but never accompanied us in the field, so they didn't witness how I communicated with people.

Former *Dallas Morning News* media critic Ed Bark included me on his top-ten list of "underpraised, in-the-trenches D-FW television news veterans." In Bark's words, "We're talking about the trusty Basset hounds of D-FW television, those durable sniffers whose beats are the streets. Some have spent more than two decades as dogged general assignment reporters."

Bark's comments were flattering, but the greatest tribute of my long career wasn't a columnist's praise or even an Emmy Award. It was in the heartfelt words of a beloved friend and colleague, photographer John Gnann. John and I had worked as a team at KDFW's Collin County newsroom. When I left KDFW for WFAA, he wrote me a touching note that served as an affirmation of my journalistic approach and who I strive to be as a human being.

Dear Steve,

I have learned two very important things that I will use the rest of my career. This is what I learned from working with you. From your work ethic I have learned to never slack off. To take the assigned story and make the absolute most of it even when it may be a dud. You inspired me to do my best at work despite any outside adversity.

More importantly, you taught me that this job could be done respectfully and with decency always. There is no other reporter I have ever worked with that I would rather walk into a widowed parent's home and talk them into an interview or just a photo. Even in something as simple as an MOS [man-on-the-street interview] you always approach people with respect. If there were more people like you in this business Don Henley would never have been able to write "Dirty Laundry." You don't deal in crap, and that defines who you are.

Many times you have heard people describe someone as a "fine Christian person." Their ignorance notwithstanding, I am sure that some of those same people describe you as a "fine Christian man." People see your decency, honesty, love for your family, and kind nature and they admire you. They put those qualities into a context they can understand and an ideal that they themselves try to achieve. In code they are almost saying, "You will like this person because they have the same values you do." But your character transcends religion. Your humanity is what others and I truly admire.

It has been an honor to work with you and to call you my friend.

With sincerity and love,

John Gnann

About the Author

Steve Stoler is a veteran Emmy Award winning television news reporter, whose career spanned more than three decades at six television stations in Georgia, Nebraska, North Carolina and Texas. Steve's assignments ranged from covering Texas politics as a legislative correspondent to serving as an environmental reporter. Steve covered almost every type of news story imaginable, from major disasters including tornados, hurricanes, earthquakes gas explosions and oil spills to high-profile murder trials and dramatic hostage situations. He is one of the only journalists in Texas to witness multiple executions. Throughout his career, Steve became an eyewitness to history. He interviewed presidents and governors. He stood on a ladder in a Midland, Texas backyard, when rescuers pulled toddler Jessica McClure out of a well after 58 hours. He covered the Branch Davidian standoff near Waco, Texas. He was one of the first reporters on the scene in West, Texas after a fertilizer plant exploded. After 34 years in TV news, Steve moved on to the "other side" of the communications world, or as his former news media friends call it, the "dark side." In December, 2013, he joined the City of Plano, Texas as Director of Media Relations. His extensive experience in broadcast journalism and media relations give him a unique perspective on working effectively with the media. Steve developed several media training courses and is a highly sought after speaker at state and national conferences. Steve serves on a variety of nonprofit boards and lives in Plano, Texas with his wife, Susan and two sons, Jordan and Jake.

CPSIA information can be obtained
at www.ICGtesting.com
Printed in the USA
FFOW03n2307140317
33497FF

9 781457 549397

1
MELISA KEENAN

WHEN THE WORLD FORGETS THAT YOU'RE A LITTLE PRINCESS

S**ometimes the world can feel like a big scary place.** My inner child is very quick to remind me how absolutely terrifying everything can be. Particularly when writing this story, there were moments when I felt like I was suffocating and perhaps I might not live if I actually shared this story. Which is why I knew it had to be shared. When women and girls go through sexual trauma, because of the Patriarchy, because of the Death Mother, because for some reason we are always to blame, we are the ones who carry all the shame. But, as Brene Brown always says from her decades of research on shame, "Shame can't stand having word wrapped around it." And so, I share this story with you today, my Sacred Silver Lining, to tell my inner child that she did nothing wrong. To free her from the misplaced guilt and the trauma that she no longer needs to carry about this event.

So as I was saying, the world is scary. And she, little Melisa, is always there to remind me how in a moment every single thing could change, everything that is wonderful about my life's current set of circumstances could blow up or disintegrate into the wind. How my health, my home, my family, my children, my marriage could all come crashing down. Change is inevitable. Everything is fragile. Everything is dangerous; the labels on the food at the grocery store with their preservatives and chemicals, the carcinogens in our products, in our water, and in the air we breathe. Just putting myself onto the freeway every day watching all the almost-accidents, that with one split hair's difference could have been disastrous, is a reminder that I personally am not in control of my life. And perhaps, therefore, I should be completely terrified and possibly live under a rock, which truth be told, crosses my mind really often. This might surprise you because as I write this, I am the CEO of a company with around a hundred clients at any given time while also following the inner nudge to take my kids out of school and homeschool them. I've also endured tremendous trauma, I've told my story on stages far and wide, and I'm an intimacy expert, which means I have openly and publicly talked about sex for the last five years with people who still think that should never be talked about. I might be one of the most courageous people I know.

That is because my inner child is also quick to remind me how magical this life, this world, this breath, and even each moment truly is. She is my anchor to play, she is the one who reminds me to take my shoes off and dig my toes into the sand, to get muddy, and to play hard. She reminds me to get down with my kids when their eyes sparkle, to freak out with them about their cool discoveries, and to snort like a pig/horse and gallop around the house like the proudest stage dancer when it's time to be wild and weird, rolling and laughing uncontrollably until my cheeks hurt and I'm crying and my abs are cramping. She reminds me to raise my hands in praise to God and open my arms out wide to life, to love, and to all the amazing things that this world has to offer. She's the one who nudges me to live bigger, love deeper, give more, bleed more, connect more, and let my heart feel more. And when something feels scary, but equally like the fire that is pulling me toward it, we go hand in hand straight into the fire. Because we know that living under the rock was never actually what we wanted to do. She might be one of the most courageous kids I know.

So here we go. I will start by telling you Sarah's story first because it is so special to me. And then, I will tell you mine.

A Little Princess is one of my absolute favorite movies. Do you know it? It's a classic tale of a little girl named Sarah whose mother has died, but who has a very close and tender relationship with her father, a successful international businessman who dotes on Sarah, his "little princess." In the story, she is sent to an all-girls schoolhouse to live in America while her father goes back to England to fight in WW1. Tragically it is discovered that her father has died and didn't take care of any of his future planning, leaving Sarah penniless. The schoolmaster chooses to sell all her things but keep her in the attic as a maid, as a charity to Sarah. Throughout the film, Sarah shows tremendous courage and devotion to her belief in herself as a true princess, the beautiful worth that her father instilled in her becomes a beacon of resiliency as she endures tremendous hardship, abandonment, neglect, and even abuse from the schoolmaster. She believes in her reality so much that magical things begin to happen and one day, after believing she would never see her father again, fate brings him to the home immediately next door to her orphanage where he is now healing from amnesia from the war. He wasn't dead after all. In the most intense part of the entire film, Sarah flees to this neighbor's house, running from the cops who have come to take her away. Hiding in the shadows, she sees her father. She is stunned but immediately cries out to him, begging him to remember who she is. Just before she is shipped away to jail, he remembers. He shouts her name and in one of the most tender moments ever caught on camera, she leaps into his arms, patting his face and touching every part of him in disbelief and complete relief that he is real. They cry and hug and kiss at the absolute miracle of it. Reunited at last.

I cry every single time. This is exactly how my daddy treated me and made me feel; I was a little princess, his little princess, barefooted running through the desert catching horney toads and rolly-pollies, but a princess nonetheless. He would say, "Hey, Melisa! Are you happy? Are you having fun?" right in the middle of something exciting, like running out to get candy at the parade, or riding in the boat and him letting me drive—he loved to see me happy. He would say, "My Melisa," as he carried me to bed at night from the spot I had fallen asleep on the couch. He would tuck me in tight with the covers and pray with me, or read to me, or bring me Coca-Cola because I had him wrapped around my finger in every way. It was amazing to be so cherished, so delighted in, by my daddy.

Except unlike Sarah in A Little Princess, when I watched my daddy die on his hospital bed in the middle of our living room floor from cancer, at only twelve years old, there was no getting him back. And so I watch this movie and think of the day when I will get to run into his arms again.

* * *

I was only seven years old. We had gone to San Diego, my momma and I, to visit her sister and spend a couple of weeks on the beach, a regular summer experience that I could remember us enjoying often. Except this time Daddy didn't come, he had too much work to do. Daddy ran his own business, Click Refrigeration, "Click" was our last name. I wasn't surprised he couldn't come with us; Daddy was a workaholic. I didn't really know what that word meant but everyone in the family called him that, and I knew it had something to do with the fact that he was always working, including often missing our family dinners and sometimes even working at 2 o'clock in the morning. He also did a lot of street drugs to maintain his erratic schedule, but I wouldn't find out about any of that until years later. He would be gone for days as he traveled to neighboring towns and cities for work. He would say, "The restaurant needs me to fix their ice machine and AC when no customers are there." Made sense to me. But Mommy seemed kind of forlorn and sad about it. She always was, when he didn't prioritize family time over work time. So we took our family vacation without him.

One day, just Mommy and I were sitting on one of our favorite beaches together. She loves to watch the waves and seagulls and walk along to collect seashells—it was something I learned to love as well.

She taught me healthy love and respect for the ocean and its salty waves. The ocean was her special place, so it became *our* special place. On this day, it was mildly busy on the beach, with perfect beachy weather. People were out milling all over the beach, grown-ups and kids alike. It was the 90s and there was lots of frizzy poofy hair and spandex going on, and as a matter of fact, my mom and I both with our dark brunette hair and pale skin sported long-haired perms, including permed bangs. Only in the 90s!

We had gone to play in the sand and waves, and I was very proud of the castle-fort I built using sticks I had collected, and our beach towels as the walls and roof. It was a real genuine tent just my size and I treated it like my princess castle! My imagination ran wild as I chatted and sang away to myself, getting lost in play as I was so frequently accustomed to doing as an only child, the sound of the loud crashing of the waves as my backup choir.

I noticed a man walking the beach who seemed to come from far, far away. I didn't think much of him at first, lots of people walk the beach. As he got closer, he said something friendly to my mom. Who knows what he said, commented on the water or the weather, or her cute daughter, something friendly.

They got to talking, he might have asked if she liked to swim or something. Somehow she shared that she had chronic back pain and he shared that he was some kind of body worker, maybe a chiropractor or massage therapist. She explained more about her pain. It was very common for momma to tell anyone who would listen about her pain, even before it got really bad and she was forced to give up her work as a nurse and rely on government disability income. As someone with chronic health issues, she was always looking for solutions. I sat quietly and watched the whole conversation happen from my tent castle. It seemed benign and friendly.

He offered to show her some things on her neck and back that could help her with her pain and she agreed. He sat down behind her and began rubbing her back and then asked for our tanning oil, which she gave to him. Then she closed her eyes and fell into his massage. Maybe she felt lonely. Maybe she and my dad's marriage had already begun suffering and so she felt desperate for touch. Maybe she was angry that my dad hadn't come and knew it was a foreshadowing of what was to come... after all, a few short years later my dad had an affair and they divorced.

Either way, somewhere in this interaction I watched my mom slip away… her body was still there but the interaction carried her spirit far away somewhere. What I sat and witnessed was first this man grooming my mom, helping her feel that he was safe, that he was a good person. I presume he saw the loneliness on her face and knew she was a vulnerable candidate. But as she closed her eyes and gave in to his massage, what I witnessed next was absolutely horrifying. He adjusted his swim trunks and began masturbating between strokes on her back. I was little, I didn't understand what was happening but I knew it was wrong. I also had never seen male anatomy, I remember seeing his testicles and thinking how much they looked like raw hamburger meat, and how much I wished I had never ever seen them in the first place.

He would stroke her back, then himself, and look right at me... I wonder if in this sick man's mind, perhaps this was more about me watching than it was about what was actually happening to my mom. I knew I had to disappear and fast. I wanted to run, I wanted to scream, I wanted to hide, I wanted to tell Mommy... did she know?

I ran into my little fort. What once was a palace for a princess was now a very tiny barrier between me and a very bad man and a very bad situation. I felt completely helpless and hopeless and terrified and just froze. I just stared at the ground and at the towel. Maybe if I couldn't see him, then he couldn't see me? In my frozen state, I felt so much shame, as if somehow I had done something wrong. Here he was, sexually assaulting my mom, masturbating on her without her consent, and I couldn't move. I couldn't do anything about it.

I don't know what happened out there, I don't know how long it lasted, but it felt like an eternity. All of a sudden, my mom started yelling. It was all a blur. Eventually, she said, "Melisa! We're leaving! Now!" She was forceful and frantic, and I felt so confused. I finally unfroze, looked out and I couldn't see the bad man anywhere. I was so afraid. I asked if we could stay and play some more, and she barked, "No!" as she frantically grabbed up all of our things. She told me to run, and we ran the whole distance of the long beach and sand to the car where we had parked.

And then we never spoke of it again. I shoved it all down. My Barbies knew all my secrets and they comforted me. Mommy was too busy dealing with her own shame and trauma to realize what I had seen and what support I might have needed. No one felt safe anymore.

That night, back at my aunt's house, it was late in the evening and we had all already eaten dinner and each of us was kind of off doing our own thing. I was playing with my Barbies all alone when someone knocked at my aunt's front door. My mom leaped up from her seat, excitedly went running, opened the door, and began ecstatically kissing the man who stood in the doorway.

I felt immediate dread in the pit of my stomach and that frozen feeling again took over. I couldn't move. I was terrified. All I could think was, "Who could she be kissing?!" The trauma set in so deeply that it affected my vision and cognition and so, when I looked up to them, I didn't recognize the man standing at the door. I felt horror as I watched my mom acting this way with a man I didn't even know.

Finally, my cousin from down the hall yelled out, "Eddy!" and came running to greet him. I looked up at him and thought… "Eddy? Like, really? Daddy Eddy?"

I hadn't recognized my own dad, my beloved daddy, who I was so close to, who called me "My Melisa," showered me with presents from his work travels, and carried me to bed at night. At that moment I didn't know him. I didn't recognize him because it was completely out of my realm of thought that it could be him. I half expected it to be the scary man from the beach, and all my greatest horrors came back to me. I froze. It's possible in that frozen trauma state, that I didn't even know my own name.

But here he was. And just like a little princess, something came over me. I lost all control and bolted to him still standing in the doorway. I leaped into his arms, wrapped my arms and legs around him tight, and began sobbing uncontrollably. I kissed him, hugged him, and patted his cheeks between tears and sobs saying over and over, "Oh Daddy! Daddy, Daddy! Daddy!" I sobbed deep heaving sobs for the next hour, heavy and uncontrollable, and wouldn't let him go. No one could calm me. It wasn't just the relief of seeing him. It was the release of ten million pounds of trauma from the day's events.

It was the strangest thing not recognizing him. But it was the trauma I had experienced that did that to me. Daddy had decided to drive down and surprise us for our vacation. But first not recognizing him, and then these deep sobs like I thought he was gone from us forever, or like he had saved me from something horrible, or like I thought he had died or something... it puzzled everyone. Everyone seemed clueless as to why I would have responded that way.

And so, with no narrative for this event, I too felt clueless about it for years. It wasn't until I was thirty-five years old that I put the two events together and realized why I didn't recognize my own dad that day. I dissociated the two memories and tucked the beach memory far, far away somewhere. I forgot they even happened on the same day or the same trip. I never understood the context. I still never understood how I could have not recognized my own daddy after not seeing him for just a couple of weeks, or why I would have responded the way I did.

Until one day, as unresolved trauma does, I was driving down to San Diego for a quick trip. And the memory of Daddy at the doorstep came into my mind. All of a sudden, it all came back to me. In my adult life, when a new memory resurfaces, no matter how dark and painful, I put my hand on my heart and thank myself for showing it to me. I know that my inner child is choosing to show me this because of the safety I have created for her in my adult life. She shows me these things because she trusts me. There were so many hard things she had to endure, she had to lock many of them away so tight just to survive. And so at thirty-five years old, the whole thing came together.

And it occurred to me, that what happened on that beach in San Diego, happened the same day as that moment, that reuniting with Daddy. And that was sexual trauma for me too. I had been raped too—raped of my innocence. Raped of my safety. Raped of any sort of decent first exposure to a man's anatomy. Raped of my comfort around strangers. Raped of my comfort around men in general. And no one to talk to about it for thirty years.

That night, as Daddy arrived at the door... I can still hear my cousin's voice calling out his name.

"Eddy!!!"

It was bright and cheery and full of excitement... and hope. It felt like a trumpet call for peace. The horn sounded, letting me know that the war was finally over and I could be safe again. The signal, letting me know that this hellish horror I had experienced, was just a moment of my life, not my forever. Summoning me to wake up from the momentary PTSD, to recognize I was not back in that place again, I was here now, and Daddy was here now.

And opposite to the scene on The Little Princess, I leaped into his arms because some part of ME had died, not because he had died. And seeing him brought me such a contrast from the fear and isolation I had felt. "Finally, my daddy. Finally, I am safe again. Finally, you're here to protect me."

My sweet inner child showed me, at age thirty-five. Maybe some part of her still has felt unsafe all these years later. After Daddy died and went away forever, it was like my safety died and went away forever too. All these years some part of me has wondered, maybe if he came back, I could be safe again. Maybe if he was there cherishing and adoring me, all would feel right in the world again.

But if I have learned anything from these many years of trauma and difficulty, my sacred silver lining from this experience is that safety comes from within. Safety comes when I, as a girl, and as a woman, tell my story without shame. When I release myself from pressures and obstacles seen and unseen. When I only pursue that which fully honors all of me. I have a beautiful husband and family and I am in emotional, mental, spiritual, and physical safety the majority of every day of my life. But as I mentioned at the beginning of my story, my inner child keeps me aware of how fragile all of that external tangible stuff really is. In this ever-changing world, everything is temporary. But what isn't, is my own love for and relationship with myself. I can cherish myself. I can adore myself. I can love up on myself. I can stand in the truth that I am a little princess, and now a radiant queen, which means I deserve every wonderful thing this beautiful life has to offer.

Melisa, you are safe, because you are loved. And you are loved, because I deliberately, purposefully, and intentionally love you.

ABOUT MELISA KEENAN

Keynote speaker and five-time international bestselling author, Melisa Keenan is the CEO of AMA Publishing and the go-to intimacy expert for high-achieving spiritual CEOs. For over five years, Melisa has helped women, men and couples with self-expression in relationships and business from their deepest authenticity. AMA Publishing has established a reputation for revolutionizing the publishing industry with its groundbreaking books and bestseller process focused on bringing forward the voice of the author. When Melisa is not in the middle of everyone's deepest soul expression, you will find her singing, playing, praying, and unschooling at her hobby ranch in Northern Nevada where she lives with her husband, CJ, and their four children.

Website for personal work: *www.melisakeenan.com*
Website for publishing: *www.amapublishing.co*
Email: *mk@melisakeenan.com*
Free Intimacy Guide: *www.melisakeenan.com/get-more*

2

CRISS MADRIGAL

I HONOR YOU

You are having twin girls!!! I was excited but still trying to process the health concerns the doctor shared minutes prior to the gender reveal. The doctor exited the room; I was puzzled. It was supposed to be an exciting day, but my excitement quickly turned to worry. My husband looked at me and said, "You wanted a girl, you get two! And they can go through this together." What did *go through this together* even mean? We had no idea the journey we were about to embark, let alone everything God had planned for our family.

My heart felt heavy. We were worried. I kept hearing on repeat, *they both have a pelvic kidney. Their umbilical cord only has one artery,* it *could be something or it could be nothing.* What did that mean? We quickly learned a single artery umbilical cord meant they *could* both have a congenital heart defect. My heart sank deeper. I wanted answers, yet our girls' hearts were too small to detect anything; I was only four months pregnant.

Four weeks later we walked into the same examining room. The scans began and the silence felt heavy. I asked how everything looked, but the nurse would not respond. Tears began to flow. Deep inside, I knew the answer.

The doctor walked into the room and confirmed my biggest fear. Both girls showed congenital heart defects that would require open heart surgery upon birth. I felt like I could not breathe, as if someone punched me in the stomach and I could not recover from it.

The next step was two rounds of amniocentesis tests to check for fetal abnormalities or birth defects. That day, I walked into the doctor's office with a glimmer of hope and left in a wheelchair in deep physical and emotional pain.

Our journey continued to evolve from that day forward.

THE JOURNEY

I suffered from anxiety since my early teenage years, and it was heavy and present. How on earth was I to manage what life had thrown at us. We were still navigating life as new parents; our son was only 18 months at that time. I thought to myself, *I'm still learning how to be a mother.* Only now I would be a mother of twins, twins that required a great level of attention.

There were days I lived in a fog. The excitement to grow our family had turned to worry, fear, doubt and I questioned if I was suited for the challenge. Until I got a flashback. I got a memory of the moment I sat on my couch days prior to our son's birth. As I watched a television show on families of children with special needs, I recall vividly what I told myself. *If God ever gave me a child with special needs, I would be an amazing mother!* In that moment, I knew God had delivered a special message to me in advance. From that day on, I knew I was equipped for the journey.

The fear was unreal. It was overwhelming. It was stressful beyond anything imagined. I tried to keep my head above water, but the waves of information kept pulling me under. My husband's brother-in-law was a pediatrician so naturally we consulted with him first. I vaguely remember our conversation. I was in a deep daze and simply looking for reassurance. Within his spoken words was a message that changed my life. The anomalies present in our daughters were out of my control; I did not cause them, and the only thing I could control was my mind, my stress, my anxiety. My job was to remain calm, otherwise my stress and anxiety would directly harm our daughters.

From that day forward, I had one job and that was to manage my mind. I knew if I waivered I would harm my daughters and they were already fighting their own battle in the womb. So, I accepted the challenge. I became the master of my mind. It was a mind game after all.

Every appointment felt heavier. The pelvic kidneys, the congenital heart defects, the second opinion, the third opinion, everything led us to a 22q.11 Deletion Syndrome diagnosis. I cried after every new diagnosis, questioning my abilities to carry out this mission, even though I was equipped for the journey. After every appointment I allowed myself to feel all the feels for 72 hours. I would cry until there were no more tears. I would pray until I could not pray anymore. I would write in my private blog and asked our prayer warriors for support. At the 72-hour mark, I flipped the switch and stepped up to the challenge. We prevailed every time. God was with me, with my family, with us! He never left our side.

Delivery day got closer and that meant I had to leave my husband and son behind to live closer to the hospital where I would deliver the girls. The Lucile Packard Children's Hospital (LPCH) Stanford was three and half hours away. I resisted the move. I acted as if everything was okay but landed in the hospital every time I went against doctor's orders. I was on bedrest for four months and that meant I could not sneak up to my bedroom on the second floor when no one was home and pretend as if nothing happened. My body took care of letting everyone know every time.

My doctor finally looked at me and said, "You have to move." I needed to be closer to the hospital I would deliver, but I refused. How could I be one month away from my husband and son when I needed them the most. I was finally told if I went into labor at home, I would be air lifted to the LPCH and put my daughters' life at risk. That was the breaking point. I packed my bags and moved away one month prior to my delivery.

I was fortunate, I lived with my brother and sister, but I needed my son and husband. That was one of the toughest months I had experienced in life. I was physically, mentally and emotionally exhausted. I cried every night as I told my husband I had no idea how I would get through another day. I could no longer move. I could no longer drive. I was confined to the couch. I felt my power stripped away from me as I patiently sat and waited for delivery day.

THE SURVIVAL

It was a beautiful sunny day in July of 2011 when our miracle girls made their entrance to this world. I was scared but full of faith. I had protected them in the womb for nearly 38 weeks, it was time for them to flourish.

Our girls were born and swiftly taken to the neonatal intensive care unit (NICU). I would not see them again until the next day. While they were attended to in the NICU, the doctor worked on me. I lost a lot of blood during the delivery; I required two blood transfusions. I felt perfectly fine, another testament God was with me and never left my side.

We were prepared to be in the hospital for weeks and six days later we were on our way home. In complete shock and overwhelm, but full of love and gratitude we drove home. Every day we showed up as the parents we desired to be. We had a vision for our family, and we stayed tethered to that vision. I did not know how things would unfold, I just knew we had complete trust, faith and belief in God.

Appointment after appointment, specialist after specialist, therapy after therapy and our beautiful girls continued to thrive. My husband is the most amazing partner God placed in my life. His calm demeanor, his soothing voice, his silence when needed all calmed my soul. He always showed up for me and our family, as he silently wrestled with his own feelings.

My father was a key player in raising our family. He always does everything with so much love. He was the only person who truly understood us. He lived this journey with us. He took care of our children from the day they were born. He is such an amazing man. When presented with the option to return to work after a layoff, he opted for his family and retired to care of his grandchildren. This man exemplified the true meaning of LOVE for a child.

Together, we survived our daughters' open-heart surgeries. So many feelings as we placed our sedated daughters on the surgeon's arms and watched them drift away. We felt better equipped the second time, but nothing prepares you to see your child after an invasive lifesaving surgery. God was the only comfort I had, and I had complete trust, faith and belief in him.

Our journey continued. I researched every possible therapy available and signed them up. My husband never questioned it; he simply supported every decision. Everything we did was to allow them to grow up as independent beautiful ladies. By the age of 12, they had each attended over 500 physical therapy sessions, add another 500+ therapies composed of occupational, speech, swim, vision, equestrian, feeding, and more. They all worked. Nevertheless, the best teacher we had was at home, big brother Geo!

Geovany was not even two years old when the girls were born. He did not understand the dynamic of our family, it just was. The love, the playfulness and encouragement were EVERYTHING his sisters needed. I hope one day he understands the hero he was and continues to be in our family. Such a kindhearted, loving boy who did not understand why his sisters needed so much attention, yet carried on as my husband and I shared our time and love with all of them.

Life continued, therapies continued, appointments continued as I attempted to have life-balance, but all I felt was my life slipping away. As I cared for our three children and advocated for the girls, I stopped living and was simply surviving. I no longer recognized the person in the mirror. I was not the mother, the wife, the sister or daughter I wanted to be. I lost my identity.

THE WAKEUP CALL

I found myself crying is despair. How did I lose control over my life? I played over and over scenes of my life and I was always an extra. I was never the lead actress in my own movie. I put everyone ahead of me, because that is what I was taught. A mother puts everyone ahead of herself, but that thought process broke me to pieces. I no longer wanted to be broken; I wanted to be whole for my family, for my marriage, for ME!

So, in February of 2020, I took the first step and hired a life coach. I was ready to find myself again. Then, two weeks later, our lives were turned upside down as we saw the world shut down right before our eyes. We navigated the unknown along with the rest of the world.

COVID-19 felt like another wave crashing down on me. It brought the unrealistic job expectations, the mental instability of my family, my own, everything was spiraling down fast. It was no one's fault. No one wanted to be in this situation. The entire world was just trying to survive.

Once again, I had to pivot and focus on my family's well-being, their mental health. Amidst survival, I enrolled in classes and took a deep dive in the mental health space. There were no therapists available and my daughter's therapy sessions took an abrupt stop. It was me again and I had to step it up.

As I sat on the couch one afternoon reading *The Highly Sensitive Child, Helping our children thrive when the world overwhelms them* by Elaine Aron, my boy sat beside me, then said "I'm a sensitive child." He did not say more and went off again. At bedtime, I asked him to elaborate, and his words marked me forever. "Why is it that you always notice other people but not me?"

My heart sank. I could not breathe. I had never felt more like a failure. How could I be pouring all my love and energy to my children, yet my amazing boy felt unseen? How could the boy that captivated my heart with his first breath feel invisible? Where did I go wrong? The conversation that unfolded that evening was beautiful, full of love and compassion. We hugged and he drifted to sleep as I fell into a river of tears and shame. I was trying to heal, trying to balance life, trying to help my family as the world changed around us, but I failed. I could not see the silver lining and it weighed heavy in my heart. Months later, a coach acknowledged how comfortable and safe he felt sharing his feelings that night.

That was the hidden message. I had instilled trust, love and comfort for him to share his feelings. That day, I allowed myself to heal from the guilt I carried for so long. I continued with life as I tried to navigate motherhood.

By January of 2022, COVID-19 reached a peak and so did I. Work became unmanageable and so did life. I fell deeper in despair as I tried to fulfill the job expectations. The weekends were supposed to be mine and for my family. Yet, I found myself working. One Saturday morning as I was up early to complete some unfinished work, I was consumed with rage and anger. I went to my bedroom in full tears, looked at my husband and said, "I'm so FU*KING mad! How is it possible that the people I love the most get my left-over energy, which is zero." That moment I knew something had to change. In order to change my life, I had to change my mind. I was no longer going to live by default. I was about to design the life I desired!

THE BREAKTHROUGH

I took another leap of faith. This time, I was not only going to change my life, but I was also going to change the life of others. I knew the method for success, I had applied it to raise our children, specifically our daughters. Now, I had to use the same method to help myself and others.

I am often asked, *How do you do it? How are you able to do so much?* My answer for a long time was, "I don't know. I just do." That was because I was an unconscious competent all my life. I did not know how my mind work great for me in certain areas and against me in others. I had already manifested things into my life with the girls because I was open to receive it, now I had to be open to receive all that God was trying to give ME. So, I embarked in a new journey and became a certified life and mindset coach.

My life was changing drastically as I continued to work with coaches. I saw the world through a different lens, which brought peace, love and abundance into my life. I continued to change my programing, which changed the way I operated. As the world changed around me, I changed right with it. Suddenly, I was consumed with an abundance of gratitude, love and appreciation at a conscious level.

I began to enjoy my corporate job again, my family appeared happier, I once again felt joy in my heart and the only person who changed was ME. I changed the way I viewed life and my life as I knew it changed right before my eyes. I was transforming, evolving and ascending to a higher version of myself.

I began to change my programing and started to DREAM again. I envisioned myself as the person with all my goals achieved and it allowed me to feel the emotions of my deepest desires and goals fulfilled. As I managed my mind, the daily stress, anxiety and overwhelm began to dissipate and an overwhelming feeling of peace took over my life. As I brought that peace into my body it went deep into my heart and I was open to receive, feel and experience all the love around me that I was previously blinded to.

With a peaceful mind and an abundance love in my heart, I began to nurture ways to keep those feelings alive. I had to incorporate habits that served me. I had to take care of my vessel that is to carry me through the rest of my life and so I focused on my health.

I began to quiet my mind through meditation and thank my body with nourishing food and movement. My body had tried to get my attention since 2019, but I could not see it. I had lived in survival mode for the last decade and my body was outwardly expressing itself. I was breaking out in hive for years without answers. My exhaustion reached burnt out and my blood pressure was at an all-time low. In that moment, I took on a new identity. The identity of Criss who could heal herself and my physical healing journey began.

My MIND, HEART and BODY were now working together, but there was still a piece missing, SPIRIT. I have always been a person of faith, but when I truly connected to spirit and allowed God to work through me, that is when the quantum leaps began. It is the beautiful synchronicity of your mind, heart, body and spirit working together to create the life you desire.

I always considered myself a God's girl but never realized that my faith was fear-based. Fear of loss, fear of failure, fear of the unknown, you name it. So, my prayers and supplications to God had an underlying sponsoring thought of fear and not love. As I began to release all my fears, love began to take over and my transformation and conversations with God became deeper.

My life has changed. I have transformed. I embraced my identity the moment I found myself again. I am creating myself anew with the love of God and a grateful heart.

> *"Life is not a process of discovery, but a process of creation.*
> *You are not discovering yourself but creating yourself anew.*
> *Seek therefore not to find out who you are.*
> *Seek to determine who you want to be."*
>
> — NEALE DONALD WALSCH

I HONOR & THANK YOU

This life would not be possible without the people who supported us and continue to support us through this journey. I have so much gratitude and appreciation for life, but there are a few people I honor and thank for helping me survive and find the silver lining with their abundance of love and compassion for me.

Geo, I honor and thank you for always showing me so much love, compassion and understanding even at your young age. You are caring, loving, protective, honest and respectful. You are such a loving and brilliant son and brother. I will always appreciate and respect your thoughts and opinions. Continue to be open and honest with me and yourself for the rest of your life. I love you with every fiber of my being and more than you will ever imagine.

Cely and Aly, I honor and thank you for coming into our lives to complete our family. You are both the most incredible warriors I know. You continue to rise to the challenge every time you face difficulty. You always impress me with your strength and ability to do things with ease even when things are hard. Cely, always stay curious and brave. Aly, always stay loving and fierce. I love you both to the moon and back, and more than you will ever imagine.

Mom and Dad, there are no words to express our gratitude. You have showed us the true meaning of trust, faith and belief in God. You exemplify family love. Dad, you have been a true role model and an angel sent to earth to help us fulfill this mission. Mom, thank you for your strength and uplifting messages when I needed them the most.

Americo, you continue to leave me speechless. Every day I fall deeper in love with you. I honor and thank you for believing in me, even when I did not believe in myself. Thank you for supporting me in all my wildest ideas even in the moments when you really wanted to say, "You're crazy!" your message was, "Let's do this." You are my saving grace. Twenty-four years by your side and I feel like our life is just getting started. Get ready to quantum leap in life, in love and in everything we continue to do in life and together as a family. Always remember, I still fall in love with you every day. Te quiero un chingo mi amor!

To Criss in 2019, I honor you for your bravery to stand up and recognize you lost and abandoned yourself in motherhood. I will always thank you for discovering the true meaning of self-love, compassion and forgiveness with oneself. This journey of self-discovery and reprogramming has opened my mind to a world of internal peace. A heart that holds all the love and abundance available to me. A body with the strength to carry me through the rest of my life. And a deep connection to spirit and God that allows me to connect with my higher self to go out and make a difference in this world.

My words tell a story and stories are meant to be told. It is through our stories that we change lives and my purpose on this earth is to change the lives of Latin@s. To help reprogram their minds to achieve break through success in life, while they embrace their identity and release any cultural barriers that hold them back.

As a first-generation Mexican American, youngest daughter of immigrant parents and founder of Latin@ Growth, I help Latin@s grow with purpose and become generational change makers. Learn to release the daily stress, anxiety and overwhelm and achieve life balance as you discover how your mind, heart, body and spirit are perfectly aligned to design the life of your dreams. Make the rest of your life, the best of your life!

> *"Experience is not what happens to you.*
> *It is what you do with what happens to you."*
>
> — ALDOUS HUXLEY

#IHonorYou
#GrowWithPurpose
#LatinaGrowth

ABOUT CRISS MADRIGAL

Criss Madrigal is a first-generation Mexican American, youngest daughter of immigrant parents, and founder of Latin@ Growth. She's a coach, speaker, author and advocate for children with 22q Deletion Syndrome. Her advocacy appeared on *The Super Parents* photography project that traveled the US and was featured on CNN Health. Her collaborations with the Lucile Packard Foundation for Children's Health and the UC Davis MIND Institute include publications, interviews, and campaigns to raise awareness for children with a variety of needs.

Criss's continued efforts to raise her children and advocate for her twin daughters with 22q brought her to a standstill in 2019 when she was forced to advocate for herself after Criss lost her identity in motherhood. *I Honor You,* is both an intimate journey and glorious wake-up call that will move the reader.

Now, as a mindset and growth coach, Criss helps Latin@s release the stress, anxiety and overwhelm of life to become the best version of themselves by reprograming the mind. If you are ready to let go of limiting beliefs, break generational chains and be a change maker, then it is time to work with Criss Madrigal.

Website: *www.crissmadrigal.com*
Instagram: *@crissmadrigal*
@latinagrowth
Facebook: *www.facebook.com/latinagrowth*

3
JENNIFER ROGERS MARKWELL

I thought I'd always work in television. It defined me. Or so I thought. I'd followed my dreams and worked as Emmy® nominated and award-winning journalist in many different (and simultaneous) roles in my career as a reporter, anchor, and executive producer. It was a fast-paced crazy existence, and it was all mine. I would not have even made it to that point without my grandparents. They acted as my parents, my rocks, and supported me in every aspect of my life.

My grandparents assumed an unspoken parental role since my mother was pretty young when she had me as a single parent. Pop and Gram were both depression era kids who grew up in big families. No one went to or graduated from college. Even though it was out of their wheelhouse, they let me run after and embrace my crazy big dreams.

Fast forward to me being the first and only in my family to graduate college. No easy feat. But, so very grateful for the journey as it truly took a village. That "village" consisting of Pop, Gram, my mother and little brother cheering from the sidelines.

In my TV career I covered wildfires, earthquakes, avalanches, drug busts, shootings, elections, kidnappings, and many other tragic stories. It seemed like those were the ones that made the national news headlines. The stories of communities banding together and really finding the silver lining or "fluff" type stories (as they were sometimes called) were my very favorite to cover. Unfortunately, most newsrooms didn't embrace those as often especially when there was another story that fell into the category of "when it bleeds it leads," meaning it was the top story or A block story in the newscast.

The money in TV was rough in my early years. I remember being on call (in addition to working a 10-12 hour day) 24 hours a day on most weekends and then again in my "off" hours. After one of those scenarios working a crazy schedule, I went through a popular fast-food drive thru and saw they were hiring for $9 an hour. I vividly remember gasping and thinking what am I doing! That was way more than I was receiving as an on-air television news reporter. But, contract after contract and news station after news station I worked my way up the food chain in both positions and salary. The hours were still long and hard.

After pushing up on two decades, I started exploring commercial work and received an offer from an international cruise line in partnership with a very large television network that were teaming up to create a global travel show. Think Anthony Bourdain with both news and food only a much lighter version. I signed the contract and was getting ready to leave when my grandpa fell sick. I lovingly referred to him as my Pop or my Poppy. He was the type of man who was quite yelley with a gruff exterior and a soft heart. Even with his tough essence, he would grumble under his breath an "I love you" to me when I forced him into a hug. When I was growing up one of his favorite stories to tell me was, he was often mistaken for Archie Bunker (actor Carroll O'Connor) from the comedy series, All in the Family. Archie Bunker was a crabby, highly opinionated (and many times vastly inappropriate), blue collar working-class family man who viewed the world with blinders as he slowly began to open his heart. Ironically, Poppy had met Carroll O'Connor in a bathroom in Chicago and they both chuckled at being each other's doppelgangers.

Now Poppy had quite a handful of health issues after retiring from the Navy and later a B2B salesman for an American power equipment manufacturer. As soon as I got the news he was not doing well, I immediately went home to be with my grandparents. Little did we know this time it would be different. Normally he would recover, and we always attributed it to him being so very ornery. I vividly remember being in the hospital with him and he was yelling about wanting coffee. We wanted him to eat some food and get hydrated with water. But he only wanted coffee and was very adamant about very loudly telling everyone. Soon after, we witnessed him getting weaker, and the doctors started to provide him medicine to get comfortable. We were all surrounding him as he passed. It seemed so surreal. He was like my dad; he was the backbone of our family and he was gone…

I've learned over the years that everyone deals with death so differently. I've seen clients extremely depressed while some others move on immediately. I learned there is no right or wrong. For us, we were in shock and so heartbroken. My grandma was completely crushed. She was alone without her husband of more than sixty-five years. Only she wasn't. I had promised both of them I would take care of them just as they did for me growing up. I had thought I'd have both Pop and Gram living with me as they got older. But now it was just my Gram.

In our complete and udder sadness, I helped Gram do all the things that you have to when you lose a loved one—call social security, make arrangements with the funeral home, get his memorial flag since he served honorably in the U. S. Armed Forces. In addition to that was making sure banks and institutions were notified of Poppy's death. My grandparents didn't have much but what they did have was spread over different institutions. We found ourselves going in front of different bankers and advisors and never felt that warm fuzzy feeling like they cared or even had my Gram's best interest at heart. She had said if we are going through this imagine how many other women are going through this. In that moment I told her I would learn everything I could. The foreign language of finance. I had no idea that my path was about to change in such a huge way. I really only had three choices. I could stay in my river and have the water keep hitting my back, I could fight the water and try and go upstream or I could go with the current and see where it takes me. That's exactly what I did. I took that promise very seriously and got securities licensed with my Series 7, 66 and insurance licensed. I knew in my heart I was meant to help women (and others) make sense of investing. This was my silver lining...

In our new normal, my Gram came to live with me. She said to me one day that she realized it was her time now. I heard her loud and clear. My goal was to have her enjoy her time and have many firsts. Everything from going to her first live concert (Coldplay), taking a cruise to eating nachos. So crazy she never tried nachos until her 80s. We celebrated holidays and stretched them out for her. Our Christmas started in October and decorations would stay up until sometimes until February. I loved her fiercely with all of my heart.

In the mist of trying to help Gram live her best life I was also trying to educate others to the foreign language of finance. I hosted workshops (and still do) on financial planning, retirement, investing, social security, Medicare, the stock market, volitivity, trusts and wills, and what the Fed is doing or maybe not doing with interest rates. My quest in serving was providing financial literacy, listening to others personal financial journeys, and helping them attain their goals.

Your personal goals could be retirement, security, creating more time to travel and spend with loved ones. A number of things.

Almost every person I have talked with over the years about their finances has a money memory. It's the psychology behind what makes people tick. Think of it as a memory that you had a child or younger self that help evolve your relationship to money as an adult. For example, one of mine is canned food at my grandparents. As I shared before they were both depression era kids and came from extremely large families. The number one goal for their families was getting food on the table. In turn, my grandparents stockpiled canned goods. I mean stockpiled. They had cabinets of canned corn, beans, meat and you name it. One day I realized that there were some cans that were bloated. I remember telling them if you are going to go out of this world it's going to be a better reason than eating a bloated can of corn with botulism. I threw out all the bloated cans. A garbage bag full. They were both so mad at me. I promised to replace them all and I did.

The second money memory for me is I tease I'm $5 shirt girl. Growing up thrift stores were a thing. I remember going to buy school clothes. Initially I was embarrassed as a very young person. Now that I have more expensive taste, I look for a $250 shirt for $5. Can I afford to pay full price? Absolutely. But I changed the narrative from a place of scarcity to better serving me now that I embrace joy in the thrill of the hunt.

My narrative has also changed around travel. I've learned not to feel guilty when spending money traveling and exploring the world. That is something that I really enjoy doing with my husband. Creating priceless memories and renewing our wedding vows each continent and foreign (to us) land we explore. This is one way we also keep our love front and center of everything we do (his idea).

Money memories continue to be so prevalent in my client relationships that I launched a podcast called "Platinum Talks Wealth." I've had the true pleasure of talking with people from all over the world. Each story is unique and different to each person. One person shared that they remembered as a small child having to dig for change in the couch, floor, the street so she could get money to pay for hot lunch at school for herself and her siblings. Another discussed hording food since there was never any in his home. Now as an adult, he buys multiples of everything to the point of food always going to waste. One guest said she would throw away her pennies in the trash when she was a kid. Her dad caught her and had to explain the value of money, even a penny. Now she teaches the same value to her kids.

One of my favorite money memory stories came from a man who said he always knew his worth when it came to money. He said 40+ years ago he had a lemonade stand and charged $5 a cup, which he realized in 1970s wasn't cheap. He shared that he only used quality lemons and top-notch sugar and also gave both a song and a dance. His mindset as an adult hasn't changed much and he continues to have a strong relationship with money.

Another shared talking with his kids about being honest about finances or being Instagram honest. They were seeing posts with people sporting the latest designer clothes with high-end Birkin handbags driving Lamborghinis. Was it real or just for show? Were they massively in debt? His goal was to potentially help his kids to create healthy honest money memories.

One man shared that while he did grow up with money, he experienced bullying. His dad dropped him off at school in a fancy sports car, and he was heavily teased, which turned into physical fights in the school yard. As an adult, he is very private about his wealth and successes.

I've had a couple women share they lived in cults and that they were taught at a young age that money was the root to all evil. So, in turn they thought people with money were also evil. They grew up in abusive male dominated households that really effected both their self-esteem and self-worth. Their stories both navigated around the process of realizing where they were and then where they wanted to be. Really changing their personal narratives so they could work on becoming the best versions of themselves. Both women are now wildly successful however still occasionally have their money memories triggered.

Another thing we also discuss in the "Platinum Talks Wealth" podcast is financial infidelities. According to Wikipedia, the definition of a financial infidelity is spending money, possessing credit or credit cards, holding secret accounts or stashes of money, borrowing money, or otherwise incurring debt, without the knowledge of one's spouse, partner, or significant other. It includes any decisions that affect the financial plan in the relationship. This topic is also a common conversation amongst clients.

A topic that was so taboo in the past people are sharing and hoping others can learn from their experiences. In one episode a women shared her partner rolled up one day in the driveway with a brand-new BMW. The car was purchased with their joint bank account money, and they had not had a prior conversation. A spouse with a gambling problem and winning-and then losing everything A business partner embezzling cash and hemorrhaging the bottom line profits of their company. A woman who realized her father had a whole separate family and was living a double life. Even the realization of when someone is not being impeccable to themselves with their own money. For example, a real Sex in the City scenario of a woman blowing all her budget on Christian Louboutin heels and didn't have money left over for her rent or her utilities.

I feel the magic behind the podcast is hope. Hearing so many stories of others overcoming their challenges in life and financially will hopefully let listeners know that they are not alone. We all have a story to tell. We want to rally behind the "underdog" and know they came out leaps and bounds ahead. They worked hard, navigated their personal journey with both grit and determination. We feel for them and in the same turn fall in love with them and their personal story of hope.

In many financial situations, communication is key. Keeping an open and honest communication with your partner, whether that be your spouse, business partner and/or even yourself. Some partners choose to keep finances separate and maybe have a shared account for common bills, while others are completely transparent. My husband is a great example of open communication. As crazy busy as we both are in life, we make time. We tease it's a hot Friday date night in our household to talk about finances. Whatever you deem best for you, just communicate.

That communication is not just for adults. Don't forget to communicate openly with your kids. We always want better for the generations behind us. Share your money memories with your kids. Talk about saving goals and saving for retirement. Many of us didn't have any financial literacy. We can do better. I started the conversation with my stepdaughter Isa at four years old. She had said she thought a boy at school was cute but quickly followed up with he doesn't have a 401k and neither did she so they can't get married yet. To clarify, that was not my exact messaging to her. However, at least I know she was somewhat listening.

Isa will share that one of her money memories is when her dad bought her first stock. Months later she was visiting Disneyland and said proudly "I own this place!" We chuckled (and still do) and said not exactly; maybe you own a tiny rock in the flowerbed on the It's a Small World ride.

Ironically, there is no real "life" class on finance e in elementary, middle, high school or college. Many well educated successful doctors, lawyers and business entrepreneurs have no idea what do to with their money or how to manage their finances. Just because you are successful at your trade does not suggest anyone taught you how to be successful with finances. That's where I really want to scream from the rooftops that everyone is worthy. No matter what you do for a career or how you were brought up or what money memory or financial infidelity that you have experienced or witnessed...you are worthy to learn and dream and have a financial future.

On my desk, there is a picture of me and Gram from when I was maybe five years old. In the picture, I'm leaning over a wall over a river trying to feed some ducks. She is holding on to the back of my jacket allowing me push past my limits all while still supporting me from the background. I remember that exact moment. I feel she is still doing the same thing for me now from the other side. That's exactly what I want to do for my stepdaughter and to empower others...

Over the past almost fifteen years I have worked at many firms. Some exceptionally big and some much smaller. I've taken the nuggets I learned along the way and launched my own firm Platinum Wealth Management. A woman run and women led concierge firm really focusing on sharing that everyone both has and deserves a seat at the table. No matter where you are at with your financial journey.

The first time I shared that message, the person I was talking with cried. She said she had always felt unworthy because she thought she didn't have enough to even speak to a financial advisor or wealth advisor. She shared her feelings watching TV commercials for wealth management firms that say to call only if you have 500k or five million—then you'd have enough money to work with them. Her story deeply hurt my heart. How is someone to get to the point of reaching their own personal financial goals if no one is willing to help? I have always been relationship-centric and am truly honored to help. You have a seat at the table. You are worthy. We (both myself and my team) are here for you when you're ready...

Another popular question I hear is where do I start? In my initial discovery meeting I really want to dive deep with you and be both raw and vulnerable to find out about you. Understanding the client's personal and financial circumstances. Next identifying and selecting goals. What's your goal? What's your dream? For some people, it's retiring early and flying first class around the globe or camping in a tent or RV and visiting national parks, or even just gardening in your backyard. Maybe starting a company that gives you the flexibility to live your best life and find a balance right now. This is your dream and no rights or wrongs. It's how you want to live life. Once your dream is established, we talk about what you have done so far. Really analyzing the client's current Course of action. Are you investing? Do you have any retirement or taxable accounts? Are you starting from scratch or starting over after a life event like a divorce? What is your time horizon of when you need money? Or when do you want to retire? After we have an understanding on your time horizon then we navigate your risk tolerance. What does that look like to you? Are you comfortable with risk or are you risk averse?

Finally, we develop the financial plan. Think of this as a road map that will continue to evolve with you as your life changes and evolves. I'm honored to have helped and still help thousands of people in their personal financial journey. It's a relationship that I don't take lightly. I've seen families navigate tragedy and the loss of a loved one to growing their families with new loved ones and kids and grandchildren.

I wish my grandparents were both still alive to witness the path they have helped me create in my life. I'm so grateful for everything they provided me with, both unconditional love and support. I have dedicated my life to continue to lift and educate clients within their personal finances and am honored to help all others make sense of investing...

ABOUT JENNIFER ROGERS MARKWELL

Emmy® nominated journalist, Jennifer Rogers Markwell, changed gears in her television career when she realized the need to help women and their finances. It started at home for Jennifer after her grandfather passed away and she wanted to help her grandmother make sense of investing. After founding the firm, Platinum Wealth Management, she regularly hosts monthly educational workshops to empower women & others to take charge of their investments. Jennifer also anchors the "Platinum Talks Wealth" Podcast where she discusses with her guests the psychology behind money memories and financial infidelities. In addition to acting as president for Platinum Wealth Management, Jennifer currently serves as a State Commissioner for the Nevada Commission for Women, volunteers on the board for Girls Scouts of the Sierra Nevada and the Pioneer Center for the Performing Arts. Jennifer Rogers Markwell was voted Sierra Nevada's Top 20 Most Powerful Women by Northern Nevada Business View in both 2018 and 2019.

Website: *www.platinumwealth.net*
Podcast: *www.platinumwealth.net/podcast*

4

JENNIFER SPOR

ANSWERING THE CALL TO DEEPER TRUTH

Like all great stories begin, once upon a time, not too long ago, there was a woman who felt a calling to discover deeper Truth within herself. That woman is me.

I had already been paving a path for myself, seeking growth and expansion on my journey and illuminating the way for others. But there was an energy that felt off. I started to notice it in my physical reality too. What used to work in my soul-led business no longer did, personal and professional relationships no longer felt aligned, and I just felt blah. My path felt stagnant, and joy was making less of an appearance in my day-to-day life. I consider myself to be highly self-aware so what gives, I thought to myself.

Seek to come from a space of love and service, check.

Surrender, check.

Trust, check,

Forgive, check.

Be present, check.

Navigate my life from my inner knowing, check.

Live intentionally, check.

There was no real obvious sign as to the root of this misalignment, only symptoms, so I decided that deeper exploration was called for.

Meditation, rest, and the Akashic Records are my top go-to practices for receiving clarity on my path forward.

This sounds so simple and it is, yet I would resist doing this as much as my soul required because I believed that I didn't have enough time, and that if I didn't spend enough time in my business I wouldn't be fully financially supported.

Crazy for someone to be so self-aware and still struggle with this limiting belief, right?

The struggle felt real, y'all.

Bottom line, I decided to take the time and space I needed for this deeper exploration despite my ego mind's constant reminder about what it believed would happen when I did. Guess what I discovered?

I realized that although my intentions were pure in how I was showing up, I was still operating within certain 3D constructs and perceptions, believing that success in the way I wanted it could only be achieved in certain ways. The personal development industry including many spiritual communities perpetuate this. It's also worth noting that spiritual communities can be some of the worst because of the conviction of their beliefs. However, regardless of this, I am responsible for my reality and what I've chose to create and choose to create moving forward. You are too.

I had a decision to make. This is a decision that was a long time coming because a long time ago I'd received an awareness that this current life for me is the culmination of all my lifetimes combined. This is the life I've been training for as an ancient soul to aid in anchoring in the New Earth and this is the lifetime where I tie up all the loose ends, where all my lessons come to completion.

It was so clear now. I decided that moving forward I would intentionally navigate my ascension journey and accomplish what I am here to do and who I am here to be.

Let me tell you, I was scared shitless to make that declaration. But I did it anyway because I am fearless. That is, my courage is greater than my fear and my faith in something greater than myself is the driving force behind everything I do and who I AM.

And I wanted to live truly free.

See, there is a difference between freeing yourself and navigating that freedom. I had been free for some time, but I wasn't living free.

Beyond the decision I'd made, I also needed to wipe the slate clean. This meant having the willingness to let go of all I'd created knowingly or unknowingly within these limiting constructs.

To create anew in all aspects of my being, free from limitation, reclaiming my power as a Divine Creator.

All of the things I thought I was doing, surrender, trust, service, etc. I was doing them within a construct of intellectual understanding and only partially embodying.

To live more deeply expressed in my Truth, I needed to go deeper. This meant facing both the light and the shadow aspects of myself. This is what ascension is, equally embracing all aspects of your being as a soul, and as a human, with unconditional love.

Onward.

What I would experience next would challenge me to the core of my being.

I drew a line in the sand and promised myself that I would only create moving forward guided by my inner knowing and Mother/Father God in my business and every aspect of my life independent of any constructs even if I was alone in my given direction.

I don't believe in sugar coating, so I want you to know that my life felt like a shit storm for a while because I needed to re-learn how to create my reality from a space of true Divine Creatorship.

Business

Finances

Relationships

Health

Nothing was off limits.

Have you seen the image of the Tower tarot card? That's how my life felt for a while—lol. I'm able to laugh about it now but it didn't feel fun at the time.

I've experienced a dark night of the soul and if there were a dark dark night of the soul, this would be it. There were days that I seriously questioned what I was doing and what was the point of me even being here anymore if I had to continue to live what I was experiencing.

Yet I stayed the path.

I visualized, healed, stayed connected with my I AM self, embraced the support of Mother/Father God and my guides, meditated, and I prayed. Boy did I pray a lot, and I was relentless.

Each day I thought I couldn't make it another day; a new day would come.

Then one morning I woke up and I physically and energetically felt lighter. The sun was even shining that morning. I changed timelines.

Then my physical reality began to show evidence of my commitment to create authentic to who I AM and from a space of Truth and Love without limits.

My existing relationships deepened,

money started showing up in abundance,

new clients and collaboration partners came in,

and my health began to improve,

and my joy reignited.

I felt empowered and FREE.

I still feel empowered and free today. I'm also still discovering other ways I'm limiting myself and releasing them. I approach my path with humility as I am an eternal student.

We are all eternal students. We all are here to learn, love, and to live fully expressed in the true essence of who are as a soul and as a human. We are all here to be free.

Know there is no right or wrong experience on our paths. All our experiences, whether challenging or joyful, are equally important. The key to our evolution is the awareness to question if we are truly living in integrity and the willingness to change what is no longer aligned on our path. And most important, to stay the path.

I'll leave you with the following question:

What are you willing to face and to sacrifice to truly walk your talk, to stand for and be what you believe in?

Some final words of wisdom:

Living your Truth is the Sacred Silver Lining.

Know that you're already whole and you have all the answers within.

To create a new world, you have to be willing to move beyond the one you're in.

True freedom is attained when you embrace all aspects of your being.

There is freeing yourself and there is navigating that freedom. Use your power to take full ownership of your freed self.

Your path is the purpose.

Advocate for truth and love above all else. This is how we heal the world. This is how we change the world.

ABOUT JENNIFER SPOR

Jennifer Spor is the CEO and Founder of her namesake company and Host of Path of the Awakened Heart podcast. She is a Spiritual Advisor, Channel, and Akashic Records Trauma Informed Master Consultant and Teacher for High Achieving Conscious Women Leaders who are here to live unapologetically expressed in their Truth and fulfill their highest destiny in this life, SOUL LED. Despite checking all the boxes off the list of what 3D society teaches it means to achieve success, Jennifer was unfulfilled in her corporate retail career and life, feeling called to make a bigger difference in the world. It was her own dark night of the soul and spiritual awakening that served as the catalyst to align her with her purpose and mission supporting others through her sacred work today. Working with Jennifer is highly activating and deeply transformational. Her medicine as a spiritual advisor and clear channel in the Akashic Records combined with her experience as an entrepreneur and corporate operations executive as well as the wisdom she embodies on her own journey supports her clients to collapse space and time to create results so powerful it feels like years of work accomplished in a few sessions.

Website: *www.jenniferspor.com*
Email: *jennifer@jenniferspor.com*
Path of the Awakened Heart Podcast: *www.pathoftheawakenedheart.com*
Download this free meditation to activate your highest destiny: *www.bit.ly/hdestiny*
Instagram: *www.instagram.com/jennifer_spor*

5
KELSIE HOLT

ILLUMINATING THE BEAUTY WITHIN THE SCARS

I believe that light is most fully witnessed when it is contrasted with the dark. One could choose to merely highlight the beautiful in their story; however, I believe that they would be missing out on the depth that was required in order to acquire such light. I want to take you through a journey, both through the dark alleys that almost consumed me, as well as to witness the small glimmers of light that would be my saving grace.

I want to begin by explaining a form of Japanese art called Kintsugi (金継ぎ). This form of art has been widely tied to symbolizing finding the beauty within the broken. Instead of choosing to discard something which has been broken, Kintsugi is the means of repairing it with gold. Highlighting the imperfections and the beauty which can be found. This means the history of the vessel is retained. Instead of hiding the fact that it has been broken, the breakage is an honored part of the journey. This can be related to the human experience and the journey of healing and recovery. When we choose to own our stories and embrace our scars; we can begin to find new meaning and appreciation for our own unique journeys. Instead of hiding in shame, it's recognizing the strength and courage which was necessary to rise from our challenges. We can choose to honor our resilience and the battle scars we weld.

* * *

Although my childhood offered some beautiful memories, it felt mostly overshadowed by years of sexual abuse. I had assumed that my innocence was lost, making the way I viewed myself very distorted. I spent a lot of time wondering if I was to blame for what was happening. I felt dirty and unworthy. I remember wondering how God viewed me, and if my parents could still love me if they knew the truth. This drastically shaped my perception of who I was.

Suicidal ideation seemed to consume my adolescent years. I couldn't sit at an intersection without being bombarded with thoughts like "*Pull out in front of that semi; the world will be better off without you.*" No matter how I tried to keep those thoughts away, it felt like they were always flooding my ability to think clearly. I was at war with myself. I spent night after night pleading with God to allow me to come back home to Him—the internal torment felt like too much to bear. However, on one particular evening, God chose to give me a simple reminder of how He sees me. I was sitting on a mountainside, my brain was numb from the thoughts spiraling inside, my eyes were red and puffy from the flowing stream of tears. I was contemplating if that would be my last night. However, in that moment, I felt a calming sensation come over me. It was as if someone had wrapped me in a warm embrace. This small reminder helped me to know that someone was aware of the silent battles I had been waging. Gazing over the valley below I realized that I was surrounded by His creations, realizing I was also one of His irreplaceable creations.

At sixteen, I entered a relationship which began innocently but quickly turned to an onslaught of manipulation, coercion and gaslighting. I made a lot of decisions that I later regretted. By the time I realized the depth I had reached, I felt trapped within his control. My caring deeply about him kept me ensnared. If I made an attempt to exit the relationship, suicide was threatened. I felt I would be responsible for his death if I left. As time carried on, his tactics escalated. It wasn't until my adult years that I came to terms with these dynamics being intimate partner violence. I thank my guardian angels for keeping me safe from many of the bizarre things that occurred. Including him chasing me down through winding canyons at high speeds, trying to run me off the road, or intentionally wrecking his vehicle in front of me.

There were other times where he would try to kill himself in front of me. Screaming in my face that *"I deserved to have that image scarred in my mind for the rest of my life."* He then forced the knife into my hands and relentlessly attempted to make *me* stab him. He felt I *should* be responsible for his death, since I wanted to leave. This was met with physical brawls, as I tried desperately to keep either of us from getting stabbed. Thank goodness for God's hand and my raging adrenaline, since he was twice my size. His demeanor would then suddenly shift. Embracing me tightly as he repeatedly assured me that *"he loved me so much."* All I could do was stand in his embrace with my entire body shaking violently as I sobbed. This was the web I was entrapped in; it was like being bound to Jekyll and Hyde.

* * *

During that same time frame, I ran away from home. The onslaught of abuse had worn me thin, and I felt like a complete burden to my family and friends. I made the drastic decision to run to someone who I had never met, believing he was a safe person. I recognize now that I was merely running away to an adult male who had spent years prior grooming me. He capitalized on the opportunity to take advantage of a vulnerable adolescent; in a later instance, he chose to rape me.

Shortly after arriving at my destination, my journey was cut short. I was pulling out of a parking lot when I got T-boned on my driver's side. With impatient drivers honking behind me and my anxiety rising, I went for it; realizing quickly that this was a deadly mistake. An oncoming van was coming much quicker than I had calculated. A glance out my driver's window told me there was no avoiding impact.

At that moment, I felt a very distinct impression: *"don't tense up."* What an ironic request, given that I assumed I was taking my last few breaths. Somehow my brain calmed, and I relaxed my body. The impact sent my car spinning across the highway, facing oncoming traffic. I must have gone unconscious, as I awoke to a loud knock on my window. With an officer yelling: *"Miss, you need to put pressure on that wound right away!"* I was clueless as to what he was referring to. A glance to my rearview mirror unveiled a large gash on my forehead. I had blood seeping down my face and pooling at my neck. Surprisingly, no glass had shattered during the impact, but my door was lodged shut. Due to suspected spinal injuries, pulling me from the passenger side was out of the question. Instead they broke my window and used the "Jaws of Life" to cut my door off and pull me from my car.

After strapping me head to toe on a stretcher and loading me in the ambulance, I was told by two paramedics that I was lucky to be alive. Stating that if the vehicle struck a split second sooner (a mere couple inches differently), it would have left me paralyzed from the waist down or crushed to death. Yet somehow, I managed to walk away with merely heavy bruising and stitches. God knew that I had better chances at not being severely injured if I didn't tense up. This showed me that for one reason or another, He still needed me around. He also knew the intentions of the man I was running away to and recognized it was going to take a drastic forced intervention to get me back home.

Unfortunately returning home meant the abuse continued. A resource officer at my school was the one who finally recognized the subtle signs. Police became involved at this point. They firmly warned me that their observations were very similar to cases which result in murder-suicide. A few months after finally escaping the situation, he did commit suicide. As with most instances of domestic violence, the web in which victims are tied to their abuser is very intricate and complex. On one hand I felt relief, as the fears of needing to watch my back constantly or worry that he would harm someone I loved were lessened. On the other, I cared deeply about him, and his suicide shattered me. I spent years tormented by night terrors and hallucinations of his death. With many years spent blaming myself, sending me to a very dark place mentally.

* * *

Due to the intensity of some of these traumas, my brain masterfully used denial as a form of protection. One portion being masked was the childhood sexual abuse. At age twenty a suicide attempt landed me in the E.R. The on-call psychologist validated that I was dealing with PTSD and had me promise to begin therapy upon release. In one therapy session I felt inclined to explain some of my childhood experiences. She looked me straight in the eye and said "Kelsie, you do realize you were sexually abused as a child, right?" With those words, it was as if a ton of bricks hit me. Simultaneously, I felt I was taking my first gasp of air after being submerged underwater for years. Someone had finally validated a part of me that had been suffocating for so long.

When I was twenty-one, I got married. Due to the presence of trauma and addiction, things were rocky from the beginning. With trust so often being shattered, this made for a very unstable foundation for a marriage and family. The effect that betrayal trauma had on me was ruthless. My self-esteem was non-existent. Shifting my energy to my own recovery offered respite, the support found in 12-step programs helped me feel less alone. During this time I had to completely reconstruct my views of God. Which aided in my ability to both rely on Him more freely, while also learning to let go of things outside of my control. I later ended up naming our daughter Serenity due to the *Serenity Prayer* and how much I relied on it during those years. Although the new learned tools and principles helped me find peace, the toxicity present in the marriage was still too much. After years in the trenches I finally requested a separation. My hope was for both of us to have space to work on ourselves, so we could come together and repair the relationship.

When I separated I had two kids under the age of four and was pregnant with our third child. To say that I was overwhelmed is an understatement. I cared for him more than words could express. However, my ability to cope had run dry. Boundaries and space were necessary, I had to put my oxygen mask on first so that I could be there for my young kids. I spent many nights on my knees sobbing through prayers, wondering how I was going to make things work. I had been the caregiver for our children, putting my career and education on hold. I felt so underqualified and inadequate stepping back into the workforce. I worked hard, but government assistance was needed to bridge the gap (with childcare expenses, medical, etc.). We were separated for a year before the answer came that it was time to move forward with divorce. I had given it my all, but it was finally time to let go. Six months after I filed, the divorce was finalized. The separation period stretched me thin, but it was a refiner's fire. It provided the opportunity to begin finding myself. I began recognizing I had worth and started shifting my life to represent that. It was the time I felt most connected with God, as I had to rely on Him with every step I took.

When I was eight months pregnant with my daughter (Serenity), we had what I'd like to call some earthly angels step in and do an incredible act of kindness for our family. Little by little, I had to learn how to let people in and accept help (this was very difficult for me). On one occasion, a friend of mine begged to borrow the keys to the mobile home where we lived at the time. Claiming she just wanted to have the carpets cleaned before the baby arrived. I finally agreed to the help and went away for a couple of days. Little did I know I would be returning to something much different.

In the short time we were away, my friend rallied a group together to completely renovate our home. We came home to fresh paint, new flooring, toilets and sinks replaced, updated furniture, etc. Normally it would sound like utter madness to completely change someone's home without permission. Somehow she knew it was exactly what the kids and I needed and proceeded anyway. I spent the next week in utter shock, allowing myself lots of moments for bawling like a baby.

They followed a bizarre prompting and I couldn't be more grateful to them for it. It was less about the tangible details and more about the glimpse of God's awareness of us through their selfless act. I felt completely undeserving of what they did for our family. However, I cannot tell you how desperately we needed it at that time. God knew how much we needed an act of kindness, an act of love, and it couldn't have been provided in a more perfectly orchestrated way.

As divorce became reality, my focus shifted to self-improvement and building a stable future. Weeks after the divorce was finalized, I began working on my degree. I knew that the journey would be slow and tedious, but I figured I may as well slowly chip away at a worthwhile goal. During this timeframe I was blessed to be connected with job opportunities that would help support me and the kids. There were many small miracles that came into play, which is why I cannot deny God's hand playing a part. Even if it was a position that required skills which I had no prior experience with, the employers were patient enough to allow me time to learn. These positions allowed me the ability to work from home so I could spend more time with my kids. School deadlines, work cases and kids were my life. I was utterly exhausted, but I was at peace.

With time and dedication, I was finally able to reach the point where I could purchase a condo in our neighborhood. This was such an empowering experience as a single mom. The prior owners were so kind and gracious as they worked with us to secure the property. It was an older home and was in need of some updates. Once finalized, I jumped right into tearing out carpet to prepare for new flooring and preparing walls for paint. There was a huge surge of freedom that came from learning how to conquer the varying projects. I am also incredibly grateful to the friends who showed up to help with so many of these projects. We were so blessed to live around people who were always eager to lend a hand. One of the first nights at the new place, I had a distinct calm feeling. It was a feeling of safety and security. It was the first time I had truly felt safe in a home. This was a place of our very own. It brought peace knowing that I did not need to allow anyone or anything within those walls that did not deserve a place within our little sanctuary.

* * *

Although I had my reservations surrounding getting remarried, I was still open to the idea if it was with someone who was a healthy fit. I had been living the single parent life for almost five years when I met Matt. During those years, I worked hard on my trauma recovery and self-improvement. I wasn't looking for someone to *"save me."* With God's help, I was determined to rebuild myself. I've been told there are some parts of relational trauma which can only be healed within a relationship. It's interesting to see all of the deep trauma that can resurface when you're back in a serious relationship. They say you often gravitate towards people, settings or situations which have a familiar feel to them, even if they are not necessarily healthy for you. Due to my efforts with trauma recovery, I was intentionally trying to push against the grain and look outside my normal. Even though this felt extremely uncomfortable. When it came to dating Matt, a lot of things were very foreign to me. He was not like my previous partners (and thank goodness). This frightened my brain though, as the unknown felt so incredibly intimidating and unsafe.

As an aftermath of trauma, I deal with PTSD and DDNOS. The way that these disorders show up for me can vary based on what or who I'm around. For example, a lot of my triggers surface more frequently within my close relationships. My husband Matt is a wonderful partner and I'm so glad I chose to take the leap. However, that doesn't mean it was an easy choice going in, or that it hasn't been a rollercoaster of a ride since being together. The first months of married life I noticed that my brain was turning to dissociation more frequently. Luckily I began another round of therapy with a new therapist who is well-trained with trauma. Although I've known for years that I deal with symptoms of PTSD, this was the first time receiving an official diagnosis. I appreciate that she took the time to do multiple assessments to gauge where my tolerance levels were at, so we could come up with a more effective plan for treatment.

Through A.R.T (Accelerated Resolution Therapy) and other methods, she is helping me to increase my window of tolerance, regarding what my brain can cope with before turning to dissociation. Trauma is an interesting thing. Our brains are merely doing what they believe they need to do to survive, they are trying to protect us. However, once the smoke has cleared and we're no longer in toxic situations, it's quite the process to slowly train your brain that you are safe so that you can learn to be present.

* * *

We are slowly learning how to more effectively show up for each other and build a secure attachment. This doesn't mean things are always butterflies and rainbows; I still have days where trauma tells me that I'm trapped and unsafe. Occasionally you may still find me rocking back and forth in the fetal position in our closet trying to calm my brain. However, I have to remind myself that this is not a sign of weakness or backsliding. This *IS* the reality of trauma recovery. My therapist often reminds me that recovery doesn't mean that those dips no longer exist, it means that the frequency and intensity of those episodes slowly lessen over time. I can easily return to a space of *"I'm not fit for marriage. I can do things on my own, but my brain is too broken to do things healthily with a partner."* That's where I have to stop and offer myself grace, compassion and acceptance. One thing that has helped with this is Parts Therapy. Recognizing there are different parts of myself which show up for varying reasons. For example, there's the part which shows up when it feels I may not be safe. This part is courageous for wanting to protect me. I can be mindful and patient, while also graciously allowing her to rest, reminding her that we are safe now.

Being with a partner who genuinely cares and chooses to be faithful and devoted is still foreign to me. It would seem that having those things now should offer my brain immediate rest and safety.

Trauma is a funny thing though, as my brain is highly trained to recognize foreign things and shift to high alert. I am grateful that I have a partner who is patient and kind throughout the process of unlearning. He chooses to take the time to better understand trauma and how my brain processes things. We both put in the time and effort to work on ourselves individually, aiding in learning to be safe and secure partners for each other. I've realized over time that this is what recovery looks like. It's not some large shiny bow you tie over your wounds when you've finally *"recovered."* It's not some glorious light at the end of the tunnel. Instead, it's the small, simple improvements recognized over time. It's celebrating the small wins. It's choosing to use the tools and resources, even when it's easier not to. It's allowing yourself (and your partner) lots of grace, compassion and patience during all the times either of you trip and need time to recover your footing.

* * *

I was recently hospitalized due to severe preeclampsia while pregnant with baby number four (Matt's first biological child). Our goal was to try to wait three more weeks before inducing labor. However, my health continued to quickly decline, forcing us to induce at thirty-one weeks instead. I consider myself to be a fairly healthy person, so to see how quickly things can go completely south was eye opening. It's given me a new appreciation for life and living. Those weeks involved so many means of medical testing, IV's and medications; as we tried to strike a balance between keeping my organs from failure, while keeping the baby safe.

Our little Harmony Mae is here now and is doing well in the NICU. She is a fighter, and we are so grateful for her. When I was finally able to go see her I couldn't help but break down crying, finally meeting the little person who I gave it my all for. This precious little human was what made it all 100% worth it. Being able to hold her for the first time was healing. As soon as I laid her on my chest she snuggled in and fell right asleep. I think we both finally felt at home in that moment. As with many of my other experiences, I cannot deny the many miracles that came into play during these times. I know God had his hand in keeping me and Harmony safe.

If I had one take-away to offer, it would be to encourage you to search for the silver linings within your own story. Hold on to those things, even if they may seem miniscule compared to the pain at times. It's within those small glimmers of light that you can find the strength to take another step. It's the collection of those things over time that can provide new meaning to life and allow you to build the resilience needed to face new challenges. One crucial step in my own recovery has been learning to forgive myself and others. Recognizing that I don't need to stay shackled to others' poor choices. I can free myself, regardless of what they choose on their end. This has allowed me to see myself and others in a different light.

For me, recovery has meant recognizing the post-traumatic growth that one can unearth among the ashes. It's choosing to find the beauty within the scars, choosing to honor the resilience and the courage it takes to pick up each jagged piece and rebuild. My hope is that you may recognize that your worth is concrete and does not falter. You are more than your experiences and you are worthy of the good that life has to offer. You deserve to thrive, not just merely survive. May you recognize just how wonderful and powerful YOU truly are. I hope you choose to wear your scars like war paint, honoring the divine warrior within you.

ABOUT KELSIE HOLT

Kelsie Holt graduated summa cum laude from BYU-I with her B.S. in Marriage & Family studies, emphasizing in human services. She is an alumna of the Institute of Healing Arts where she learned techniques for facilitating trauma processing. She is a graduate of UCMT and is licensed as a massage therapist. She works as the Class Coordinator at Bridle Up Hope. Kelsie enjoys teaching about the beautiful symbolism of kintsugi through classes and workshops. She's a contributing author in the book *Warrioress Rising* and looks forward to sharing more about her journey of self-discovery and trauma recovery. Kelsie is especially passionate about helping others to feel seen, heard and valued. She has participated in multiple video projects focused on raising awareness surrounding trauma recovery. She is passionate about advocating for survivors.

She lives in Utah with her husband and four kids. She feels most alive when she's out exploring in nature; she's always eager for an adventure that involves hiking, cycling, kayaking or horseback riding.

Website: *www.kelsieholt.com*
Email: *hello@kelsieholt.com*

6

LAURA MARTÍNEZ MCDERMOTT

WHAT MAKES HIM "TIC?": A JOURNEY THROUGH MEDICINE, FOOD, AND WELLNESS

We were supposed to blend in like any other spring break family in Palm Springs.

Downtown Palm Springs was dotted with tall green palm trees lining the streets. The city was nestled at the base of the mountains where the warm sun slowly set behind them. Both sides of the streets were lined with vendors selling items such as homemade lavender soaps, scented candles, wind chimes, and bright, modern artwork. The sweet aroma of nearby freshly popped kettle corn and the scent of warm roasted nuts tickled my tastebuds as vendors quickly bagged up the treats for sale. Local show banners flapped in the dry desert air announcing upcoming shows and events. From each street corner we heard music from local artists who played for their eclectic and captivated crowds, guitar cases lying open to collect spare change from passersby.

My young family was embracing a week away from school. We came to Palm Springs to spend time together and for our family to relax and connect. These closed-road markets were fun to navigate and served as a staple tradition in the desert. We liked to wander around as a family and saw one musician playing both his accordion and harmonica simultaneously. As we pressed on, another vendor was drawing henna tattoos, while their music played from a speaker. We did not need jackets because the mountains captured the heat of the sun and wrapped the desert in a blanket of warmth for our evening adventure.

I remember marveling at the strength of our small and beautiful family. I was pushing our baby girl, Maddie, in her stroller while clutching the small hand of our three-year-old daughter, Marissa, in mine. Marissa's blond braids swayed as we walked, and I watched her eyes dart from scene to scene. Our five-year-old son Mitch held his dad's hand attempting to lead our family through the busy crowd. We paused briefly to watch a few break dancers with their beat box draw in a crowd. Slightly ahead, Mitch tugged on his father's hand as he saw an open play area. My husband looked at me for guidance and I nodded my approval for Mitch to dash ahead and play. I released our three-year-old daughter, Marissa, to join him. We watched as Mitch's brown curls bobbed enthusiastically in the bounce house. His large almond shaped green eyes were wide with excitement. His childish laughter filled the colorful tented playhouse. His younger sister, Marissa, jumped happily near him, smiling at her older brother.

I remember the stillness of that moment. It was like a polaroid picture, until I saw Mitch's movements become jerkier. He started making small grunting sounds. His leg kicked in an odd direction, uncontrollably. His noises grew louder. His head shook oddly. We watched as this continued for many minutes. My husband panicked. "What if he is having a seizure?" he stated worriedly. Although in my heart I did not guess that was the case, I certainly was not going to speculate as Mitch's body movements were different and frequent. What was going on with our son?

Earlier in the week I had noticed some slight twitching from Mitch but did not think much of it. In the bounce house, his symptoms appeared to be ten out of ten. It was hard for us to watch, and we were worried about him. "Let's go to the Emergency Room," my husband suggested frantically. Reluctantly, we gathered our young children and hurriedly walked back to the hotel to drop the two younger girls off with their aunt who was also staying there. We then took Mitch to the local hospital in town. Was this really happening? Thoughts ran through my head. Cold air and stark white walls gave me an unwelcome chill as we entered through the hospital lobby door. What an abrupt shift from the fun, colorful, and lively outdoor desert street fair. I remember wishing we were back at the fair. I was scared. Luckily, Mitch's vitals checked out fine. I was relieved. At this point it was almost 9:00 p.m. and Mitch was getting sleepy from being in the sun all day. He yawned and rubbed his eyes as he leaned in closer to me. "What do you think is going on?" my husband asked the doctor. The ER doctor wore stereotypical white hospital garb, and through his glasses, shrugged at us and suggested additional testing—both an MRI and CT scan. I panicked. It was apparent that our son's imminent health was not in danger and that we could take him to our own pediatrician when we returned home from spring break. "Babe," I suggested gently addressing my husband, "May we please take him to our own doctors back home? He is not having a seizure and I think he will be okay until then." This one moment stays with me and I am thankful for having a mother's intuition, especially at that moment. Putting our young son through a battery of medical tests in an unfamiliar place so late in the evening just did not feel like the right plan. The three of us left the hospital.

Mitch's onset of both motor and vocal tics came on strong and continued daily when we got home. His arm would jut out, or he would do a little hop, make a squeaky sound, a grunt, or shake his head for no apparent reason. But other than this unusual new behavior he was the same, happy, bright, and outgoing boy. When we got home, our pediatrician evaluated him. He then referred us to a pediatric neurologist. We took Mitch to see the specialist the following week. What stands out the most in my memory was the way the stern doctor declared to us with a glare, "Your son has tics, he needs medication. It is most likely Tourette's." She said it authoritatively. "Tourette's?" "Medication?" It was a lot to take in since I was unfamiliar with those terms. Fortunately, once again, my inner voice told me I should listen to what she said, gather information, and do my own research. I glanced down at our handsome young boy, admiring his wide-eyed curiosity, thinking of his bright wit, creativity, and energy. I considered the side effects of the medications she proposed. Weight gain, lethargy, muscle relaxation? I was not opposed to medication, and knew it had its place, but it certainly was not going to be my first course of action for our young son. The doctor seemed angry when we declined. Thanking the doctor, we left the office with Mitch, not accepting her prescriptions for medications. We did not return.

We had a son with tics. The tics were severe. We still needed a solution. We needed help. If we were not going to start with medication, then what steps could we take to help him? This was a pivotal moment in our family's life. This is when my journey toward natural health and wellness began.

Frantically I dove into research mode. This was really the first time I had heard the term "Tourette's." Maybe I had seen something on a TV show once, but I did not really understand it. I began to look up any information to help me better understand the condition. With my own mother's urging I contacted the Tourette Syndrome Association and with their recommendation I booked an appointment with Dr. Cummings, a renowned specialist in the field of Tourette syndrome at the City of Hope in Los Angeles. His first available appointment was in a few months.

I became a scavenger of information. Between nursing my baby girl and shuttling my toddler and Mitch to preschool and kindergarten I scoured the internet conducting research, the library reading books, and reading anything I could get my hands on that mentioned or explained Tourette syndrome, or involuntary motor and vocal tic disorder. I learned more about the condition and learned natural treatments that were working for some individuals. Much of the material I read regarding natural treatments pointed to diet patterns, supplements, exercise, and lifestyle that could reduce the symptoms of Tourette syndrome. This long list included things like not using artificial food coloring, avoiding preservatives, and staying away from added sugars. I wondered: could that really make a difference? I was skeptical. But I knew it was a good place to start and in my desperate attempt to help Mitch, I did a complete pantry and refrigerator overhaul. I poured out colorful crunchy sugared cereals, boxes of rainbow fruit chews, sweet apple juice boxes, and I even tossed out the pink and white circus cookies the children always loved to eat. Doing this, I started to improve not only on our son's diet but also our family's diet. I replaced these unhealthy items with whole fruits, vegetables, nuts, seeds, whole grains, and other natural snacks. It was transformative for all of us.

As we started making the shift toward more healthy food and diet changes, I noticed a remarkable change in Mitch's tics. Within a few months they reduced by about half. It reminded me of what Hippocrates once said: "Let food be thy medicine and medicine be thy food." So, I began to realize the health and wellness approach I was taking was working and devoted more and more time to it in between taking care of my other young children.

By the time of our appointment at the City of Hope we were doing well managing Mitch's symptoms and becoming more comfortable with his condition. At the appointment Mitch and Dr. Cummings joked together, and the doctor found him precocious. Mitch's tics were about five out of ten now. They appeared less noticeable, calmer, and less abrupt. "There are always medications available," the well-admired Dr. Cummings mentioned to us after his examination, "but it seems like what you are doing is working for your son." Tears came to my eyes. I felt grateful. The doctor agreed and recognized that Mitch did not have to be medicated. He did not seem concerned about Mitch's abilities to thrive and felt Mitch would be just fine. A new wave of hope washed over me and my family. We left the City of Hope feeling grateful. I had a new goal: to stay current on food nutrition, improve on this plan, and ensure that Mitch's confidence was high despite his diagnosis and tics.

Silver Linings are funny things. The idea of silver linings may actually date back to 1634 and was apparently used by John Milton in *Comus,* when he was quoted as saying: "Was I deceived or did a Sable Cloud turn forth her silver lining on that night?" As a mother, I have had many sleepless nights. I had three young *babies,* really at that time.

One with a condition I barely knew much about. While I was relieved to learn that Mitch did not need medication and would do well without it, it was daunting now to learn that I was the one he depended on. I began to toss and turn at night, filled with concern for Mitch, for what I knew, and did not know, and of course, this new diagnosis of Tourette syndrome. What would happen? How will others see him? Will kids make fun of him? Some days were better than others. Eventually, I just dug in, and my positivity overwhelmed all the fears I had for what could be. I decided that I would learn everything I could about Tourette syndrome, create an environment at home where he and the family could thrive, and control what I could control. Despite what I had to balance and juggle in the home, I knew with love I could do anything.

For the next several months, my passion for natural health flourished as I started shopping at different grocery stores that offered healthier whole, one ingredient food options, among many other things. To inspire Mitch's confidence, we joined the Tourette Syndrome Association and helped Mitch become an advocate for himself. We sent him to an ambassador leadership program through the association and Mitch learned how to make light of difficult situations and explain his Tourette syndrome to others by becoming an ambassador for the association. He would stand up in front of his elementary school classes each new school year, filled with 20-30 curious students all interested and eager to learn what Mitch had to share about his condition. He would let other students know that he was not trying to be "annoying," but his tics were involuntary. He explained that he could not help making the sounds or movements. Mitch brought his own healthier snacks and treats to classroom parties at school, ones that would not trigger his symptoms. By being an ambassador for the association, he was given special Disneyland passes. This was a huge and exciting perk for Mitch, and our family spent many days during those years enjoying the theme park. His diagnosis made him more resilient. Instead of letting it affect him, he embraced his diagnosis and other kids respected him for it. As Mitch became more comfortable with his condition, he grew more confident, and the kids gravitated toward him. He became school President in elementary school.

As time went on, I became more knowledgeable about Tourette syndrome. I became more aware of how food played a role, epigenetics, and the genetic component of Tourette syndrome as well. I was especially observant of our other young children too as they grew, and my husband and I educated them on their brother's condition and building compassion for others. But it was not always easy. Sometimes, with Mitch's tics, he could not control what he blurted out. He was impulsive at times, and this was hard on his younger sisters. They had no prior experience with this condition, so we all learned together. We learned to understand that Mitch could not control his tics and what he said or did sometimes.

My passion for health and wellness continued. I started to cook more meals at home. Our young children began trying new foods with the motto of "You don't know if you don't like it if you don't try it." I read in one of Dr. Fuhrman's books that a child must try some food many times before they develop a liking for it. Questioning more and more about what was going into our bodies and the impact it might have on our health, I carefully chose a diet and improved our lifestyle. Witnessing the amazing benefits of diet and nutrition I began to read more on the differences a healthy diet and lifestyle makes on life and longevity.

Over the years, our family grew. We had a fourth child, a girl, Mia. When she was in elementary school, I decided to get my health coaching certification from the Institute of Integrative Nutrition. I wanted to help others outside of our family achieve what we achieved. Having witnessed the benefits of better energy, immunity, and health, I knew with this certification I could help others get the same results. I started coaching individuals with diabetes, obesity, cardiovascular issues, and other chronic health conditions. I worked as an individual health coach and as a corporate health coach with companies to help improve their employees' health and education related to nutrition and lifestyle. Partnering with individuals and organizations gave me even more energy to continue helping others, researching more, and doing more. The results were inspiring. I worked with individuals with various forms of cancer, seemingly irreversible diseases (which were reversed and improved), and individuals who just felt "unheard" or "unseen" by traditional medicine paths.

My passion for natural health and wellness continued to rise. I voraciously read any book I could get my hands on about health, nutrition, and functional medicine that dove into the roots of what was happening in the body. Excitedly during this time, I also sketched out a drawing for my home vegetable garden and hired Harvest to Home to build it. This company came out and helped me create and maintain an organic vegetable garden in our back yard. This garden became a spiritual haven for me and my family. Our youngest, Mia, helped dig holes to add the first new plants. Growing fresh green herbs inspired me to do even more home cooking and experience new healthy recipes calling for fresh nutrients, such as basil, oregano, and thyme. One of the beds was dedicated primarily to herbs, another contained fresh berries, and several garden boxes change over seasonally with vegetables like snap peas, tomatoes, broccoli, and cauliflower. My home cooking improved as I began utilizing the fresh seasonal produce in new recipes and dishes for our family and friends. I learned to make things like crunchy kale chips and hearty vegetable soups for colder months. I began experimenting with all our fresh garden harvests.

As a mother of four grown children today, when I reflect on the challenges we faced with our son's initial diagnosis, three words come to mind: thankful, grateful, and blessed. I am thankful for the positive path it set us on to improve our health and well-being. I am grateful for the amazing resources we were able to obtain from an incredible community of supporters through Tourette Syndrome Association as well as our family and friends who supported us during the challenging time.

I feel blessed.

Today, my twenty-eight-year-old son Mitch is a hard-working entrepreneur, married, and aware of how stress and diet play a role in his condition and make a difference in his life. My three daughters have all been active witnesses and participants of their healthier lifestyle and they too see the way food plays a role in health and prevention of illness and disease.

I am clear on my life purpose: to educate and inspire others to make changes in their lifestyle to improve their health and longevity. I am currently completing my Master of Science in Integrative Nutrition at Bastyr University in southern California. It is never too late to continue to learn, grow, and help make the world a better and healthier place. It is imperative to understand preventative health and nutrition to improve one's longevity.

It is with pride I can state Mitch has never been on medication for his Tourette syndrome. This was not an easy road. Giving him medicine would have been easier. Learning how to restructure our diet and lifestyle took time, years really, practice, and the formation of new habits for all of us. But it is now the road I take to help others make a difference in their lives.

Today, my garden thrives, full of fresh herbs, seasonal vegetables, blueberries, strawberries, citrus fruits, and avocados. I am now a surprisingly good cook too. I use fresh vegetables and herbs from our garden to make homemade pasta sauces or Pico de Gallo... I especially love making and eating guacamole when the avocados ripen. Fruit salad is a daily staple in our house because I understand how nutritious the phytochemicals are in addition to the vitamins, minerals, and fiber the fruits provide. Daily I squeeze ripe Meyer lemons into water glasses and make fresh homemade lemonade out of them, like my father once taught me. The bees fly happily in and out of the garden, along with the monarch butterflies, and the hummingbirds all do their part to pollinize the garden greens and work with the natural rhythm of the world.

I sat across from Mitch recently during our mother-son date, which we have frequently. I watched him closely. When we are together, I often watch him as I used to while he was growing up. His gestures always give me clues about whether he is following his diet closely or not. This time, I watch as he touches the rim of his black glasses adjusting them to sit better on his nose. His green almond eyes are now wide with pride as he shared with me about his recent new client, an innovative company looking to recruit some solid talent. His dark curls sit short and tight on his head, and I notice a slight tic as his eyes glance upward as he speaks. These days, his tics are minimal. Sometimes they are exasperated with stress, lack of sleep or some other dietary trigger. But I can tell from just a slight tic that life is great for him. I catch a flash of his wedding ring as he raises his hand to adjust his glasses. He got married last summer. He shares with me his vision for his future, for his company, and for his life. In this moment I see a flashback of my young, outgoing, witty son. He has not changed. Nothing has stopped him. Certainly not his unmedicated Tourette syndrome. Now I am the one on the other side of the table beaming with pride.

It can be done.

I saw a quote on a tea bag once that said, "The only thing that can limit you is believing that you are limited. Become limitless." The idea in this quote resonates with me. We must face life's challenges head on with vigor. Sometimes it means taking a not-so popular road. It might be hard at times, but you end up learning from the experience and become better and more self-aware.

When I reflect now, I am grateful. I remember our first experience in the hospital, the fear resonating against the stark white walls, the authoritative gestures towards the MRI and CT machines, the demand for medications, the judgment. I am grateful for trusting my instincts, for the support of my husband. I am grateful for coming up against and being forced to navigate the challenging roads to create a new path with our son, and for paving a road that led us all to health and a deeper understanding of our bodies and "what makes them tic." Our four children have a better appreciation for others' differences, compassion for those struggling, and a knowledge there is always more than one way to arrive at a solution. As a mom, I have been able to share with my children how to find resources, seek support, research, and lean on others in times when life presents challenges.

Candidly, before this happened, I had always questioned times in life when a situation like this presented itself. The times when we were going along and then suddenly, a big wall presented itself. Was it a message? Do we stop here? Do we turn around? Or do we find a way to climb over the wall and get to the other side? I do not take that same approach anymore.

Today, I see the walls differently. Walls exist to give us pause in life —a moment to catch our breath, gather our resources, and create our own path.

ABOUT LAURA MARTÍNEZ MCDERMOTT

Laura Martínez McDermott is a Certified Integrative Nutrition Health Coach, advocate, and educator for preventative health and wellness. As a Coach for over a decade, McDermott has worked 1:1 and in groups with individuals who have been diagnosed with various forms of cancer, Tourette syndrome, liver and pancreatic diseases, cardiovascular diseases, long COVID, dementia, and many other chronic health conditions. As a proponent of continuing education, McDermott recently decided to pursue a Master of Science in Integrative Nutrition at Bastyr University. Her mission in life is to inspire individuals to improve their health and longevity through diet, nutrition, exercise, sleep, community, and stress management. In her spare time, she enjoys cooking, travel, and tending to her garden, as well as spending time with her husband Rod, their four children Mitchell, Marissa, Madeline, and Mia, and their extended families and friends. She currently lives in southern California and spends time as "Captain" on her boat "Our Happy Place" seeking out dolphins, whales, or watching sunsets.

Website: *www.Lauramcdhealth.com*
Instagram: *www.instagram.com/lauramcdermotthealth*
Facebook: *www.facebook.com/laura.mcdermott.359*

7
MELISSA LEE PARENT

THE GIFT IN DEATH

Thursday, February 17th, 2022, around 8 p.m., I died, and it was the best thing I did not know I needed. Yes, you read that correctly, I died, and it was a gift that I call my great reset. Before I dive into how dying was a gift, I need to share some of the back story.

People often ask what my catalyst was, the one thing that prompted such change, growth, and healing in my life. The thing is, there is not a single moment but instead several aha moments. Moments where I was sick of my shit. Sick of repeating cycles. Some of these moments are bigger than others, but they all impacted me in some way that led to the next aha moment.

In 2017, I was fresh home from my last deployment and though it was non-conflict, I was a mess. A friend took one look at me and her lovingly bold way said I needed some fucking help. In December of that year, I spent twenty days with her in Maui doing yoga and I started cracking open in the best way possible. I knew I needed to move to the island. When I got home, I immediately submitted paperwork to the Air Force to part ways. Though my move happened in sixteen months, the transition was not smooth. Initially I worked between eighty to ninety hours a week selling art and bartending.

Finally, I secured a Department of Defense job doing almost the same work I did in the military.

The pay was great, but I was not happy. Don't get me wrong, I was grateful but not happy. Working there opened many opportunities but I didn't leave the military to do the same shit job only with better hair at a nicer location. Much better hair. This did not stop me though from continuing my healing journey. Honestly, that lovely paycheck helped facilitate it. I started learning more about meditation, different types of yoga, mindful consumption, energy work, and even became a reiki master. The more I worked on myself, the more I disliked bartending and working for the DoD. So here we are in this incredible and unpredictable path. I would heal to a point then feel stuck, a thing would happen that would catapult me to the next phase of healing, then the next. Seemingly random moments divinely leading new heights. In this randomness I was connected to a friend that led me to plant medicine. We are not talking about herbalism or recreational use of psychedelics. We are embracing the mindful, intentional use in sacred settings for deep healing. Some of this healing was subtle but most blasted through like the Kool-Aid man.

Oh Yeah!

Six months before my death, I bought a 99 Jeep Wrangler TJ as a secondary vehicle and project for myself. She is a delightful beasty that I named Alakoa, loosely translated from Hawaiian it means Warrior Spirit or Spirit of the Warrior. She is a stunning bright blue, straight six, four-liter engine, with a manual transmission. The first thing I did was take off her doors and top. It is Maui, Alakoa needs to be nakie. She quickly became my mental health vehicle in so many ways. I was driving her to a plant medicine ceremony one day, and the highway goes up a steep hill. About 1500 -foot elevation gain in nine miles. I was cheering Alakoa on—Jeeps aren't known for their speed or aerodynamics—when I had a lightbulb moment. What if I talked to myself the way I talked to my Jeep? What if I encouraged and cheered for myself the way I did Alakoa. Mind Blown!

It may have been during that ceremony or perhaps another that I realized not only had I been neglected as a toddler in foster homes, but I had also been sexually abused.

Friday, February 11th and we are going to start getting a little woo with this story.

That night I was attending another plant medicine ceremony; however, this one was a bit different than what I was used to. I was stepping into the assistant role and there was someone attending that I had a bit of friction with. I debated internally to the point of making myself sick, and finally I decided to throw it in the fuck-it bucket. Mentally, I told myself I wasn't going to let that ahem person hinder my healing. On my way out the door, my stunning Medusa crystal and hand carved wand demanded to come with.... So they did. Who am I to argue with spiritual things? Off we go in Alakoa ready to face the thing that gave us so much angst throughout the day. Except nobody showed up! All of that anxiety for no reason. My mind had created a scenario for no reason, as if that isn't applicable for the rest of our life experiences. I ended up having the most profound and beautiful plant medicine experiences that cannot adequately be put into words. I will say two things about it though.

One, I sat with the question of do I sell Alakoa. She was turning out to be a bigger project that I had anticipated. The answer I got was no, she was going to be a source of abundance.

Two, I manifested everything that would happen over the following week.

Tuesday, February 15th. That DoD job that I did not love? We had mostly been working from home due to COVID restrictions, thank God for getting paid to sit at your computer in your underoos. It had been determined that we return to the office but COVID vaccination was required in order to do so. Well, I believe in people doing what is best for their body. For me, it did not feel right with my background or family medical history to get the vaccine. Bright and early that day, I got a phone call telling me that I no longer worked for the Department of Defense.

That same day, I received a random package in the mail from a friend and that surprise package was a sheet of affirmation stickers very similar to the affirmations I post daily on my social media stories. One of the stickers said, "I am Abundant." Immediately, I went out and put that bad boy on the center console of Alakoa.

Here we are, back at September 17th, my personal D-day. I don't remember much about how that morning started outside of coffee was definitely involved. Coffee is pretty much the elixir of life and humanity. The plan? Drive up that steep hill to my mentor's house to spend the day playing in the dirt, cutting back her behemoth lilikoi vine, and contemplate my next phase. Once again on my way out the door, my Medusa crystal and wand demanded to go for a ride. Also, for some reason, I also decided to leave extra food out for my cat, pack an overnight bag, and grab my laptop. I had no idea why but once again, I was not going to question the urge. It was a stunning Maui day with the sun shining bright, with enough of a breeze to keep the heat at bay. There was so much healing and release that day. We talked story, I laughed, cried, raged, mourned, and processed. It ran so deep, deeper than the loss of my job. There was the liberation of not caring about my security clearance for the first time in eighteen years. The reckless abandonment of cutting, pulling, clearing overgrown brush without hearing the criticism of my family of how precise I should be when pruning. Tears for the loss of stability and joy for no longer feeling the need to perform. When I left, my heart was full and my spirit was high.

Two days later I woke up in the ICU unable to move, in agony, not understanding what was happening or knowing where I was. My last clear memory was sitting at a red stoplight. My precious Alakoa and I had been in an accident. I had random flashes like seeing someone I recognized and saying "I know you." I remember bright lights. I remember telling someone they did not need to shave so much hair. I remember repeating to myself that I was safe; it was just a journey. I am safe. It is just a journey. I am safe. It is just a journey.

I had to pee but could not move and was so confused. So confused and lost. I remember how mortified I was when I told the nurse I had to go and her kindness when she explained that I could. Apparently I had a vacuum catheter called the purewick. For days, I had to be rolled to my side in the hospital bed to go to the bathroom before I was strong enough to be assisted to the toilet. As the mental fog cleared, I started to get answers. It was unknown what caused the accident or how I was found, just that the Jeep was on its side and I was not conscious. I had sustained the following:

- Traumatic Brain Injury
- Fracture at base of C1, through C2 (hashtag), part way through C3
- Multiple ribs were fractured with mild displacement
- Contusion R posterior bottom lung
- Fracture L Hip
- Fracture L pelvis
- Fracture R sacrum
- Fracture R iliac wing
- Laceration along right front hairline. 8 staples
- Laceration of the right foot. Stitches
- Six months later we discovered that I had a Lisfranc sprain with possible fracture in the right foot.
- One year later we discovered that I still had debris in the right foot as well.

So where in the fuck is the silver lining?

The most obvious? I was alive. That break of the neck that I sustained is called the hangman's fracture. The name speaks for itself as far as the potential severity. While some people are able to wear only a brace while they heal, I could not. Due to the extent of the break, multiple fractures in one bone both vertically and horizontally, I got to be bolted into a halo. Another miraculous silver lining? None of the broken bones had moved significantly either. Several months later during physical therapy I found out that if my C2 had shifted a millimeter. I potentially would be dead or paralyzed.

The next immediate silver lining? Remember how I mentioned I had left my cat extra food and packed my laptop when I left the house that morning of the 17th? Welp, for whatever reason I still don't understand, nobody had been notified that I was in an accident or that I was in the ICU. My phone had not yet been recovered from the crash site; however, when I got to go on my ambulance ride, the paramedics swooped up my overnight bag with my laptop. Being an iPhone and MacBook user, my text messages synced directly to my computer. With that, I was able to notify close friends that I had a little head boop and my cat probably needed to be fed. Outside of keeping my cat fed, I did not expect much support. That is not a reflection of the people I have in my life but my own perception believing that I was not that closely connected to most people. I was so blissfully wrong.

Not only did friends look after my cat, but they walked the field where I had my accident, found my phone, and got my Jeep out of the tow yard. Toiletries were delivered to me in the hospital, journals for me to write, the owners of a local diner I am a regular at even brought me food. Though we were not allowed visitors, there was always support. After a few days in the hospital, I was told that I would not be released unless I had care at home otherwise I would have to go to a long term recovery facility. I, in my stubbornness, was absolutely NOT going to the recovery facility so I told a little fibbers saying that yes, I totally had help at home. I live alone. My ridiculous thought process, I can take care of myself and figure out the rest.

First, I would like to point out how that belief was not a good reflection of my IQ.

Second, blinging silver lining here, my friends Cambria and Chantel came in like fucking saints.

These two incredible souls live a few streets away from me, and while we were friends and close, I didn't even stop to consider how close. While I was in the hospital they cared for my cat, watered my plants, and cleaned my home. After being in the hospital ten days, they swooped me up when I was discharged, patiently drove me around to get my prescriptions filled only to find out the next day they could not be due to hospital error. Cleaned the infection I had developed in my foot while in the hospital, cleaned my halo holes in my head, kept me clean with body wipes because I could not bathe, helped me dress, made sure I was fed, patiently tidied my house because I made messes trying to be independent, took me on small adventures to get me out of the house, the list goes on. They weren't my only support either. Chantel is active in her church, and though I am not a parishioner, members of the congregation were bringing me food and helping around the house after she had shared about my boop. My hairdresser came over several times to wash my hair with the hose outside and braid it because I couldn't. My meditation teacher drove an hour each direction with her six-month-old son to spend time and have lunch, twice. From virtual strangers, casual acquaintances, to close friends, I was so fucking supported that I was overwhelmed with gratitude. My mind was blown.

Where was my family in all of this? I waited until I was discharged from the hospital and home a couple days before I called them. Not because I was trying to hide or be proud or stubborn either; I did not have the emotional bandwidth for that call yet. The previous October, I had gotten into a large conflict with the mother who raised me, not biological. Nothing new but it was a doozy. Everything I did came with a lecture, criticism, warning, advice, and so on. Everything. Even at thirty-eight it was constant. Rarely was there acknowledgement of what I was doing without some additional comment. It felt like I could do nothing right or enough. I was never enough. That no matter what I did, she was always questioning me, my path, my choices. We hadn't talked in months, not even over the holidays. I finally decided to tell her because of my grandma. When my grandma was admitted into the hospital for the final time, my mom did not tell me until a day or two later. In so many words told me that I could not do anything anyways. When they decided to remove oxygen, they did not call me the next day to tell me if she had made it through the night. I had to call and ask. Remembering that feeling, I could not do the same thing to her. I worked backwards with the news kinda like "Hey, so I no longer work for the DoD. I was supposed to graduate magna cume laude last week but I was in a Jeep accident. By the way, the Jeep was mine. I spent ten days in the hospital, broke my neck and a few other bones. I'm ok though and home now." About a week later she arrived in Maui and was here for two weeks. I spent quite a bit of time watching her while I was lying on the coach and realized something HUGE. All those years of criticism, of not feeling like I was enough or worthy? It was not about me and it was not about how she viewed me. All of the lectures, warnings, and comments were first, made out of love and second, a projection of her own stuff. It was not me. I also realized that though she may not be the most affectionate, it was not because I wasn't loved by her, but instead how she was personally wired. Over thirty years of internalization, limiting beliefs, and programming were understood in that moment. She came to help me recover from my accident but instead, that realization was the greatest healing I could have hoped for.

It was after Mom left that the incredible support I mentioned previously really came into play. I kept having this vision followed by a knowing deep in my core. I would see an angelic creature sitting in a tree watching the accident and keeping my body safe while an energetic part of me dissipated. One of the incredible humans that came to help me also facilitates deep energy healing. I was receiving a particularly powerful and vulnerable session with her when I fully realized my death that day. When I had been sexually assaulted in foster homes as a young child, the original essence of Melissa was tucked away into safety and the Melissa that had navigated life until this point had emerged. She had been the energetic buffer between childhood trauma, abusive relationships, and military service. Through the healing and growth that I had experienced over the last couple years, that version of Melissa no longer fit. She had done her job, done it well, but it was time for her to pass. Time for the original Melissa to reemerge. The only way for that to happen was for me to die. Some may see it as woo or far reaching, but I know I am not the same person that I was. My Medusa crystal and wand were never found. Maybe they were part of it.

I was off of crutches in just over seven weeks and out of the halo ten and a half weeks. Nobody, including the doctors, understands how I was able to heal so quickly. I do though.

In my reset, my entire perspective shifted. Even while I was in the hospital, I was filled with deep gratitude and confidence. Gratitude that I was alive and confidence that I was going to heal. That is not to say that I did not have down days or that I could not acknowledge things sucked hairy monkey balls. Trust me, I had some emotional breakdowns, tears, rage, and frustration. Cause let's be honest, this was far from ideal and I knew there was a long road ahead of me. That did not mean however that the entire road had to be difficult. I would envision my bones being mended and my body being healthy. It would have been easy and completely understandable for me to stay at home, on my couch for however long I felt I needed. Instead though, I left the house as often as I could. I was like that excited puppy ready to go for a ride. I also had a sense of humor through the entire process. If you are familiar with Hawaii, you know that getting your picture taken with parrots is a huge tourist attraction. So what did I do? I went to the other side of the island where they were and not only did I get a picture taken with a parrot, but I also put one of those beautiful creatures on the halo, balanced myself on my crutches so that my hands were free to hold one in each. I may have had some small issues with spatial awareness with the halo and bumped into walls, corners, and cabinets. Our solution? We put tennis balls on the corners. When a friend, who also drives a topless Jeep, offered to take me out for adventures, many people questioned the wisdom of this, I just said at least I have plenty of head room. When I was more stable on my feet, I would take waddles on the beach. As I felt safer, I would waddle in my halo around the block.

I ran a marathon eleven months after the accident—it was not my first but it was different than the rest. My entire relationship with running and fitness changed after my boop. Before, I ran with force, pushing, with a fuck you attitude to prove that I still could after I had developed chronic sciatica in the military and was told I should stop. One day I was on a long run and my internal dialogue shifted. I stopped saying asshole things to myself under the bullshit guise of motivation. I started encouraging myself. I started praising myself. I acknowledged that my running and fitness looks different and that is ok. I am different. I started running out of deep gratitude and love for myself. For what I could do, not punishment.

As for Alakoa, she survived and the "I am Abundant" sticker is still on her center console. She was still drivable after the accident but with some body damage. Sound familiar? It cost more to fix her than what market value said she was worth. Many people questioned why I would spend that money instead of getting a new Jeep. To me though, she is priceless. She and I bled together. She has become a symbolic extension of myself. Talking to her, cheering her on the way I learned to talk myself. How she is still going strong no matter what life throws at her. Not giving up on her, fighting for her the way I want others to for me. The way I fight for myself. Loving and caring for her the way I was loving and caring myself.

The greatest silver lining of all with my great reset is learning life is about your relationship with your mindset and perspective.

I am stronger than ever but softer than I ever could have imagined. I no longer have a hardness to me or a desire to keep people at an arm's distance. I am not scared to surrender or be vulnerable. To embrace my passion and fierceness instead of watering myself down out of fear. In breaking, I have learned that I am whole, worthy, and enough.

I have learned unconditional love for myself in all forms and all forms of me are worthy of love.

Silver does not always shine. Sometimes it is dull, sometimes it is tarnished, sometimes it is oxidized, and sometimes it is just plain tin foil. In every situation though, that silver depends on your perspective.

8
PORTAL TO MAUI

AUGUST 8TH, 2023. THE LION'S GATE PORTAL.

A day that has forever changed the island of Maui and her people. At 12:22 a.m., the first major fire was reported and evacuations started in Kula, known as the Upcountry area. While the situation was concerning, we all had faith it would be contained quickly. Morning dawned and the rest of the island started their day unaware of how significantly their world would shift in a few short hours.

Trade winds are common on Maui, especially during the summer months, and it is not unusual for them to blow anywhere between 10-30 mph. On that day, the conditions were dry on the island and the winds were higher than normal. Hurricane Dora, though 700 miles away, was relentlessly spinning as a Category 4 storm. She spun longer than any other storm in the area in over fifty years. Dora created a windy low-pressure system to the south of Maui that pushed against the high-pressure system north of Maui. The result? A funnel bringing significantly hot weather, low humidity, and gusting winds across the island. Gusts that were reported to reach peaks of around eighty miles per hour.

In Lahaina, on the west side of Maui, nearly opposite of Kula, a downed powerline sparked a brush fire at 6:37 a.m. Due to the fire's close proximity to a residential neighborhood, evacuations were ordered for the immediate area, and the fire was reported to be fully contained by 9 a.m. This same neighborhood had been evacuated months prior due to a separate blaze. Throughout the day, the winds whipped across the island, especially in Lahaina. Homes started to sustain damage, school was canceled, electricity and cell service was intermittent.

At 3:30 p.m., either the previously contained fire flared up or a secondary fire started—it is unclear which. The homes nearby were once again ordered to evacuate; however, residents in other parts of Lahaina town were instructed to shelter in place. The section of the highway nearest to the fire was closed. Between the high wind gusts, drought conditions, dry lawns due to residents being under water restrictions, and neighborhoods with homes in close proximity, the fire grew rapidly and was soon out of control.

When firefighters attempted to battle the blaze, they were thwarted by a lack of water pressure for reasons that are still under investigation.

And so, the fire continued to spread, leaving people with little to no warning to evacuate.

Maui has the most advanced alert system in the world, yet it was never sounded. That is also under investigation.

The flames jumped major roadways moving from the outer edges of Lahaina and closer to her historic heart. Within minutes, hundreds of homes burned. Some people received text alerts while others did not. Many did not know what was happening until the fire was upon them. People attempting to flee on foot and by car were surrounded by flames. Traffic was jammed. Front Street was closed in both directions, survivors report that the police had roadblocks in place. There was no other way out of town.

Around 5:45 p.m., just over two hours after the fire flared up again, the flames had reached the shoreline. Buildings, homes, businesses, cars were engulfed in flames. Some were exploding. Survivors were trapped and their only escape, their only hope for survival, was to jump into the ocean and pray as the town burned.

Meanwhile, while the rest of the island knew that there was a fire in both Kula and Lahaina and that there were evacuations in place, many of us were unaware of just how dire the situation was. We knew the highway connecting Lahaina to the rest of the island was closed and it happens often enough for us to not be alarmed at first. There was no cell service however later that day, drone footage showed much of the area engulfed in flames. Another fire had started Upcountry in Olinda (near Kula) then a fourth in Pulehu that moved towards Kihei at the south end of the island. We all were on edge. That night, my neighborhood was ordered to evacuate as well. While I did not think there was a big risk of reaching my home, there are also only two ways to exit. It was a risk I was not willing to take. The smell of smoke was thick in the air and as I was driving to the central part of the island at 1 a.m., August 9th, I could see the flames glowing in the distance. It was the third major fire in four years.

My cat and I hunkered down in my SUV in the Costco parking lot for a few hours. I knew it was a safe, well-lit location, and I wanted to ensure that my gas tank was full just in case. By 6 a.m., my evacuation order was lifted, and I knew the community was going to the support of everyone coming together.

In 24 hours, thousands of Maui residents had been displaced. Initially, over a thousand were unaccounted for. Thousands of buildings destroyed. Homes and businesses lost. The historic town of Lahaina, the original capital of Hawaii, had burned. Some of the state's oldest landmarks had been destroyed. Maui had experienced the deadliest fire in the United States in over a hundred years. The county's emergency response was not prepared to handle such a catastrophic event.

As I look back at August 8th, it was emotionally charged. More emotionally charged than I realized at the time. When I woke up that morning, I discovered through Facebook that a friend had been evacuated in the middle of the night. She had vaguely posted around 2:30 a.m. stating sarcastically how joyous it is to be woken up by firefighters and loading horse, two ponies, a dog, plus her ninety-year-old mother up in the middle of the night. I called. I called often but it kept going straight to voicemail. Throughout the day, I reached out to our mutual friends hoping they had heard from her, but they had not either. I was nearly frantic and battled with myself on if I should drive up, but I did not know where the fire was precisely or where she had evacuated to either. All I could do was pray that no news was good news at that point. I will never forget the tears of relief I felt when I saw her following Facebook post telling us she was safe. I also had friends that lived in Lahaina that I could not reach. Friends that were like my own family. I had to hold the faith that they were ok but to be honest, I was constantly checking my phone. Checking for messages, checking social media for updates, and checking the news. Desperately grasping for any kernel of information. We even posted on social media asking if anyone had seen them. When we finally found out they had made it to a shelter safely, they did not have enough fuel to drive out. I am not sure how they managed to get fuel, but in the middle of the night, they bravely drove a winding, single lane, road on the back side of West Maui where much of it has cliff drops. We found out days later that their home was lost in Lahaina, a lifetime of memories, family heirlooms, and mementos of their grandchildren. They were told that it would take anywhere between five and ten years to rebuild the condo complex. Twenty days after the fire, they moved off island to Florida.

And here friends, amongst this tragedy, is where the silver lining begins.

It was a new day and the ENTIRE island morphed into go mode without hesitation or prompting.

People immediately went to the stores to purchase necessities for those displaced. Within hours, shelves were emptied, and employees could not keep up with the demand to restock. We were thankful when we saw an item was sold out because that meant that need was being met. Businesses became donation drop off locations for those items to be distributed to evacuation shelters. Shelters quickly became overwhelmed with donations and people wanting to help. Restaurants started cooking meals to be delivered to first responders, survivors, and volunteers. Cooking is a coping mechanism for a friend who lived in Lahaina, she was on the South Side of the island when the fires broke out, she had no idea if her home stood. While she waited to hear, she cooked eight pans of fried rice. I will never forget the look on an Uncle's face when he saw me walk into the shelter with those pans. His eyes immediately filled with tears and when he helped me carry them in, he looked at me with wondrous gratitude and whispered, "It is still warm."

There was no limitation to what we would give to support. When a gap was discovered, it was quickly filled without question. Through the chaos, there was a unifying cohesiveness. This selfless unification was not limited to the people of Maui though; all the islands immediately came together. People of Lanai and Molokai, who are small and have very little as it is, started bringing supplies over by boat. Those that were on Oahu and the Big Island purchased airline tickets simply to bring over what they could in checked bags.

Friends, family, and strangers from both the mainland and internationally started donating funds directly to those of us on the island so that we could continue purchasing needed supplies directly. Amazon wish lists were created should people want to purchase items instead of donating funds.

We still had minimal contact with Lahaina though. There were small pockets with cell service and power. We knew it was bad. Footage from boats and drones started reaching social media. Traffic in and out was limited; the main road was closed for safety reasons.

By August 10th, we still had virtually no outside support and instead of being discouraged, efforts quadrupled. If we could not access the West Side by car, we were going by boat. Dozens of boats and jet skis rallied. When we could not access land by harbor or pier, we did beach landings. We would create fire lines or daisy chains, standing in the water and sand to pass supplies off to those on shore.

People started creating their own support hubs and relief centers, even those who had lost everything, including their own homes and vehicles, and some were still searching for missing loved ones. These hubs were popping up in parks, front yards, and parking lots, there were no limits.

Another few days passed, and we still were lacking external support. Why? We still are not sure, but all we knew is that our people needed help. So, we dug in deeper.

The people of Molokai started fishing and hunting more deer, processing it, to bring over much needed meat. Farmers donated their produce. Restaurants went from preparing hundreds to thousands of meals a day. Generators and Starlinks were donated so that we could start creating sustainable contact. There was not a single person on this island that was not impacted by the fires nor was there a person that did not contribute towards the relief efforts. For weeks, most of the support came from the local level.

We lovingly refer to it as Kanaka FEMA and Kanaka Costco.

Then we noticed a shift. At some point through this, volunteers had arrived. Yes, there were organizations like World Central Kitchen that came and were vital game changers. I am referring to individuals. People from neighboring islands and the mainland dropped everything to come help. Help in all forms. We had people ranging from retirees, off duty emergency responders, construction workers, medical support, warehouse management. Average people coming together to create a monumental difference.

I channeled my military experience into helping my community. Initially, I was purchasing supplies, delivering those purchases plus whatever other donations I had collected to the support hubs Upcountry. Driving back and forth several times a day. After three days, I was able to join people running supplies by boat to the West Side. Each day was filled with purchasing, collecting, loading, delivering, and unloading. We would repeat this as many times a day as we could. I was sharing as much information as I could on social media to help bring awareness to what was really happening and how desperately we needed help. After two weeks, I heard from a casual friend asking if I could help him. Instantly, I said yes. He had been delivering pallets of ice, water, and any other supplies he could get directly to impacted neighborhoods and relief hubs. For nearly a month and a half, we ran six days a week. We distributed at least six pallets of twenty-pound bags of ice, a rough estimate of 8000 pounds of ice per day. One neighborhood we walked the streets, gridding back and forth, passing out ice and cases of water because their water was contaminated. On one of those days, a much older Aunty gestured to me, calling me over. With a bit of a language barrier, we learned that she had no soap or toilet paper. So I ran down to a neighborhood hub and grabbed some for her. Two days later, I discovered she was out of Depends. Off we went running. Every few days, we would leave a couple packages for her next to the door.

Our deliveries were not limited to ice and water though; we would haul any supplies we could. Spam, rice, milk, eggs, air purifiers, literal tons. We are still delivering supplies three to four days a week to impacted neighborhoods and six different locally organized/operated relief hubs. We are greeted with big smiles and hugs every day by the people who do not get to drive away from this tragedy at night. I take pictures of what their current needs are and reach out to my network to see what we can find, donate, or purchase. We talk story, share how the other hubs are doing, and how we can help one another. An initial community hub was set up directly on a small boat ramp and you could see Molokai in the distance. Several occasions, we arrived while they were unloading supplies that had come over by personal boat. One occasion was a rare and special gift. We were making one of our regular stops when we saw three boats from Molokai arriving. I learned that much like older western culture, they were asking for permission to come ashore. The smiles and joy from both those on the boats and the land reinforce the connection the people have to one another.

One of the community run hubs is very family centric. One night a week they have a movie projector and popcorn machine set up for the kids. During the day, a bounce house for them to play. There are also two Uncles that have been displaced living there with their two-year-old rottweiler, Shadow. Shadow is a gentle giant that I get to love every morning that we are there. He has gotten to know the sound of the truck and my voice. As soon as he hears us coming, he will perk up and wag his adorable nub tail. We even keep treats in the truck just for him because every pupper needs treats. At each of these locations, there is a personal connection. Every location asks if we need food, coffee, or water, yet we are the ones coming to support them. Our last stop of the day always has either an otter pop or popsicle waiting for us when we are done.

You see, in nearly fifteen years of combined military service, I have worked disaster relief around the world. Never, at any point, have I seen a community come together like I have here. It did not matter if you were Native, local, transplant, or mainland volunteer. We are all one ohana, one family, caring for one another. Often, cars honk and wave as they drive past because they recognize the truck. They yell thank you out the windows or pull up in their cars as we are loading ice to deliver. In many places, violence and looting erupt after a disaster; that was not the case here. In fact it has been the opposite. Individuals are managing to get fishing supplies donated for children and adults who lost everything. Same for tradesmen who lost their tools. Instruments for both professional musicians and the casual enthusiast. The list goes on of people donating time, goods, and services. It brings me to tears every time I think of it. The overwhelming humility and gratitude I have, not only witnessing the true aloha spirit, but also to be part of this community. I have met so many incredible souls that I would never have connected with if it had not been for this tragedy. People who were either casual connections or strangers are now family. I have never felt so at home. I often refer to myself as the transplant, jokingly call myself haole. Now I am lovingly corrected, told that I am not haole or transplant. Now called ohana by kanaka and kapuna alike. The humbling gratitude and honor of those words brings me to tears every time.

While not as shining, a different silver lining aspect of this fire and the community coming together is also awareness. Often, when people think of Maui, they picture lush jungle and stunning beaches.

They are not wrong, but there is a side that many do not see. Many do not see the profound and distinct differences between the local population and tourist centric areas. Redirection of water supply and water rights is an ongoing issue in Maui. As you drive local neighborhoods and agricultural land, one will notice how much of it is dry and overgrown. Much of the island is on water restrictions. In contrast though, one resort in Maui uses nearly half a million gallons of water daily and the average golf course consumes 200 million gallons of water per year. The average home 52,600 gallons per year. As I volunteer on the West Side almost daily, I see the distinct line in the communities between the dry residential areas and the green tourism driven regions. County parks that had not been watered in nearly a year. One area burned, the other did not. Could some of the fire damage have been avoided if there was better access to water?

A second notable distinction between residential and tourist central areas are the power lines. See, many of the power lines in residential areas and towns are still above ground and not well maintained. It is estimated that over thirty power lines were downed by the high winds. Should one look at resort areas such as Wailea, Napili, and Kanapali, most lines run underground. On the few occasions they run above ground, they are well maintained. Logical solutions considering our notorious trade winds.

With thousands of people displaced, we are now facing the issue of housing. Before the fire, there was already a shortage of affordable housing on the island. Emphasis on affordable. Maui has one of the highest costs of living in the nation where the average home to purchase is over one million dollars and the average condo to rent is $3500 a month. Minimum wage is $12 an hour. Now here we are, only two months after the fire, displaced people are searching for homes to live long term while they rebuild. They are being removed from temporary solutions like resorts and condos to accommodate tourism. In a 2018 study, one in seven residential units are used as vacation rentals, 60% of condos and 52% of homes are sold to nonresident buyers. Where are people going to live?

While tourism is an important part of the Maui economy, seventy cents to every dollar generated in Maui comes from tourism. In tragic times like COVID and now this deadly fire, the island is economically crippled. Through this adversity, we can look for more sustainable ways to support the island. Outside of financial sustainability, there is also sustainability of our natural resources. Each year, Maui sees three million tourists, but her local population is only 165,400 people. At what point is the land overburdened? We are already paving over paradise to accommodate the demand.

As I sit here, I cannot help but notice today is exactly two months since the fires started. They still are not out. Many parts of the affected areas still do not have clean water, and some neighborhoods do not have power. Many residents have not been able to return to their home to sift through the ashes. Thousands are still in temporary housing. However, the West Side of the island has been opened to tourism. Unofficially, over 6,730 acres have burned, 2,300 buildings destroyed with 86% of them being homes, at least ninety-seven deceased with people still unaccounted for. There are grassroots organizations like Brown Kross Hui, Manuahi Community Outreach, Maui Rapid Response, and Hungry Heroes Hawaii supporting every day.

The greatest silver lining? We are no longer an island divided. We came together to support one another in the community. We stand together raising awareness of the harsh realities that come with living on the island. We stand together as one voice. That this is one ohana. Ohana at its core is a family connected by love, respect, character, actions, mindset. We are one ohana showing the world how deeply we live the true aloha spirit.

ABOUT MELISSA LEE PARENT

Melissa Lee Parent is a Master Reiki practitioner, shamanic healer, energy worker, median, and transformational mindset coach helping people break free from their trauma, limiting beliefs, destructive habits, behaviors, and cycles.

Melissa believes that we are all looking for Moksha (moke-shaw) in some form.

When finding Moksha, we release the attachment to the beliefs, stories, mindset, and habits that do not serve us.

In her own healing journey from childhood trauma, military service, sexual assault, and a near-death experience, Melissa embraced the multifaceted dynamic that is Moksha. She realized that we all have the power within us to transcend our limitations and can achieve liberation from our subconscious. These unhealthy beliefs come from unconscious programming we receive throughout our lives. Once we identify this harmful programming, we get to shift our perspective of these stories and release their hold over us.

Melissa is the founder of Lions Pride Healing, a non-profit dedicated to supporting Veterans and first responders. Melissa is also a founding facilitator and member of the Hale La'a Church that believes in the healing power of Earth-based entheogenic sacraments and ceremony. She is an endurance athlete and outdoor enthusiast living in Maui with her cat, Tinkerbell.

Email: *Melissa@TheMelissaLeeParent.com*
Linktree: *www.linktr.ee/TheMelissaLeeParent*

9
NATALIE BIGLER

WALKING ON WATER

INNOCENCE

She is a Child—innocent, pure, loving, believing. The world is her playground; eyes full of discovery, courage, and openness. Her voice always sings, her body loves to dance. She is *free.* She embodies effortless joy and beauty. When she laughs, she makes everything she touches live.

Wholeness is her birthright, crystal pools of life-giving stillness in her soul. Her essence is unchangeable, eternal, basking in the love of the Father of Lights. She resonates with all the illumination in the universe, connected to everything—mother earth, sky, her ancestors —limitless oceans of stars and love.

FEAR

I am confused when he touches me. *Why is this happening? Wasn't I supposed to be safe with you?* I was supposed to trust him, but everything felt wrong. Fear escalates as he holds my mouth, so I can't scream. Raw pain is mixed with absolute horror. Fragile beauty in me fractures into a million shards of glass. An illusion, a reflection of me but no longer whole. The living flow of my soul abruptly stops as waves of terror wash away my innocence. Walls of forgetfulness surround my heart to protect.

I am sinking beneath a million oceans of darkness, drowning in the unknown blackness of an unseen, unheard world. I open my mouth to speak, but all words are choked out by the miles and miles of water. *When will it end? When will it end?* I sink to the bottom, *I cannot breathe*. Memory and time blur into each other in this endless, eternal night.

SHAME

I awake on an empty beach, unsure how I survived. I slowly become conscious of the sun stretching to touch my face and back. I should be dead, but *I'm alive*. Sand covers me along with thousands of scratches —reminders of past pain, but without any recollection of it. Everything within me feels rearranged in a tangled mess without the truth.

I look out across the wild sea, missing my home. In the waves, I see flashes of distant, swirling memories. Suddenly, a young girl crosses the sea on her white stallion; her laughter echoes in the splashes and spray. We are eleven and best friends; freely playing in ripples of joy. My heart and body heal; the shadowy darkness below the surface fades. As suddenly as she appeared, she disappeared. *Last night she was killed instantly in a car accident.* With no warning, slammed to the ground, I am drowning, choking on wave after wave of silent grief. Suddenly the world feels too big for me, larger and somehow insurmountable. As much as I try to orient myself, I cannot figure out where I am. I feel lost.

I turn away from my childhood paradise, no longer safe there. A towering jungle of twisted vines appears before me; I must cross it, find shelter, make a fire. It's so dark! I find others on my journey who seem to have torches I can hold, but I keep getting burned. My mind continues to hear raspy voices of shame constrict around me like dark vines around my neck, choking out life. *It's not safe to speak, to be seen, to connect. You will be abandoned.* I need connection more than air, and search deeply for the truth about God: finally, honestly seeking a relationship with Him. Light rays break through dark clouds when I hear his gentle voice whispering to my heart, *I am here.* I begin to trust him, finding myself again.

PAIN

When I meet my husband, I promise myself not to get too close; I'm scared of this warmth of growing love, of abandonment and loss. But Isolation is cold, so I ask God if It's safe to get in this boat. *If you choose this, I will support you.* We joyfully marry, but a growing darkness makes me feel uneasy. As a university student, I am awakened in the night by a sudden, clear voice in my mind. I am learning to trust that voice, even if I can't see the why.

Change your major to marriage and family therapy.

I could never have anticipated the tidal wave that followed. My new husband confesses, haltingly, to pornography use for many years. Salty waters of grief and pain flood in as I try to hold the ocean back inside and tell it to stay. *Would truth destroy me, destroy us?*

I spend all my energy now warily watching, holding my breath. My body is running a marathon. I build taller walls to hold his secrets, but the churning waters hold no clarity. The terms *sexual addiction* and *betrayal trauma* feel like life sentences. *Is this really my life? What did I do wrong?* I feel unprotected, my children now in tow. *I must protect them!* My body reels from the impact of the lies. I desperately grasp for safety, holding on tighter and tighter to control. Maybe my world won't fall apart if I could keep everyone together. I reach for God's comforting voice in the deep, but fear and isolation are deafening as the swells of pain wash over us. I can't hold the pieces; it's too much to carry.

Truth comes out, drop by drop. *No one else should have to hold all of this.* I am hurting all over, but I smile at my neighbor, my friend, my child. I don't want to be the one with all the leaks, the one causing problems, the subject of whispers and closed-door conversations—so

I never share all the weight of the secrets and sadness. The crashing surf is relentless; I can't catch my breath. Compassionate loved ones, counselors, and coaches bail with me now as my husband commits to inpatient treatment.Behind my soft and vulnerable heart the life drips, drips, drips out of me... like uncontained water seeping from my body, my eyes, and my weary knees as I crawl.

"More Buckets!" I yell as the water keeps rising.

The cyclone of fear reaches hurricane force. Desperate pleas for rescue cry from my heart every second for relief from this impossible situation. I have seen many miracles, but this one does not come. *God where are you? Can't you see we need healing?*

Silence.

A massive tsunami hits my home and fills it to the very top. My perfectly cleaned and arranged home is now floating wildly, everything inside colliding. My children are flailing everywhere. I am swimming, fighting, grabbing everyone and everything I can see with my outstretched hands. My children are shaken, bruised, cut all over. I should have been able to protect them! Why did I not build a stronger house? How could I allow them to feel this same pain and fear? It's not fair to them. *I did this. I did not protect them.* The words hit my heart like steel shafts. All the past trauma comes to the surface in torrents of grief and anger. I know we cannot survive the next hit. *There is no high ground. Where can we go for safety?*

I am angry with God, allowing it for the first time. This was not my plan! *This was not the design I had for my life!* I scream, sobbing. *Why does he not answer my prayers?* There is no God, there are no miracles. I fully expect his judgment, his wrath.

I must be broken. Look at all the wreckage.

I am finally quiet enough to feel. I am shocked when all I feel in return from God is pure love. I hear Him whisper gently. *Let go of your pain. I can hold it, make this journey possible.* I want to trust him, but I'm terrified. I start to trust, then retreat back to what I imagine is solid ground.

All I had known was tight, rigid, controlled. There was misery here, yes, but predictability. It was nothing like the uncharted sea deep within; its wild swells and sweeping waves beckon me to journey beyond the terrifying, oh so expansive gulf of darkness.

TRUTH RISING

Sometimes, one defining moment in life shifts everything.

I watched him drive away, fearing it might be the last time. I slowly slumped onto the cold tile of the entryway, only sensing darkness and cold as I felt the life drain out of me. I was helpless, abandoned by my estranged spouse. Slowly, I was drowning in a poisoned ocean of fear and shame. Coming to consciousness many hours later, I realized I'd been there all night. My babies were still asleep in their beds, gratefully having not stirred during the night. My body, a victim of frequent, undiagnosed muscle weakness attacks, couldn't do it anymore- it was failing, heartbeat slowing, next breath uncertain. With the early morning chill coming through the open door, a realization struck me like lightning.

*I am not Ok. If I die, they die.*These lies, the swirling, maddening, insanity and chaos, must STOP.

I knew I needed to do something incredibly courageous or die trying. Years of silence are finally broken by my sober words. For the first time in my life, I open my eyes to the truth, and speak my truth, without minimizing the pain and damage. The walls of lies kept me separated from God and others; they must come down! I knew I had to be radically honest with myself.

I was still here, I was worth finding. It was worth any effort to recover and heal, worth any price. There was value in simply BEING. Nothing could diminish from my true nature, my truth. I get to live!

What if all this energy poured into proving I was good enough could be channeled instead to create the life I want? Why was I allowing expectations, trauma, and events of my life to write my story? I was fighting for something I thought I was losing, when perhaps it needed to be lost. All of the darkness, anger, rage, and ugliness within me *was not me.*

I had to challenge all the lies in me, risk believing the truth, for it to take root. Truth was rising out of the darkness like the stirring of a tiny flame. I honored it first in my body, then mind, then soul. I held it close to me, grounding myself in truth. The wind could no longer put it out; it was fanning the flames.

The crisp morning air spoke of fall as I drove in a rare solitary moment. The beautiful colors of transformation began to illuminate the edges of my consciousness. In that sacred moment, I felt an almost imperceptible shift in my soul. My favorite christian music filled the car; the words filling the deepest portions of my heart. Living water revives my parched soul.

Unexpectedly, effortlessly, my lungs breathe deeper than they have in years. My mouth turns up in a wide grin, the deep, rich sounds of my belly laugh filling all the empty spaces in the car, and my soul. I almost stopped at the sound, so easy and free. *Was that me?* It had been so long since I remembered the sound of my own laughter. It was music to my ears. Even though my life appeared to be smoldering ash, something breathes new life into my soul. I feel life and peace flowing freely. I finally caught the vision of living in authenticity and alignment with truth; it felt like solid ground.

I am gently reminded that healing is a process, not an event.

LOVE

My mental health was at its most fragile point. I had endured over thirteen years of betrayal trauma, major health difficulties, and several miscarriages. In my latest attempt at pregnancy, my little girl was almost full term, but nagging feelings of quiet dread enveloped me. Her life was a tiny spark of joy amidst such horrendous torment. Our special connection was literally keeping me alive, but I still felt our lives were hanging in the balance. My worst fears were realized when one morning a sharp twinge in my womb catapulted me off my bed, I knew something was terribly wrong. I felt a terrible stillness instead of the baby's movements; deep down I knew that someone had died in me.

There is no heartbeat.

At the doctor's words, my whole world disappears in a flash of fire and flood. *Is he talking about my baby or me?* The little life that had kept me alive for so long was now gone.

The ocean broke open; waves and waves of grief spilling out my eyes, my groaning mouth, the depths of my aching soul; mourning years of untold deaths. The nurse asked me to don a gown to start the induction. Another layer of shock hits me as I realize I will still have to endure the travail of labor and give birth to my unbreathing daughter. It was more than I could bear. Another wave washes over my soul. I am suffocating.

Suddenly aware of the stark feeling of being utterly alone, I felt my body drop on my knees on the cold hospital floor. I petitioned the God of heaven for the strength to do what I could not do alone. *I can't do this alone.* There was no way around this, only through. No matter what comes next, I pleaded with God to not let me not feel this insatiable isolation. I begged him, *Please be with me.*

She is silently born. My tears silently fall. While I hold her close in the moments after, I feel encircled in a tender, sacred light. She was here, free. For a moment in the darkness I find heavenly rest, a pinpoint of light and peace within the chaos.

SURRENDER

There is something that happens to you when you do not have capacity to hold another ounce of pain. Like the fuller fire, it burns away all the incremental impurities of human frailties and ego, anything temporarily disappears–all left is the eternal.

My arms and heart are empty. The funeral shroud wrapped tightly around my body like a cocoon. I feel a strange relief to have a visible reason to grieve. Others could cry with me, comfort me, and understand when I didn't have it all together. I held her blanket, her bear, but the pieces of my shattered heart were gone.

What is this life for anyway? How is it possible to feel this much raw pain and still survive?

My grandmother died very young. She was involved in an accident that left ninety percent of her body burned, but she still lived for several months. Without modern medicine, she endured unimaginable pain without any way to numb it. As she slowly died. She never allowed her young children to visit her hospital room, afraid of them seeing her disfigured. Instead, she watched them from the hospital window where she was out of their sight. They never got to say goodbye. They never saw her again. I have a room inside of me like that, and I had not let anyone near it. I would not even admit *myself* as a visitor, not wanting to see myself in this state, but I was dying. I connected more deeply with her than I previously had with any human. She became an angel for what was to come, the most difficult part of my journey.

I was in agony, covered with deeper despair and darkness than I had ever known or thought possible. I was stuck in a perpetual nightmare; I couldn't wake up or get relief in sleep, but to endure that kind of torment was the very definition of hell. The thought of living for one more day seemed impossible. Anguished, I cry out.

Wouldn't it be easier if I just disappeared?

I wouldn't let anyone really see the deepest part of my heart, the ugly crying, moaning, wailing, screaming, crying, angry child within. I feared the deepest vulnerability of seeing myself in that state would scar me forever. Years of suicidal idealization culminated in a plan to end my life. With unseen angels help, I make one last desperate call to the suicide prevention hotline.I remember realizing the biggest tragedy in the story of my grandma's death was she was alone in her pain; not allowing herself to be *seen.*

There are more than just one type of scars.

SURRENDER

Fear is a powerful Illusion. The energy of fear is the most misunderstood force in the universe. *If you let fear keep you from living, you are already dying.*

Suddenly, and not so suddenly, I realized I had experienced everything I was afraid of. What was left to fear? *Suffering was all the energy I spent resisting fear.* The pain was the empty spaces between—silent impenetrable walls I had erected to protect my heart from the experience of fear; numbing me, closing me off to love, and suffocating the little girl inside. Suddenly, she cries out:

I EXIST! I EXIST beyond this egoic version of me!

This time I didn't want to die. I wanted to really *live.* Something cries out from the ashes like a phoenix rising from the flames.

Some miracles are not the ones you ask for. She would whisper with butterfly wings. *Mommy, I am here. I am with you always.* She comes to me, delicate, beautiful, free. She is alive in the fragile creature who is wrapped up in a funeral shroud and turned into goo before emerging in new life, with colors so brilliantly divine, no one could say she is not God's creation. She teaches me ever so gently about surrender, transformation, death, and rebirth.

I was ready to let myself, God, and others in.

I am done fighting for the illusion of what I thought I wanted. I commit to give the only thing I have left to give. My fighting for a freedom I already had, focusing on everything I didn't want. I am the only one who can give myself permission to see my experience and myself through the lens of love. I can keep holding onto all that holds me back—what I've seen as reality—or I can trust God and give it all to him. I am tired of living in fear, fighting. I am ready to accept whatever God has in store for me. In the most unexpected stretch of soul, realizing I am being called by God to surrender control and believe in His radical goodness; anything He wills is for my good. I lay my life and will down in a final act of surrender. It is no longer mine.

Take it all, take my life.

TRANSFORMATION

If there existed this depth of darkness, surely there must exist another realm of light, so exquisitely bright as the stars in the night sky. This reality was unfamiliar but no less real to me. I didn't know where it was, or how I would get there, but I would find it. I would embrace it. traverse boldly the sea of darkness in order to know light. I would be healed by it.

I had experienced so many different versions of hell over my short lifetime—all the while heaven was within my grasp. Nothing is wasted. Nothing is accidental. There is a purpose behind the pain, the fire, the engulfing storms. The experiences were never meant to hurt me. They are exactly what was needed to peel off another layer of hardened crust around my once tender heart, exposing my core to the light. I accepted in love the paradoxical experience of holding within me both fear and love, darkness and light. I can choose which experience I want to have, at any moment. The power to choose was always before me—love came from inside, not my outside experiences. Overcoming my fears meant embracing them, holding them, seeing them, loving myself through them. Freedom is *always* on the other side of fear, just past the unknown.

We are designed to transform,stretch, break, die—reviving as new creatures. To go upon the sea, walk with faith, let go of control.*Trust,* even in death. Redemption is the purpose of who we are, of who God is. His divine flow is in us, giving us new life, transmuting burdens of darkness to sacred, powerful light and love.

With God, nothing is impossible.

No force on earth or hell could keep me from journeying to that light. That path was love; it is love.

HOMECOMING

The child stands on a churning sea, unafraid. She knows me, loves me, and has been waiting for me. She pulls me onto its surface; her white dress blows in the foam. The spray hits my face; we laugh. The darkness turns to dawn around us as we step across the water. Miraculously, it holds me. *I am weightless, supported.* The water flows with power through me now. I dip my hands in the ripples and splash the bright droplets as I spin, dancing atop the waves. My laughter sparkles across the surface.

The storm turns to stillness, the water turns to glass, as the sun breaks across the surf. In the beautiful colors of the morning rays, I see my reflection clearly for the first time. I see beauty within me dancing around me, a thousand playful butterflies in all different shades of iridescent blue light. The light emanated from me, from the bottom of my toes to the tips of my fingers. The jewels beneath the water glitter in the morning light. This is who I am. This is what I was always meant to be. LOVE. LIGHT. PEACE. JOY. The journey into the most vulnerable places in my soul and heart have produced this shattered light, with a thousand facets of brilliant prisms glowing on every surface. Rainbows dance, laugh, and reflect in every drop of water, in all the mist.

I no longer needed to be afraid. I could walk on these waves; I could find this space again when the water rises and the wind whips across the deep. I was never lost. I am the farthest thing from alone. The light and love I find in another is an expression of what is within me. God never left me. He is here with me now, holding my hand. He never abandoned me in the thick, black sea. I was washed from head to toe from everything that was not Him, and *was not me. I am clean.* He is this power inside of me, the transformation of this fear into brilliant light. There is an essence of the feeling of flow, creativity, life giving and sustaining power coursing through my veins. It is the divine within each one of us.

Every time I feel the swift sea starting to pour in, I open my arms wide and say, *dance with me!* I am one with the water, the wind. It was never meant to hurt me or drown me. You are here to wash away the dust and tears; renewing my soul. You are here to remind me I was always enough, and the miracles don't lie in the absence of darkness but the paradoxical position of contrast to the light. And all the beauty held within my soul already existed before; it can never be erased.

I Live. I am seen. I am Love. I am Light, Eternal Existence. I am FREE.

Nothing could make this truth burn brighter. I pull this little child close. I hold her near, breathing in the smell of her hair, the glow of her face and bright eyes. I feel her heartbeat in tune with mine, her voice whispering, speaking, singing songs of love. Her perfect, whole body dancing. I reach for her hand and spin freely with her. We are no longer separate. We will never be apart again. *We are ONE. healing,* gratefully, parallel with my spouse, children, family and posterity. Miracles rippling out to eternity. *We are walking on water together.*

ABOUT NATALIE BIGLER

Natalie Kaye Bigler is a true visionary, a leader in the field of transformation. Co-founder of Truth Rising Coaching, she is a professional life and betrayal trauma recovery coach, partnering with her husband. Together they guide individuals and couples through the intricate journey of healing from sexual addiction. Certified as a therapeutic art coach, she empowers breakthroughs through connection that creates lives and relationships founded on love.

Through 'Sacred Silver Linings' Natalie unveils the art of transformation, by sharing her own sacred journey, inviting others to discover their own divine essence. As CEO of Illumination Studios, she lives in the creative space of professional photography, fine art, and illustration. A native of beautiful Southeastern Idaho, she now lives in St. George, UT, with the loves of her life: her husband Matthew Bigler, two beautiful girls, and two fun little boys. She lives for sushi, outdoor adventures, travel, and beautiful music.

Website: *www.truthrisingcoaching.com*
Instagram: *www.instagram.com/truthrisingcoaching*
www.instagram.com/illumination_studios_artphoto
Facebook: *www.facebook.com/truthrisingcoaching*
Pictorem: *https://www.pictorem.com/profile/Illumination.Studios*

10

TANYA RACHELLE FAGETAN

'GET A GRIP- SPLITZ GRIPPER'

Get a Grip. Hi, my name is Tanya - what the Universe has taught me through movement about Life, Loss, and Love.

My tears had been flowing for days and weeks nonstop. I didn't have any more tears left in me to cry. I lay across an unmade bed grieving in anguish over a lost love relationship. I glanced at the closet door mirror from across the room and caught a reflection of my face and limp body. My skin was ashen gray and I had extremely dark circles under my eyes. I thought to myself, "you look like a corpse, Tanya." It scared me to see my intense unhappiness and pain in such a vivid way. My heart was broken, and I felt shattered. It had been several weeks since the end of my romance. It was real, it was deep, and it was over.

Untreated PTSD and alcoholism contributed and had taken love and my love away from me and out of my life. I was not handling it very well. I tried to keep going but my soul felt shattered and lost. Although I would keep going through the motions of moving forward in life my heart closed. Not only did my heart close but I would slowly quit living my life full of the beautiful movement I had always enjoyed since I was a child- ice skating, yoga, skiing, ballet, dance and more.

At the time I had been a successful yoga instructor for several years and knew there were effective mindfulness practices for everything, and I knew it would have been effective for dealing with the issues, but since the romantic relationship was intense but short, I was only able to introduce it to my lover as a brief possible solution. Following the untimely ending of this relationship, my own life would then follow nearly two decades of pain and effort. I tried it all. Relocating, working on my career, changing career fields, dating, marriage, divorce, eating, not eating, and overeating to the point of gaining a significant amount of weight. So much weight—the girl who once modeled and participated in local scholarship beauty pageants hid from cameras. The path seemed steady to unhappiness and loss of physical movement and abilities as I had known them. The weight gain was so severe eventually even my beloved yoga practice became nonexistent.

My own health and self-esteem took a toll. I no longer was the 'tall, slender brunette' leading yoga classes in California and across the country. Life kept rolling and I kept going but the truth was inside I was in intense emotional pain and the more I did in life to try to counter these feelings the worse I felt. I put on a smile. I laughed. I dressed well. I pursued another career path. I tried making myself love again. That did not work and made things even worse. The reality was I continued to gain weight, and internally feel isolated from a meaningful life. I lost two things I loved most in my life, yoga and the man I loved.

It didn't get easier or better for quite some time despite living and trying. I became a full-time caregiver for my beloved mother who had given me so much love and provided opportunities for me throughout my life. My mom was my best friend my entire life. Few girls can say they had no major conflicts with their mom, but I can. She was a nonstop supporter of mine. I watched her gracefully struggle with stage four cancer and in the middle of her treatments I too was diagnosed with cancer.

Being blessed with great health all my life, I had never spent a night in the hospital since my own birth, yet I awoke after major surgery alone in an oncology unit. Seeing the word 'oncology' on a sign on the cold pale blue walls, I asked myself, 'how did I get here, like this?' This was not the life or place I had envisioned for myself while going through young adulthood. I always thought I would have a loving long-term marriage and a handful of beautiful children. Yet I faced the first hours after major surgery alone in an isolated hospital room with tubes and needles in my body watching the clock hands pass time- five and ten minutes at a time.

2:00 am. 2:10 am. 2:15 am.

The only thing I knew that could give me peace and relief from both the intense emotional and physical pain was my own breath. The words from my favorite yoga instructor, Rich, played over in my mind. 'Always come back to the breath.' It was one part of my yoga practice I could do in the hospital bed while I was unable to move my body. So, I began. To breathe. Moment by moment, I watched five then ten minutes pass into a few hours.

The deep rhythmic breath comforted me. The simple act of breathing is movement. The sustaining life force of the breath I have within me helped. It helped me calm my mind as it rapidly ran from every disappointment in my life I had encountered. It stabilized me as I anxiously anticipated the unknown future. I wish I could say this was the magic moment I changed my life to regain full health and vibrancy, but it wasn't. No, my life's journey of progressiveness would show me I would still need to learn much more through a period of unemployment, the tragic suicide of my lost love and other life happenings. For life never stops. It does not wait for us to Get a Grip. Both the good and the difficult keep rolling simultaneously. I knew there had to be a path to get from where I was to who I hoped to become—and in my case, again. The soul's messy and unpredictable journey is inevitable; it is essential to our quest to live a life we thrive in.

Immediately after surgery, the hospital gurney I was on rolled past the oncology sign and every small bump in the hallway felt intensified. This surgery represented having to endure once again, the emotional pain of the reminder and finality of not being able to bear my own children—a major life disappointment. Hours earlier, as I was being prepped for surgery, my doctor asked me if I would be willing to have my surgery filmed and broadcast for other physicians and medical students. My doctor was a pioneer in the DaVinci robotic surgery technique and wanted to shed some light on the complicated process. My personal modesty and first thought was 'no way, I don't want anyone to view this very personal event,' but I felt prompted to change my answer and say 'yes.' I felt if another woman could be helped or help to save their life by having another doctor learn this technique then yes, I would allow it.

Learning and progressively and efficiently moving through life has been a theme throughout my life. Early memories include my mom driving me to ballet lessons after school in our family van while I changed clothes ducking down in the back seat so we could arrive on time for my lessons. I spent early morning hours before school at a cold ice arena practicing figures and skating. My mom supported me in every endeavor, sport, and activity. I am eternally grateful for her sacrifices. Keep moving forward. Ice skating during a performance feeling the breeze across my face and shoulders, my chiffon skirt floating behind while the deep bend of my knee and my skate blade edge carves into the ice feeling the curve of the edge and movement. Gliding movement forward. Forward in life, always.

The dark times and space in life can be our greatest teachers for progression and transformation. Dark times exist even in a blessed and charmed life. Private moments alone can be intense when facing our innermost thoughts and feelings. In a world that is quick to judge physical weight and appearance and criticizing others, being kind to self is one of the most powerful tools for transformation. It was easy for me to want to hide away from life and not be seen as I felt great shame for the way my body had transformed. I no longer felt free and able to move or dress fashionably—I loved clothes, fashion, color and fabric. At times the world can be cruel, and even after significant weight loss it can be cruel. Criticism, thoughtless comments, probing and inappropriate questions and even compliments about how much better I looked 'now' can cause self shame. Comments or looks about loose skin at times caused me to feel shameful of what I did to myself or allowed to happen to me, but I now wear it with honor as it is part of my journey and life story.

I wish I could identify the exact moment where I felt the real motivation to transform and regain myself. The simple answer to that is it's a compilation of moments culminating in many small moments where I decided to make changes in my behaviors. The Silver Lining in life can be found in the everyday moments and times where I worked on and made positive choices to move my body and to nourish it healthily. The moments where I chose to laugh or think of happier more beautiful things versus the things I had lost. The moments I chose to meditate and seek spiritual healing. Time is the most precious asset we have. It means life, and once gone it is never coming back.

Working out and training was never difficult for me as I loved physical activity and enjoyed going to a gym. Shame and embarrassment were another story. Walking into a gym being the largest female took courage for me and more than a few baggy T-shirts! What I found though was time on the elliptical trainer that gave me energy and time to listen to upbeat music moving my body, sweating, and eventually finding my way to my yoga mat again.

The first time I did yoga after major surgery, muscle memory kicked in. In vinyasa style I jumped back to plank pose flowing into chaturanga (a yoga style pushup) then into upward dog, and I felt such intense pain from the surgery along the entire front side of my body. The surgery left internal scar tissue, and the feeling was unbearable for a moment but after a breath or two my mind began to calm, and I began to enjoy it instead of fearing the sensation. After being absent from yoga classes in a studio for some time, the first studio class I took I placed my mat in the far back of the room not wanting anyone to notice I was there. Formerly being referred to as 'Gumby' and then not being able to touch my toes was not something I felt proud of. Yet, my breath and the words of Rich echoed in my mind, 'Just breathe and connect the breath with the movement.'

When I was a teenager, days after a coveted skating performance an incredibly wise friend asked me, 'Are you getting what you wanted?'

I had practiced, longed for this performance, sewn my skating costume, and done all the preparatory work for this performance. It was something I wanted in my heart so deeply and I had spent weeks preparing. After feeling the exuberance of the performance, I remember skating to the side of the rink and taking a moment to myself to take it all in. I still recall the sounds, the temperature of the air on my skin, the vibration of the audience on the other side of the curtain and the feeling I had in my heart of real happiness.

We are all unique, complex beings with secret dreams, fantasies, mysteries, and longings we want in our lives. We are who we are, and, when we are allowed to be our most authentic, vulnerable, real selves, 'We've only just begun,' as the Carpenters' song goes, to set free the potential electricity buried deep within us, waiting to be released. If we understand the importance of this expansion or progressiveness, not only for ourselves but for our partners in life, then we have begun to grasp the energy of a lifelong commitment. Life becomes a thrilling adventure.

"Love is an activity, a power of the soul."

— ERICH FROMM

Over the course of three years, I lost four of my closest confidants and family members to death. Life is an eternal circle, and the course of life occurs for all of us but as I experienced each of these losses another hole appeared in my heart. Death and loss occur to each of us, so I was not singled out, but the timing seemed personally intense. These were profoundly deep and meaningful relationships and as each one transitioned to the next phase of our existence I was left here on this earth to live and continue my journey. To flourish without my closest loved ones seemed an unimaginable task yet, I knew they would want me to do just that, flourish. Each of them taught me different things but mostly it was about love.

One of the highlights in my transformation period was the discovery of my enjoyment of cycling. A girlfriend introduced me to cycling and she was my first 'cycling coach.' Her gentle but strong teaching reminded me of my yoga instructor Rich. She encouraged me to ride ahead of her and circle back as I was stronger than her, but most importantly we had fun and laughed. I needed laughter more than anything. She taught me more than she knew about life because she brought something back to me that had been missing. Fun and joy! I had recently lost my mom after a long brave battle and many years of being her primary caregiver—something I would do again in a heartbeat, but that gift did not come without personal sacrifice and trials. Cycling gave me movement in one of the most exhilarating ways!

Four months after starting to cycle I participated in a local ride called the 'Edible Pedal 100.' It was held with nearly 800 cyclists and the setting was a beautiful fall day starting and ending at historical Bower's Mansion located in Washoe Valley in Northern Nevada. Edible Pedal sought to promote healthy lifestyle choices by producing an annual event that focused on fitness and eating right. It gave everyone a reason to ride a bike and to model a lifetime fitness activity. The philosophy of growing food and riding a bike teaches a real-life lesson in 'hard work pays off' and the hard work on this ride was going to pay off. 'Ride well. Eat well. Give back.'

Alone, during the early morning hours on the brisk fall morning of the ride I drove myself to the starting point. I watched the sun begin to rise over eastern Nevada and took a breath of the fresh air of the pine trees I dearly love. I had spent many hours and days as a child learning to swim and picnic at this venue and my heart was full of love and anticipation for the day ahead. I unloaded my bike from the rack and put my race bib on, #263. I have never done something like this, and I was doing it alone, so I thought.

I got on my bike and began the ride solo. The first moments I looked up at the pine trees, took a deep breath in and dedicated my ride that day to two people I dearly love. One, my mom, could not be with me any longer because she passed away months earlier and the other, a reconnected love who would continue to teach me more about love and life than anyone else ever has.

One of the highlights of my day was stopping for a moment at the halfway point to refill water bottles and #261 and #262 walked by me and said hello. I did not know the couple, but a chance meeting would give me strength and encouragement to keep going. It seemed serendipitous out of 800 people I would get to see and meet the bib numbers next to mine and I instantly did not feel so alone. They disappeared as quickly as they had appeared.

Hopping back on my bike, I continued to the last part of the ride up Combs Canyon. This section is a 2.32-mile stretch with a steady but grueling 526 ft climb. During the last 8 miles of a 54-mile ride my legs were not ready for this torturous climb. The muscles began to fatigue and the first thing I thought of was to come back to my breath. Keep looking forward a bit ahead of the front of my bike but not too far and push one pedal down then the other and do not stop. The muscles in my legs were on fire and I felt like I couldn't keep going. I gently felt a breeze over both my right and left shoulders carrying me along. The presence of two specific angels guiding and keeping me moving forward in life was profoundly powerful. Next thing I knew #262 came out of nowhere and rode alongside me for about 30 seconds. As he steadily passed me, he said 'keep going' then moved ahead and disappeared out of sight. I knew at that moment there were no chance meetings. We are always being looked out for and guided but we must first exercise faith in action and then perseverance.

I reached the top of the climb, and as the descent finally started, I squealed and cried out-loud, 'I did it, I did it!' At the end, the ride was a total of 54.33 miles in 3:51:56 hrs. I did it!!! The most challenging physical movement I've ever done in perhaps one of the most emotionally trying times of my life.

'Get a Grip' in American English slang refers to keep or recover one's self-control. Yogis will know about grippy sticky mats to practice on, which allow your feet and hands when sweaty to remain firm and grounded. Life is not about self-control but rather about living and flowing like a river. A life in balance means to pick up speed and slow down as necessary, taking turns as life weaves around and through rocks, and flowing yet remaining steady. Splitz Gripper Yoga & Wellness was founded on the fun nickname of Splitz because one of my favorite poses is the splits and being flexible is both an acquired, through consistent practice, and a genetically gifted attribute.

I have been blessed to find my passion and to be able to cultivate a sense of purpose and interest in life, which brings me energy. Being passionate about something leads to contentment, Santosha, and happiness... which leads to ageless beauty. Yoga heals—not just the body but also the heart and soul. Yoga is about you. Physically, it increases endurance, strength, and flexibility. Mentally it helps reduce stress by bringing in mindfulness and meditation and helps you find stillness in a chaotic world. Spiritually it helps you evolve to your highest potential and connection to God and the universe while living in a space of gratitude and peace.

How you move is the result of an intricate dance of muscles and joints, strength, flexibility and even mood. Posture, too, indicates strength and flexibility. Many elderly develop a hunched back due to years of slumping as well as unhealthy bones, but those who stand and sit upright with energy and strength always look younger. Slumping, shuffling, and hunching are habits that accumulate over the years, but they also indicate physical weakness, low energy and often a depressed mood.

"Love will turn pain into medicine."

— RUMI

Being open means being teachable. I unknowingly cracked open my heart again years ago while attending a very chance Al-anon meeting. I had not planned on going to the meeting, and I did not plan on participating. I attended to support someone else in need, but it was my heart that was healed and finally opened. When in the circle, I was invited to say a few words of support and my intuition led me to say some things that I thought would help others, but instead they were words I needed to hear myself. The message was me speaking about and encouraging one to keep their heart open despite difficult life circumstances. I realized my heart was not open to life and love again. I listened to the inner voice within and said to myself 'if and when real love presents itself again, open your heart to it.'

My yoga practice and teaching has been restored. A Silver Lining is that it is even better than just being restored. I have grown and learned how to use yogic philosophy in my asana (physical) practice as well as guide others in both asana and spiritual practices. The love I receive daily from yogis who practice with me and attend my classes is undeniably the most rewarding thing I have ever been able to do.

> *"Grow old along with me! The best is yet to be, the last of life, for which the first was made."*
>
> — ROBERT BROWNING

As I enter the later years of my life, aging and emotional progression continues. Making peace with aging is a spiritual practice. And to find peace with our age, we ultimately need to connect with that part of us that is wise and more mature. The team of people you choose to have in your life is very important. Take a realistic and objective look at those folks. Determine who you need more of and who you may need to dial back. Your inner circle can make or break you. My open heart has brought in more love in unimaginable measure. Romantic, strong, and deeply connected.

I have received love from yoga students who give me more love, hugs, and laughter than a dozen of my own children ever could. When I walk into a full chair yoga class with chairs set up and yogis waiting for me with the biggest smiles on their faces, applause for my arrival, laughter during class, and grunting and groaning—my chair yoga classes are not easy!—I am content. More importantly, the quiet and stillness during savasana, the final resting pose, when hearts are calm, minds and bodies still and there is peace.

There is nothing that cannot be overcome. I have faced challenges life has presented, with resolve and strength. At times with more grace than others. I also believe wholeheartedly life is meant to be enjoyed, and that we have a duty to ourselves to manifest our greatness and live the life we came here for. I love to travel, explore nature, eat delicious food, and hang out with friends. This is how my Yoga & Wellness retreats were born. They are wellness retreats for those who are ready to step into their highest selves and have a blast doing it.

Movement heals. I have experienced it for myself, and I have witnessed balance improve, strength increase, and laughter expressed freely. The love and connection I feel with yogis in my classes and retreats has been immensely meaningful to me. Knowing my life's experiences—challenges and joy—can help others feel good in their bodies no matter the age, stage, or physical ability. Regaining health, vibrancy and love is the greatest gift.

During life challenges—and yes, some continue as life always does —I often say to myself 'look what I get to do on a daily basis.' I share health, wellness, and hope with others. I am a lucky girl; indeed, an incredibly lucky and blessed girl. An English proverb: "Fear knocked at the door. Faith answered. No one was there."

Namaste.

ABOUT TANYA RACHELLE FAGETAN

With an eye towards the future but steeped in wisdom from 27 years as a practicing yogini Tanya Rachelle Fagetan, also known as Splitz Gripper, is a Yoga and Barre Instructor, Author, Inspirational Speaker and Entrepreneur.

She is certified in Barre, Vinyasa Yoga, Pilates and is a certified Mindfulness Coach. Her background was in dance, figure skating and she loved snow skiing near Lake Tahoe as a child. Her innovative Chair Yoga classes have been a hit and are always full.

Tanya grew up in Reno, NV but also counts places like San Diego, Atlanta and Arizona as her home. She received her BS in Communications and minors in Clothing & Textiles and Sociology from the University of Maryland. Tanya has a diverse background and has been in Human Resources Management and Real Estate, but her passion is wellness. When she's not practicing yoga, she can be found quilting and adding to her growing stash of colorful fabrics and unfinished quilt projects.

Keeping her eyes open to see silver linings in life is a gentle reminder to 'get a grip' and hold on tight to a vibrant lifestyle- better things are times are on the way!

Website: *www.tanyafagetan.offeringtree.com*
Email: *yogabytanya@yahoo.com*
Instagram: *www.instagram.com/yogabytanyarachelle*

11

ADELLE BRIANNE

A month before my wedding date, I hired a relationship coach. It wasn't an easy or cheap choice. I followed my intuition after the carefully woven tapestry of my life began unraveling. I was having trouble loving myself after my partner left me the day after his 50th birthday, with no communication about his intentions or our future.

Engaged for two years, we were in the midst of planning a fabulous wedding, featuring my entertainment company, at a beautiful venue overlooking the Pacific Ocean. Out-of-town guests had already booked their travel, and we'd lined up most of our vendors. No amount of texting, calling, emailing, or praying inspired this man to reconnect with me despite five years together. I was crushed.

On our first call, the coach advised me to accept that my relationship was already over. She gave me specific suggestions on moving forward. The steps include listening to affirmations to improve my self-worth and inner dialogue, doing a practice to forgive myself and my ex-fiancé, moving the rest of my belongings out of his house as soon as possible, and blocking him and removing him from my phone.

Up until the moment I got on the coaching call, I held space and hoped for his return. I'd already begun digesting the coach's resources and wrapping my head around a new belief. My ex-partner had been emotionally unavailable and a workaholic for our entire relationship.

Enlightened by this new perspective, I also felt validated. I had four years and dozens of pages of therapist-supported journaling in which my notes describe a desire for receiving more quality time, affection, sex, kissing, family vacations, camping, hiking, etc.

At the beginning of our courtship, I lacked the discernment necessary to realize he couldn't fulfill my emotional and physical needs for intimacy. I accepted him without assessing that we weren't a good fit on a deeper level. I didn't know which behaviors were misaligned for my sensitive soul.

Looking farther back in journals, I found evidence that I've chosen emotionally unavailable men for two decades. I recently discovered that I was avoiding feeling my feelings for decades! I also held judgment and shame for any negative feelings and believed anger or fear are bad. I had no healthy way to cope with my own anger or triggers for most of my adult life and my inner critic was consistently mean to me.

"There is no sacred silver lining," the bitch whispered to me, "you're fucked."

"That's not true," a wise voice whispered back.

"Do the next right thing," my dad reminded me after I texted him informing him I canceled the wedding. A tear rolled down my cheek reading his text. It was the perfect thing to say.

Reassuring messages kept popping through as I detached from visions of walking down the aisle in a gorgeous wedding dress followed by a romantic honeymoon and living happily ever after.

I forgive myself. I forgive my ex. I release him, clearing space in my world for the new me and for the future me. I am amazing and lovable, and I create my destiny. I believe in silver linings and happy endings.

"What you seek is seeking you."

After I waited for a silver lining to shine hope upon my tears and prayers, I realized it was with me all along, night and day, wagging his tail.

Snoop is a tri-color Pomeranian whose coat of fur at first glance is a mixture of white and tan yet features a subtle silver layer around his neck and face. He arrived in my life as a four-month-old silver and white puppy whose undercoat disappeared as he grew. Now his distinctive fluffy coat shimmers on a windy day and you may catch a glimpse of the silver lining that brightens my world.

If someone walked up to me earlier in my life and said, "You're gonna get a dog when you turn forty," I would've been surprised and dismissive at such an absurd statement.

"That doesn't sound like me." I am a cat person not a dog person, or so I believed. After a few scary experiences with big dogs in childhood, I was never attracted to them as pets. I tolerate dogs when their owners are my friends or family members. For forty years, I mostly ignored them without a second thought.

As I began to cope with stress in new ways in my thirties, I found a very soothing stimulus on Instagram. Pomeranians. O.M.G.

Glorious fluffy balls of energy! I tapped into the healing energetics of dogs. Many already know they can provide a yummy experience for humans, but since I avoided dogs for so long, I was clueless. Watching these addictive creatures online led to the inevitable. I started pondering being a "Pom Mom" myself.

Learning about their behaviors, personality traits, and the strengths and the challenges of owning this type of dog didn't deter me, though it brought up a lot of negative thoughts. I didn't want to be judged for getting a purebred dog. But it was already too late. An internal switch flipped from OFF to ON. My heart and soul wanted a small fluffy lovable Pomeranian.

Parallel to this shift inside my spirit desiring a dog was the evolution of my romantic relationship. I was engaged to a hardworking divorced business owner. I'd begun living with him and his two children as soon as the pandemic restrictions went into effect. It was a beautiful time in life.

Being stuck at home was blissful. We were homesteading in paradise. My man and his teenage son dug up a massive section of dirt on the side of the house and created a plentiful garden with food to nurture us. I planted wildflowers that bloomed everywhere. We got a black kitten, fulfilling my desire for a witchy feline. The next year we got another kitten, and the two cats became besties. It was my first time getting pets with a beloved and my first experience navigating motherhood.

The imprint of investing in my lovely tween daughter's wellbeing and watching her gain self-confidence will never leave me. It was incredible witnessing and supporting her growth. Supporting and loving her felt effortless. I love seeing her eyes light up telling a story and expressing her opinions. Hearing her laugh hysterically with my niece made me very happy.

I bonded with our teenage son through honest conversations about real life. He's tall, strong, creative, musical and devoted to his physical and mental development. He's one of my favorite people on earth. I was a proud mama the day he got his driver's license borrowing my car. I regret not telling him how much impact he had on my life and how much I simply adore him. I love him and wish him an incredibly happy and wonderful life.

Belonging to a family for two years was a huge blessing. I said repeatedly that "I won the Stepmom Lottery!" because the kids are so great. Christmas as a mother was amazing. Tears fall as I relive the feelings. I was a mother. In all actions, I was a wife. I was fulfilled.

It's over.

At times intuition must override all other protocols to bring forth one's ultimate destiny. Now I am a mother only to my inner child. Nurturing and responding to my wounded inner child who needs me to show up when she expresses herself is my only parental duty for a while.

Spirit stepped in and corrected my life's course clearly and powerfully, hearing my inner child protesting loudly. My inner child needed me to show up and take care of her.

I sought therapy for a decade for my fight-flight episodes and learned breathing techniques, meditations, time-out, and other suggestions from a dozen therapists. Yet I could not develop a consistent pathway to resolve these situations safely and without escalating into fight-flight. Thankfully I finally figured it out with the right guidance, but only after so much despair, rage, sorrow and grief flowed through me.

Now I feel empowered. I show up for myself. I know how and when to pause and place my hand on my heart and my tummy and connect with my own power. I soothe myself if I'm crying, and I allow myself to feel anger, disappointment, frustration, loneliness and other feelings without judging them or stopping them. I am ready to FEEL . . . and so I shall heal.

This shift is huge. In many past relationships I needed external support when my inner child came out. I became triggered when I did not receive physical and emotional support for my inner child's needs. So much healing and growth comes from tending to the little girl inside of me who needs to feel safe. This is as much her story as it is mine.

The little girl inside of me was kicking and screaming and wailing at the top of her lungs, "What's going onnnnnnnnn?" (Imagine the band 4 Non Blondes as they sing that line from their hit song *What's Up?)* That's the energy of my inner child for the past year or so. That song embodies the energy I'm writing about.

An essential and amazing gift that I desperately needed and cried for so many times has arrived. I pursued this gift in therapy for over a decade, yet I could not understand or manage my emotional triggers.

This present moment is a gift and so am I. My own presence is a gift in my life. I'm tuning into myself again, after detaching from my own feelings for many years. I'm feeling my feelings in my body. I'm learning. I must practice really feeling instead of analyzing or dismissing or ignoring or judging my feelings.

One must face the consequences of bringing our own unhealed trauma to relationships. Although I went through agonizing self-doubt and horrific stories of unworthiness during this recent personal transformation, I am free now from self-loathing. I know that I did my best. There is no regret, no remorse; only growth and transformation.

This year's surprising turn of events led my internal dialogue to sabotage and overthrow my wisdom protocol. I cried and punished myself many days on end for too many months for being allegedly unworthy, unlovable, unforgivable, and out of control. My self-worth was seriously shitty.

One learns through the action of gardening and growing plants that fertilizer is an amazing gift to a plant's life. At times we are understandably resistant to fertilizing with what is obviously readily available. Perhaps it's the smell, or how it arrived, or something else.

"I did not order this," I kept thinking after he left. I rejected adding this experience as potent fertilizer to my life's garden even if my garden was starving.

This garden is the metaphor of my own self-love, self-care, and self-worth. I am nowhere near mastering gardening but I'm not ignoring free fertilizer anymore. I'm currently deep in the stinky pile of poo digging and distributing. In reality, I'm cultivating a positive daily mindset and shooing away invasive untrue thoughts lingering from limiting beliefs based on fear.

I'm going to make it through this big, unexpected transition. I am already reclaiming my joy and navigating confidently again. My head and heart have supported me through grieving losing the family I loved for five years. I'm done crying!

In writing this chapter, I asked myself, "Who am I to share any wisdom, when I've howled silently and cried spontaneously in front of strangers so many times wondering when this emotional tsunami will finally calm its raging seas and allow me peace."

Who am I? I'm crushed yet crushing it. I released three multi-author books this year, propelling my career to new levels. I achieved my first five-figure month booking an international client who found me from a Google search. It's my first six-figure income year. People who've known me for years keep complimenting my brand and mentioning my success when I see them around town. Acquaintances would never suspect I cried daily during the last quarter when I also released a YouTube video every day for ninety days.

It is perfectly alright that I'm changing rapidly and who I was yesterday is not who I will be tomorrow. I'm reforming inside my chrysalis. I completely trust that I will emerge anew to faithfully pursue living the life of my wildest dreams.

I wanted a gorgeous companion to wake up beside, go on long walks at the beach, and to fill my days with love. I have all that! I traded my fairy tale ending for a furry tail! It's certainly a 'happy ending' seeing his cheerful tail and adoring eyes every day.

Accessing my feelings also means I can trust my wisdom now more than ever. I pay attention to the stories I'm tuning into, the beliefs I'm embodying, and the self-talk guiding me. I take more pauses. I breathe. I release.

I encourage others to do a self-check-in right now. It's time to fertilize your new garden. You're ready. You've got this.

Embrace the metaphoric shit in your own life that you've been ignoring for too long. Yeah, it's uncomfortable but your garden flourishes once you start using the fertilizer readily available.

The beauty of gardening, like the beauty of self-care, is that no one can do it better than you. There's no right or wrong. You're actually an expert gardener. Trust yourself. Your soul's got this! Show up in love. Let the light around you nurture you when you're in times of darkness. Release any judgment about the shitstorms that wrecked your intentions in the past. Trust there's powerful information—keys to your healing that your future self is offering you—when you feel and express your feelings.

ABOUT ADELLE BRIANNE

Adelle Brianne is an international bestselling author and website expert who's built and managed hundreds of websites over the past twenty-five years. She enjoys helping women launch profitable websites that are easy to manage.

In addition to writing and designing, Adelle is a consultant and coach who teaches digital marketing strategies online. She earned her bachelor's degree in advertising and multimedia design from the University of Oregon. Her passion for serving women began as an undergrad while working as the Public Relations Director of the YWCA and volunteering at the University Women's Center.

Adelle and her Pomeranian SnoopDog live on the island of Maui where she also performs as a character actress for her company, Dazzle Entertainment. She enjoys making tie dye clothing and gifts and playing ukulele at the beach.

Website: *www.amazingandhelpful.com*
Instagram: *www.instagram.com/amazingandhelpful*
YouTube: *www.youtube.com/@AmazingAndHelpful*

12

BRONWYN

FINDING MY VOICE

"These cracks are getting harder to hide
And the secrets weighing heavy on my mind
That these days are getting harder to face
Cos every move I make is just another mistake"

— (*OPTIMISTIC* LYRICS - RELEASING 2024)

So many things about these lyrics and when I wrote them seem crazy to me now. It was April 2020. It was the first song I'd finished in three years. At the time I put my writer's block down to my perfectionism, which isn't entirely wrong, but there was so much more to it. I was a people pleaser and so disconnected from myself. Of course it's hard to know what to write when everyone else is dictating your songs, and, you let them.

We'd just started the first lockdown in New Zealand. I was both enjoying having a break from my five jobs and hating it simultaneously because I'm a workaholic. If you'd heard or read those lyrics, you'd think I was really sad but I thought I was somewhat happy. If anyone saw me then they'd probably agree I was happy too. I was twenty-five, relatively healthy, working a variety of jobs that I mostly enjoyed alongside gigging. I had obtained good local success with the original country pop music I'd put out so far, along with my national tours.

But everyday I was dreaming of moving to Nashville and touring the world.

I'd successfully healed my epilepsy. I had also come off the anti-depressants I'd been on for years. I was living at home still for the sake of saving money. I was always good at looking at the bigger picture, and any frustrations I experienced living at home I left in my guitar case. Work as much as I can, save as much as possible, and then fly... that was my vision that got me through. Smiling through sleep-deprivation and racing from one job to the next was as easy as singing to me. Yet these lyrics fell out of me like they already knew what it would take me a couple more years to understand.

People pleasing was the only way I knew how to navigate every aspect of my life. Music was the exception. It's hard when your accountant dad tells you to stop doing what you love even when you're five because it's not productive and you'll "never be able to make money from it." I breathed music as long as I can remember. I learnt ten different instruments effortlessly by the time I was thirteen, most of which I could still play (at least basics of) today. I never did stopped playing like he wanted me to. Every time I tried I'd catch myself singing again without even realising it but I wanted his approval so desperately that the resistance from disappointing him meant I never enjoyed music as much as I used to, until recently.

My mum didn't have many friends so from four years old I was the person she would confide in. I always wanted to help so after a while it became natural for me to go and comfort her before she even said anything was wrong, which was more regular than the incessant bags under my eyes. Pleasing both my parents weighed on my soul more than I understood..

At school I was a crippling perfectionist. Top of the class was the only place I felt somewhat comfortable. If I wasn't there, my whole world would collapse and it did every time I got something wrong. I had a hard time making friends and spent a lot of time on my own.

Sleep was a huge issue since I was five. Before that I remember waking up naturally at 6 am to watch cartoons with my sister but after that I couldn't get to sleep til the early morning and struggled to get out of bed. My parents put it down to me starting school and my brain not wanting to stop learning. I didn't learn the real reason until twenty-three years later.

When I was around eight I started making weird noises in my sleep that, after a year of doctor's, hospital visits and tests, we learnt were seizures. I was officially diagnosed with epilepsy when I was ten and started taking medication to treat it. Two years later I was diagnosed with depression and started on anti-depressants as well.

I remember teachers looking at me and treating me differently after my initial diagnosis. I don't really remember telling other kids or their reactions until I was twelve. My initial epilepsy specialist believed my seizures were puberty related (as if puberty isn't already stressful enough?!) and made a plan for me to come off my medication. It didn't work. Not only did my seizures come back but I also started having them during the day, including during class. I remember kids mimicking me when they thought I wasn't looking and calling me a cat because during my seizures it sounded like I had a fur ball. I hated my life. I was put back on the medication, but it wasn't as effective this time. The specialist tried to tell me I was too stressed and needed to work on that to prevent the seizures but I didn't want to hear it. It would be hard enough for an adult to accept that they were essentially the reason for their seizures, let alone a twelve year old. I just got more angry and stressed. I was sent to several therapists. My only real take away from the therapy sessions was being told to stop hating myself and the world and just "be happy." Easy, right?

I went from being able to keep my diagnosis quiet because I only had seizures in my sleep, to having to tell everyone. And of course the one time I forgot to tell someone was the time I had a seizure. People didn't understand that my seizures were minor and I got sick of them treating me differently.

Fast forward to last year, just two years after I wrote the song *Optimistic.* After thinking about it for over a year I decided somewhat last minute to book a one-way ticket to the other side of the world. I had always wanted to move overseas because NZ is simply so small and far away from... everything. I tried a couple of times but things fell through and then the pandemic happened, and I knew I had to go soon or I never would. I had enough savings to last me approximately six months without working and decided to trust that by then either my music will have taken off or I'll have found a remote online job to help me stay longer.

> *"Am I crazy? naive maybe? well it's too soon to know. I guess that all we can do is sit back and see how far this goes."*
>
> — (*WISH ME LUCK* - SONG OUT NOW)

Everyone thought I was crazy for this decision, but I was used to being a bit of a black sheep. Every now and then the people-pleaser in me would crack and go "crazy" like in 2017, I quit my job and spent several months living out of my car and singing and couch surfing my way around the country.

> *"Everybody thinks I've lost my mind. They think I'll come running back on home, just give it time."*
>
> — (*QUARTER LIFE CRISIS* - SONG OUT NOW)

Mexico and the UK were the only places that weren't discriminating at the time I was deciding (after my last specialist told me I'd never come off my medication without having seizures and proving him wrong since 2018 I had no intention of taking unnecessary medical treatments again, especially ones with such little research on them), and since my long-term goal is to get to Nashville, USA, for music, I chose Mexico. It was the closest I could get..

Because of my medical choices I had to take a longer route to Mexico but forty-eight hours of traveling and no sleep later, I arrived in Playa Del Carmen. Another reason I chose Mexico was that I hate the cold but I definitely didn't anticipate it being as hot as stage lights baring down on me 24/7, 365 days of the year. I expected to sleep like a baby after all that travel and stress of arriving in one piece but I wasn't used to sleeping with a fan or AC so barely slept at all.

The initial weeks in Mexico were a blur. I was somehow excited to be here and numb at the same time. There were lots of intense thunderstorms, which was quite a change from the weather in Dunedin and kept me home more than I would've liked but I also needed the rest. I only knew a couple of people here but made an effort to get out and meet them and meet others when the weather allowed. I only knew a handful of words and phrases in Spanish and relied heavily on my translator to get around and settle into my new life.

When I couldn't go out, I stayed at my apartment and took online music lectures or filmed singing videos to post online. I connected with a videographer early on and we managed to get out and shoot some nice videos for my song "Wish Me Luck" in between the storms. We talked about how we were both starting over pursuing our passions and were nervous about whether we could make them work and cope away from home. I thought we were both in a confident enough place that we'd both be sticking it out here when I last saw him but a couple of days later I saw on his Instagram that he decided to go home to the USA and hasn't pursued filming since. It's times like that that I'm glad NZ is as far away as it is, otherwise that may well have been my story by now too.

My sleep went up and down over the coming months. I was getting out and making friends and connections. I met some Aussie expats that adopted me as one of their own. I got a tan for the first time in years. I wasn't making the progress in my life and music that I wanted but I was still hopeful something would click soon and felt like it's more likely to happen here where I'm pushing my comfort zone most days than back home where I know I'd just throw myself back into work and forget about what I really want which was to have a successful music career and live in Nashville.

I tried reiki and breathwork (and enjoyed them so much I decided to train in these modalities, both as a way of helping myself move forward faster and to help others in the future) as well as hypnosis and even plant medicine but while I was making some small general progress, I still felt like I had this massive invisible block in my life. I still wasn't writing and after a while I stopped sleeping all together. Between the terrible exchange rate and my unanticipated therapy bill my savings were going down fast. Despite using all the healing and relaxation techniques I'd learnt I started having panic attacks in the middle of the night. Finally, I called home and was about to book my return ticket.

A breakthrough came during a self-hypnosis. I remembered a recurring nightmare I used to have about a wolf-man coming down the hill to our house while I hid in the lounge. My sleazy uncle's name came to mind as I remembered it and I had a feeling there was more to it than just a random nightmare but without more memories resurfacing I didn't want to jump to conclusions.

> *"Well I'm tired and I'm blue*
> *But I'll keep fighting yeah I'm not through*
> *Sometimes it's hard to move on*
> *Feels like all my hope is gone*
> *But I can always adjust the script*
> *Cos I'm not broken I'm just a little chipped"*
>
> — *(JUST A LITTLE CHIPPED* - SONG OUT NOW)

In a last-ditch attempt to avoid going home and work through whatever was behind the nightmare and blocking my sleep and life in general I booked one last therapy session.

Everything changed in that therapy session and the sessions in the following months. I remembered all the forgotten details of being sexually assaulted by that Uncle multiple times from the age of five (when I stopped sleeping). I started to piece together so much of my life and things made so much sense now that I remembered what I had been through.

I had a lot of mixed reactions from my family when I told them the news. My Mum was crushed but believed me instantly. My Sister didn't want to know about it. My Dad didn't believe me and didn't want me to talk about it to anyone, especially Nana and he definitely didn't want me reporting it to the cops. Initially I held off on both because it felt like the only reason I wanted to do either of them was to spite him but after a while of still not feeling like I was healing despite finally having my answers I decided talking about it more openly and reporting my Uncle might be my only option to move forward.

I found a contact for the NZ police and reached out to them. They talked me through the whole process. I was worried about telling Nana. It was hard for her to hear me over the phone from Mexico and since she would find out soon with the police investigating, Dad ended up telling her. I wasn't sure if that would be better or worse than telling her myself. She always thought the best of my Uncle so I really didn't think she would believe me or talk to me again. Dad said she was reluctant to hear it at first but she came around almost more than he did.

Fast forward to the present day, August 2023, and I've just returned to Mexico after a brief trip home. It was the first time I'd seen my Nana in over a year. We tried talking on the phone a couple of times in the early days of my move but she struggled to hear me so much we stopped trying. I wasn't sure if I should bring up the assaults with her or just leave it but I decided I needed to mention it at least briefly. I didn't say much but whether she realised it or not, she gave me so much closure that day.. I barely started bringing it up before she said my Uncle was creepy and sleazy sexually. I would've taken that closure but she kept going. After fighting my Dad about whether these events had actually happened for almost a year, she then said that my

Dad had always been quite naive and that's why he doesn't believe me. Words can't express the impact that brief conversation had on me.

It's still a work in progress but I've slowly been making improvements with my sleep. I've finished a couple of songs that I'm making plans to record soon. I'm finally on good terms with my Dad again. The police investigation closed. They didn't have enough physical evidence to arrest my Uncle given there were no witnesses and due to the time that has passed, but I feel better knowing he's on their radar should anyone else come forward with information about him. They said they believed me and that he has the traits of a predator.. Hearing that felt like the biggest weight was lifted off me.

I am starting a new chapter in my life. I've launched a healing business and started helping others heal with reiki, breathwork and EFT (emotional freedom technique). I'm working with clients who've experienced anything from burnout to sexual assault. I've taken part in a TV show. I've gotten to contribute to this book and am in the process of writing my own. I performed live for the first time in a year recently and could feel the difference all these hours of healing work have had on my voice. I am so much stronger and have even started to make plans to move to Nashville which, for a while there, I felt like I'd never be ready for.

Most importantly, I feel good. Happier than I've been in a long time. And I mean genuinely happy. Not just thinking I am when really I'm too busy to realise how I truly feel. I don't know when I'll get to Nashville but I know it'll happen when the time is right. In the past I would've been embarrassed to be running a business for something that isn't music but doing both healing work and singing excites me more than anything I've done before! Each time I try to choose one I end up changing my mind a week later so why not do both? Music is also powerful and healing after all. It's been a journey and it's still evolving but it's safe to say I've finally found my voice! And these lyrics are just beginning…!

* * *

"I survived every road block and detour so far
That place where I'm going, yeah I know it by heart
But how I'm gonna get there, that part isn't clear
So I'll just keep going and trust It'll appear

Cos even when the world keeps pushing back,
Even when I lose sight of the track
Even then the goal is still the same
If anything it strengthens my aim
Even when the light all turns to dark
and I can barely feel the beating of my heart
Even then I know I'll make it through
And that's what it all comes down to"

— (*WHAT IT ALL COMES DOWN TO* LYRICS - RELEASING 2024)

ABOUT BRONWYN

Bronwyn (Bronwyn Halley) is a successful contemporary country singer songwriter from New Zealand. Her EP "All In" reached #9 on the NZ album charts and her original music has seen her travel and perform all over the world. Having spent the last ten years bringing joy to people through her music, it was only a matter of time before she found more ways to help people. Over the last few years, she has undertaken training and become a practitioner in reiki, breathwork and EFT. After experiencing her own profound healing journey, she now wants to share what has helped her with others. She is currently living in Mexico, where she is writing songs and honing her skills as a healer before she moves to Nashville, USA, in 2024 to work on new music alongside her healing work.

Websites: *www.simplybronwyn.com*
www.simplybronwynhealing.com
Spotify: *www.open.spotify.com/artist/4Kc4UcILUCWT9Fy-JJ24iqm?si=3z8R_0GlS1GyFSegq2KFtw*

13
CHELTZEY NEWMAN

I always had a desire to be a mother.

When I was a kid, I could often be found with a toddler-cousin on my hip or babysitting for neighbors. I even worked in numerous daycares. I loved kids!

It took my husband and I a few years to conceive our firstborn, but when she joined our family, motherhood seemed to come naturally. We enjoyed two and half years adjusting to this new adventure called parenthood, when baby number two arrived on scene, and with her, the shocking experience of a dream becoming a living nightmare.

My newborn was an absolutely perfect baby. She was beautiful, smart, and quite happy, but I sometimes feel robbed when I think back to her infant years and don't recall many clear memories.

We didn't fully understand what was happening at first. I had dealt with both anxiety and depression since I was around twelve to fourteen years old, so I was familiar with the signs, but this experience was complicated with added layers. Hallucinations, spiraling thoughts, a lack of serotonin and restless sleep prevented me from getting the very thing my brain was starving for … the thing that would help me bond with my baby.

I don't remember when the hallucinations and spiraling thoughts began to haunt me, but I was aware that I needed some help. My husband had just started a position with a new company, though, which did not end up being the dream job he thought it was going to be, and I didn't want to add any stress to his plate.

I found myself isolated—a stay-at-home mom in a new town, with no real friends in the area. Before I knew it, and without realizing it, I was staying home more and more and getting out less and less.

As someone who had always loved gardening and cleaning, my home began reflecting the state of my mind. We had weeds six-feet tall in our yard, and inside the house, messes were piling up in the corners of rooms, and eventually out into our living spaces.

It was easy to brush it off. We had just had a new baby after all. Parenting two kids was harder than one. I just need some time to adjust.

Yet, I knew, deep down, that it was worse than I was letting on, as I would lie in bed at night with my heart racing and barely function each morning as my husband got ready to leave for work.

The yelling started, and I remember feeling as if I were a complete and utter failure. I had never raised my voice to a child before. I knew better! Yet, it happened, and every time it did, I grew in resentment and disdain for myself. Eventually, the yelling wasn't enough. The emotions in me were so strong, I felt as if they were literally going to kill me. Taking the next breath was becoming a challenge in and of itself. First came thoughts of how to end the pain. Consuming thoughts. Then came the physical abuse.

I will never forget the day my two-year-old screamed at me from her bed, "Mommy, please stop hurting me!"

I sat on her floor, with the baby in her crib and all three of us cried and cried for what seemed like a very long time.

I remember talking to my husband about what was going on at home while he was at work, but I don't think he realized how bad it had actually gotten until bruises and scratches started showing up on the kids.

I remember him confronting me about it. He grew extremely concerned and implored me to call him or my mother if anything was getting out of hand. I remember him begging me to put the baby down and get out of the house if I was feeling out of control. He and my mother began to come and check on me to make sure the kids and I were safe. I was feeling worse than ever knowing that they were both taking a lot of time off of work to check up on me.

It helped some. At least, I knew that my kids were safe, for the most part, but it wasn't sustainable long term, and I was now growing resentful of them for babysitting me.

I prayed to be changed. I hated who I was and what I was becoming. How could my life have taken such a drastic turn? This situation was something I read about in the news, not something I (the fun-loving, good-natured, perfect-for-kids, dreaming-of-motherhood girl) could possibly be living out!

I remember reaching a point where I felt so numb when I would peel myself out of bed in the mornings. I felt as if I were Bill Murray in Groundhog Day. Cycling through the same day, over-and-over-and-over again and again. It was a miserable way to live, and I often wondered why I kept waking up. Then, as the day would go on, the numbness wasn't enough. The body craves emotion and spontaneity, but when you're caught in a cycle of asking yourself "what's wrong with me?" and "why do I feel like this?" It doesn't leave much room for the creativity, excitement and dreaming of a person who loves themselves.

By the grace of God, I somehow held on to a semblance of faith. I continued to pray, in faith that, maybe this life would be full of suffering and misery, but if I endured, I would hopefully experience some justice and respite, eventually. Not an optimistic outlook on life, at all, but the principle of faith stands strong; even the faith of a mustard-seed could move a mountain, and, though I didn't see it yet, God was moving mountains in my life.

I had been praying to be changed. Despite all of the pain I had experienced in life, I always felt that I was receiving answers to my prayers. I didn't always understand the answers, though, and this time was no different.

The answer I was clearly receiving through my prayers for respite and to change was, "just make the best of everything you have!"

"HOW?" was my response.

"HOW do I even do that? WHAT does that even mean?"

I began asking myself those questions regularly. How does one "make the best of everything they have?" and "what does that even look like; to make the best of everything you have?"

The answers to these questions weren't clear in the beginning, but looking back, I can now see that these questions were being answered little by little. The repetition of me asking them began occupying the space which once held the questions of "what is wrong with me?" and "why do I feel like this?" The very act of becoming occupied with these new questions changed the focus of my attention, and the results that were showing up in my life.

I was still struggling with my children, but I started taking better care of my home. I remember the first time I heard Admiral William H. McRaven's commencement speech entitled *Make Your Bed* and that little seed of light inside of me grew into something more. That speech moved me to action. The very next day, I peeled myself away from the comfort of the space between those sheets and turned around, without hesitation, to make my bed.

I don't remember how long it had been since I had made my bed, but after a few weeks, I started seeing the fruit of McRaven's teachings. I began feeling a sense of dignity and a desire to clean up my living space. At first, making my bed was all I could do. The dishes still piled up, unwashed, in the kitchen sink, and weeds still grew ten-feet-tall in our yard, but when I went to bed at night, I knew that I had accomplished something that day.

Eventually, the dishes stopped piling up as I began to make them a priority as well. I started to take pride in our little home and the piles and rubbish that had been growing into our living-space began shrinking as I worked my way through them.

It was at the kitchen sink that my life would take a drastic turn for the better.

I will never forget the afternoon I stood there, washing dishes with my phone running a video-app on autoplay for some background noise while my children napped.

A documentary on Andrea Yates started playing.

I recognized the name. I had heard it on the evening news as a child. I never could have known then how much I would relate to this woman who seemed to have nothing in common with me at the time. Listening to her story, though, opened my eyes to my own story and how similar they were. I knew right then that I needed help, NOW.

My husband came home from work that night and I practically dumped everything on him. I asked him to call CPS, and when he said no, I threatened to turn myself in. He was scared that our children would be taken away, and he instead set up an appointment with our bishop to first seek his counsel.

We met with the bishop the next morning and, though I was incredibly frightened at the idea of letting the news of my behavior leave the walls of our home, within moments of opening my mouth and telling my story, I felt as if a weight had been lifted off of my shoulders.

For the first time in months, I felt myself take a big, deep breath of air. I didn't realize how tense my body had been for so long until I became aware of it relaxing. The simple act of allowing others to help us carry this burden released so much of what had been pent-up inside of me.

My bishop kept in touch with us to hold me accountable to keep my children safe and arranged some family counseling. I felt that the measures we were taking, combined with the personal study and practice I was doing, intuitively, were truly beginning to make actual change in our lives.

Shortly after that initial meeting, while I continued to seek guidance through prayer and intuition on how I could make the best of what I had, an idea sparked in my mind one day.

I must process a lot of my issues through water, because I was back at the kitchen sink washing dishes when my daughter came and asked me to wash her hands. She put her fingers under the tap and instantly drew them back, exclaiming how hot the water was. I thought, how interesting it was that something unbearable to her was normal to me, as I had acclimated myself to the hot water.

The wheels of my mind began spinning and I started studying the primitive response of fight/flight in the human brain. I became acquainted with the inner-workings of my mind and decided one day to turn my shower-time into a controlled laboratory experiment—to test the limits of MY OWN primitive responses by forcing myself to stand under freezing-cold shower water.

The first day didn't go so well. I turned the water on first and could feel the cold mist before my body ever got close to the stream of water. I talked myself out of the idea the moment my toes touched the water and goosebumps broke out across my body.

I was determined, though, and I felt that this idea was Divinely guided.

The next day, I waited until I was in the shower, with the curtain drawn, then turned on only the cold-water handle. The water first hit my back and I felt absolutely out of control of my body. Instantly, I started hyperventilating and gasping for air, but I didn't count this as a failure as I somehow found myself outside of the stream of water. This was feedback. Something was happening that was causing my body to move against my will, and I was determined to understand not only WHAT was occurring, but if and how I could strengthen my cognitive mind to remain in control.

I unfortunately don't know how many days it actually took to accomplish this, but within a few months, I could stand under the cold stream for twenty-five seconds, with deep, controlled breathing. I was seeing through practice that this deeply neutral state of mind was becoming my new norm.

I was more present and patient with my children. I noticed, surprisingly, that my driving had also changed. I had never thought of myself as a rage-filled driver, but I was noticing a difference in my reaction time and stress levels in the car, as well. My sleep improved, and to this day, I can fall asleep within moments of lying down.

When stress appeared, rather than tensing up and getting ready to fight, I was defaulting to that deep-breath in such a way that I now could sense that the conscious-part of me that I would call "self-awareness" was now consistently present in the frontal lobe of my brain, rather than retreating to the posterior area where I used to make my decisions from my amygdala. Now the moment I sense my consciousness retreating, I can call it forward through my deep breathing, and the angry monster I once was, I no longer become.

I used to hope no one was walking by as I ran from one side of my house to the other screaming at my children. Now our doors and windows are open and passers-by will most likely hear laughter and singing pouring from within the walls of our home.

Over the past five years, as I have considered all the changes I have made, I would say the greatest change has been in my identity. I used to consider myself a failure, and it showed through the actions I was taking in my life. That identity yielded resentment, fear, worry, anxiety and a horrifying lack of confidence.

I often thought to myself, "what is wrong with me? How could I possibly be such a failure?" and the experiences I had through life seemed to be bringing more and more proof that there was something wrong, and I was a failure.

Still, there was an innate feeling inside of me that I was made for a purpose. This feeling was what kept me praying and seeking my divine Creator, even when some of my prayers seemed to be going unanswered. There were times when the desire to understand purpose was the only idea I could cling to that kept me going, despite feeling as if everything around me in my life was futile. This little seed of light somewhere deep, deep inside of me that whispered to keep going so that I would one day understand the purpose behind all of these experiences.

I have learned that desire combined with faith are extremely powerful when it comes to belief and identity. I found God through intuition, and in finding God, I found myself. Not the self defined by the hurt and experience of this world, but the self that is created in divinity. Pierre Teilhard de Chardin taught that we are spiritual beings having a human experience. I believe one of the ultimate tests of this experience is whether we will lean into those innate whisperings. Will we come back to our true identity, or will the weight of the experiences of this life lead us to forgetting who we truly are?

Will we allow our experiences to shape the questions we ask about our lives, or will we cling to those inner whisperings that don't fit conscious reasoning? While experiencing my dark night of the soul, I became aware of how the questions I asked about my life shaped the very experiences I found myself having.

We humans can become fixated on searching for the solution, which will always seem just out of grasp when life is approached this way because our focus is on the lack of a solution. Instead, perhaps we should change the questions we are asking about life. For example, rather than asking how to leave the darkness, which naturally turns our attention to the darkness, perhaps we can ask how to see the light?

One of my biggest desires was to one day become a mother. I couldn't have imagined that experiencing such a desire would bring so much darkness to my life. That experience taught me that desire, combined with faith can yield transformation and that transformation comes about through clarity of purpose.

If you wake up one day and realize that your dream has somehow become a nightmare, ask yourself what this experience is meant to teach you. What is it that you have yet to learn about yourself? Where is your current focus? When you ask these questions, trust that you are Divinely created and there is an innate ability within you to draw the answer you are seeking. The gift of the effeminate is to connect with God through intuition. Go make use of your gift! Then, the next time you find yourself in the throes of darkness, could you be so brave as to ask "what's the best thing that could happen today?"

ABOUT CHELTZEY NEWMAN

Cheltzey Newman is a Spiritual-Emotional Educator and the founder of Key Mindset. Her superpower is helping others produce clarity and purpose by learning how to ask really great questions about life. Cheltzey is passionate about the simple things in life. Growing up and choosing to put roots down in extremely small-town Idaho, USA, Cheltzey is passionate about adventuring in the Idaho back-country with her family, volunteering in her beloved farmland home-town, homesteading in her backyard, building a family business with her husband Andrew, learning everything she can about an array of topics she finds interesting, cooking healthy homemade meals, and "un-schooling" her and Andrew's three cute kids.

Facebook: *www.facebook.com/cheltzey*
www.facebook.com/groups/1208977119274440
Youtube: *www.youtube.com/@cheltzeynewman*

14

DEANA MORSE

BLOODY GUTS

"Some stories have to be written because no one would believe the absurdity of it all."

— SHANNON L. ALDER

My journey to finding wholeness began in an exam room that felt like every other exam room, cold and devoid of personality. A solid wooden bench built into the wall sat beneath an informational cork board that showcased diagrams of the human body alongside informational brochures describing various treatments for intestinal diseases. Sitting in the exam room at only twenty years old, I was already living on omeprazole and antacids. I had chronic heartburn, indigestion, abdominal pain, cramping, bloating, diarrhea, constipation, and internal bleeding.

The gastroenterologist walked into the room and shut the door. He sat down on a round swivel stool and rolled it closer to the exam table. "Your colonoscopy revealed your hemorrhaging is due to an ulcer and irritable bowel syndrome," he said flatly. Then he proceeded to blather on about no definitive testing and something about IBS still being a mystery. He used a lot of big words just to tell me that he had no idea what was wrong with me and that my intestines were inflamed. As the visit with the doctor concluded, he casually mentioned that stress could be a contributing factor and handed me a little white piece of paper for prescription grade ibuprofen.

Really? I was bleeding out my guts and all the gastroenterologist did was give me a prescription for *ibuprofen*? Side effects of ibuprofen include *hemorrhage, hypertension, upper gastrointestinal hemorrhage, upper gastrointestinal tract ulcer, and dyspepsia.* Let's get this straight, the expert prescribed me a medication that could have exacerbated my internal bleeding, ulcers, and indigestion. Those were the same symptoms from which I needed relief. How insane!

I never filled that prescription—but let's pretend I did, and I began to suffer from hypertension as a result. High blood pressure can be life threatening, so it is not unreasonable to think my doctor would have wanted me taking amlodipine to regulate it. Bad news, edema is a side effect of that medication. I can imagine him whipping out his prescription pad again for spironolactone because that would reduce the water my body was retaining from the amlodipine, and that would lead to another medication and so on and so on. Even I could recognize it was a shitty treatment plan. The only thing the doctor said that resonated with me was that stress could be the source of my hemorrhaging, so I replaced him with a psychiatrist.

American culture and TV programming had successfully conditioned me to believe in the pop-a-pill quick fix. So, when my new doctor was more interested in managing my emotional stress with bupropion and escitalopram, that was fine by me. Taking a pill to eliminate anxiety and sadness from my life rather than taking the time to deal with it was my kind of solution. Unfortunately, all it did was hollow out the spirit in my heart. I felt nothing. The anxiety and sadness disappeared, but so did joy, and what is the point of life without joy?

During this time, I was still having the same digestive issues showing up in my body: heartburn, upset stomach, diarrhea, constipation, and hemorrhaging. I later learned that those are also side effects of the antidepressants I was taking. Somehow my intuition was beginning to connect dots that my conscious mind did not fully understand. Was it untreated IBS, emotional stress, or side-effects from medication?

Frustrated, I dumped the psychiatrist, flushed the antidepressants, and reclaimed my soul. My joy returned but my anxiety and depression did too. With my intestinal health still in distress, I pushed through the pain and pursued the American Dream. By the time I was thirty, I was a married homeowner, small business owner, and mom to two beautiful daughters. With all of that on my plate, stress was only building in my life, and due to my inability to cope with all of the negative emotions I was feeling, I prescribed myself alcohol.

Emotional regulation with vodka is like a Jack-in-the-Box. I was just stuffing down the emotions I didn't want to feel under the lid. Instead of antidepressants, I just used alcohol to paint a happy exterior; a joyful facade for everyone to see, including me. That appeared to be working until I got so wound up on the inside that I would randomly explode. I became volcanic, uncontrollable, and unreasonable. Despite these random outbursts, I continued to drink. In fact, I actually escalated my drinking. It doesn't take medical expertise to know that vodka is not kind to your innards. It is well known that the side effects of alcohol include hemorrhaging, ulcers, and dyspepsia. Needless to say, my intestines were still bothering me.

So, let's recap. The gastroenterologist's solution was to treat my IBS with a pill that could cause hemorrhaging, ulcers, and dyspepsia. The psychiatrist's solution was to mask my anxiety and depression with a pill that could potentially cause hemorrhaging, ulcers, and dyspepsia. Then there was me. My solution was vodka and that is known to cause hemorrhaging, ulcers, and dyspepsia. Enough was enough. I had to find a solution; I couldn't live this absurdity any longer.

"Take the time it takes because it takes less time."

— PAT PARELLI

Enter Shelly. Shelly was a nurse practitioner who left traditional medicine to start her own clinic with a holistic paradigm. There were no quick fixes with Shelly. Her approach was new to me, but I immediately resonated with her authenticity and her deep understanding of the mind body connection. As she asked me various questions about my health, my body completely relaxed. I didn't even feel the needle as she inserted it into my vein and filled vial upon vial with my blood. However, she didn't need to see the results of any blood test when it came to gluten. She suspected it was causing a disruption inside of me, and her suggestion was to eliminate gluten from my diet for two weeks. It worked. The hemorrhaging stopped.

After this, I became obsessed. I wanted to learn all I could about what I was putting into my body. A bit of research taught me that just days before harvest, farmers around the world spray their crops with desiccant agents to lessen the work for the combines. These are herbicides used to evenly dry out crops. Desiccants should be familiar to you. They are those little square moisture absorbing packets marked "Do Not Eat" and come in packaging such as shoe boxes.

The liquid form of desiccant sprayed on crops is called glyphosate. When you suck the moisture out of any plant, it dies. Dying wheat is easier to cut than vibrant, thriving wheat. The process is used on barley and oats as well. It is troubling that our farmers are more worried about the efficiency of their machines than the destructive effects herbicides have on our bodies. Many countries, including Austria and Germany, have banned glyphosate. So I ask, do I have a gluten issue or a poison issue? But I digress.

Shelly also suggested that I get a Carroll food intolerance evaluation to adequately address deeper concerns with my diet. She recommended a naturopath and gave me a referral. Results in hand, I listened as that doctor explained to me that I didn't produce the needed stomach acids to properly digest fruit. It is embarrassing to admit, but this particular issue gave my breath such a horrible stench it could kill a small goat. My relationships suffered—*obviously*. It is no exaggeration when I say that I was brushing and flossing my teeth multiple times a day. I tried mouthwash. I tried many, *many* mouthwashes. I even invested in an entire oral care system that guaranteed to fix the stink.

It didn't work because the issue wasn't *hygiene*; it was my stomach. I just couldn't digest fruit, so whenever I ate some, it just sat there. Rotting. Fruit isn't always eaten alone either. For example, adding lemon to my fish or pears to my blue cheese and walnut salad created utter chaos in my intestinal tract. Even the smallest bit of fruit with my meal would cause *everything* to rot, the solution was to eliminate it.

The Naturopath explained that I should also avoid coconut, olives, avocados, and their oils. He showed me how to read labels and warned me about certain ingredients such as the preservative citric acid. He even had me check my spice cabinet. Allspice, nutmeg, and cloves were also irritating my guts. He was adamant that I eliminate ALL fruit. When I followed his instructions completely, my need for antacids went away and so did my bad breath.

I continued on my path to wholeness with Shelly. When the six pages of my lab results came back a week later, she took the time to walk me through what everything meant. She explained how imbalanced hormones such as estrogen and cortisol combined with low levels of vitamins B_{12} and D were affecting my mood. She made meticulous notes on every page so that I could refer back to them when I got home.

Although addressing these things along with the gluten had eliminated my hemorrhaging, my digestive issues had not completely gone away. Then Shelly began educating me about the link between emotion and illness. She suggested I see a psychologist to deal with stress related depression. So I did.

> *"Genuine feelings cannot be produced, nor can they be eradicated. The body sticks to the facts."*
>
> — ALICE MILLER

I spent an entire lifetime bottled up and there was no more holding back. At that first session with the psychologist all I did was cry, and I kept crying. I was inconsolable. Over time, the doctor showed me how I had throttled my opinions, choked my spirit, and tied my guts into knots. For years I morphed myself into whatever I thought those around me expected and that caused a lot of overwhelm, frustration, and resentment. No wonder I was depressed!

Depression is just repressed anger, and since healthy emotional regulation was never modeled for me, anger was especially scary. When I stopped stuffing my negative emotions, they began to bubble up everywhere. It was messy. It was *very* messy. The most random things triggered me—commercials, sporting events, potted plants. My emotions were just intense, especially if I had been drinking. I randomly went into fits of rage followed by bouts of crying.

I was introduced to meditation as a part of learning how to regulate my emotions. I had to feel my feelings regardless of how scary or painful they were. It took months of mindful practice to learn that emotions are not bad. They are just feedback. Over time, my nervous system began to calm, and my digestive issues went away.

> *"Our wounds are often the openings into the best and most beautiful part of us."*
>
> — DAVID RICHO

When I was in that gastroenterologist's office all those many years ago, I thought all I needed was my body to be fixed. I didn't know it then, but what I really needed was wholeness. Wholeness of mind and body because they are interconnected. Two halves of a single whole. I learned from the first two doctors and alcohol that masking symptoms never works. I learned from Shelly that simply addressing the physical side of things such as diet and nutrition wasn't enough to heal my insides.

Externals like diet and nutrition are certainly culprits to many diseases and those things cannot be ignored. I learned from the psychologist that neither can our emotions, we have to feel them. We have to deal with them. It was only after addressing both halves of myself that I completely healed.

There is beauty in pain, and I now see it in an entirely new way. Pain, whether physical or emotional, is merely feedback that something needs attention. My bloody guts taught me to listen. Now I pay close attention rather than cover up my pain or stuff it down. That is the silver lining to my story.

MEET DEANA "D" MORSE

Deana Morse is a speaker, coach and author who specializes in helping people learn the power in listening to their own intuition to navigate a healthier lifestyle. She motivates and gives others hope for healing.

Deana grew up in a small town in Minnesota then moved to the west coast with her family at fifteen, where she met her husband. They married and had two beautiful daughters. Working side by side, they have successfully owned and operated a small business for over twenty years. Deana's internal bleeding and diagnosis at such a young age put her on a path toward wholeness where she learned that mind and body are intimately intertwined.

Contact Deana to learn more about the tools, techniques, and resources she uses to advocate for better health for your lifestyle.

Website: *www.deanamorse.com*
Facebook: *www.facebook.com/deana.morse*

15
ELLIE JONES

WITH DEEP HONOR, I SEE YOU

Hi there, loves, thank you in advance for reading my chapter.

Matshona Dhliwayo said, "The world's greatest teacher is pain."

My silver linings have manifested as lessons learned, gifts of wisdom and connections made with others through authenticity. With each shattering of my heart, I have been left to pick up the pieces, and much like the Japanese art of Kintsugi, putting it back together. Instead of using gold, silver or platinum powder and Urushi lacquer, I used self-compassion, connection, authenticity and wisdom. Hmmm...maybe I should call these my sacred gold linings instead…

I came to Earth right as the Autumn Equinox was beginning in September of 1980. As a young girl I was a firecracker mixed with sunbeams and as such my mom called me her sunshine. It was quite fitting with my blonde hair and infectious smile. I had BIG energy. Always on the move, curious and full of empathy. I was interested in the WHY of things from the beginning. A natural born investigator that would read my share of mystery novels and become quite the explorer, fearlessly running through cattails as tall as I as I was, my destination, the river. Books, rocks, music and adventure in the great outdoors would become my best friends, and they helped me survive the chaos of my childhood.

The legacy I had been born into was pure survival. My family was TOUGH, in the Ayurvedic philosophy you'd say they had a lot of Pita (fire), and it was my father's mission to make sure he toughened me up. Life had shown him that the weak don't survive in this world.

Tall, dark and handsome, his green eyes seeming to pierce your soul, paired with charisma, determination and sharp wit, he was a great storyteller and people either loved him or avoided him. As a boy he knew the brass end of a belt and the back of a drunken hand more than he knew the safety of love.

In the 70s, his mother, my grandmother Beverly, stole his money to buy alcohol. Money he'd worked all summer for so he could buy himself new shoes with no holes in them, for the coming winter. His mantra, "All women will hurt you" still echoes in my mind to this day.

Sadly, Beverly had endured molestation at the hands of her brothers and own alcoholic father into her adult years, and alcoholism was her means of survival.

My grandfather Vernon, his dad, was an entrepreneur who worked hard to provide. His own tendency toward the bottle, gambling and rage, partly born from finding his baby brother drowned, at age three. His mom dying a few years later of a broken heart.

In the late 50s when my mother was born, her parents were in deep grief. Her older brother had died from pneumonia at nine months old not long before my grandmother Marian got pregnant with her. To say her mother was checked out was an understatement.

Mom was tall and beautiful. She had the voice of an angel and paired with her tenacity, resourcefulness and striking blue eyes, she was a force. Her intensity rivaling my father's, and when they disagreed everyone in a three-mile radius knew it.

My grandfather Lewis, a well-respected banker, also an alcoholic, abandoned the family when my mother was a young teen. My grandmother Marian shut down, leaving my mother and her siblings to fend for themselves and eventually they were separated and taken to live with various families in the community as foster children.

Her early twenties found her holding a positive pregnancy test. She was ill prepared for motherhood and considered aborting me. Honestly, I wouldn't have blamed her if she had.

By now she'd witnessed my father's temper and was already questioning marrying the handsome Marine she had met at a Mormon Church Halloween dance only two months prior.

As a young girl I would witness my father raging, laying hands on her and throwing her across the room. On one occasion he threw her toward the couch, her back cracking on the corner of the hardwood frame, rendering her unable to walk for two weeks. This was all they knew. They were repeating generational cycles and patterns.

One of my earliest memories was being told I was the glue that held my family together, that if it wasn't for me, they would have gotten divorced long ago. For years I prayed they would. I didn't want to be "the glue," the reason they stayed unhappily together.

Countless times my father would come get me from my room during one of their fights and storm out of the apartment, cursing at my mother as he left and then telling me, "I'm divorcing your fucking mother when you're eighteen." This would become my normal. My nervous system attuned to uncertainty, chaos, pain, terror and shame. The same emotions that had been passed down for generations. No wonder my ancestors were alcoholics.

Between the ages of six and eight, my uncle molested me multiple times, which led to thirty years of deep-seated self-hate, never feeling worthy or good enough, hyper sexuality, chronic people pleasing and intensified the panic attacks I was already experiencing.

I clearly remember at age seven riding my Big Wheel in our apartment's parking lot. I was dressed up in my favorite dress and shoes, my hair in a neat ponytail, yet my thoughts were not on looking pretty. They were imagining what it would be like to be inside the dumpster, my gaze fixed on the garbage truck emptying it at that moment. I felt like trash. After all that's how my father talked to me. His abusive words flooding my mind as I imagined myself being dumped into the truck with the garbage, feeling the terror pulse through my veins.

I would later learn that these traumas and experiences created patterns of survival within me and some of these patterns were self-sabotaging. I operated from a place of people pleasing and giving more than I ever received in hopes of being loved and safe. Earning love was all I knew.

Fast forward to 2002. My friend Sabrina was talking to me one summer evening.

"Ellie. Ellllliiiieee! Helloooooo. Hey, where did you go?" I blinked, and her waving hand started coming into focus, her eyes concerned as they met mine. I had done it again, something called dissociating, yet another new word I had recently learned. I hadn't gone anywhere, well at least not physically but my mind was a million miles away.

I was twenty-one and had just had a therapy appointment. I was the only person I knew that went to therapy that didn't have REAL problems. My parent's voices in my head saying, "It's just a little dysfunction, you don't know what hard is." Then my thoughts returned to what the therapist with the kind eyes, had said.

She had taken her yellow notepad and drawn two lines going different directions on it and then put a stick figure that represented me where they intersected. She told me that I was at a crossroads in my life, and I needed to really weigh my choices and choose wisely. My boyfriend had recently cheated on me and given me an STD and then threatened to kill me if I tried to leave him. She told me that statistics showed he would likely follow though based on his track record, and my next choices were a life-or-death matter.

So, there I was at a crossroads, feeling ill equipped to handle the decisions I was faced with making. All the toughening up that my father had put me through only silenced my voice and all the belt whippings I endured at my mother's raging hand made me less resilient.

I was frozen. Six years old again, hiding in a corner, fear paralyzing me, shame constricting my airway and tears streaming down my face. Somehow, with the strength of angels I left him, he stalked, assaulted me and I got a restraining order against him in the end.

At age twenty-two I took huge steps to breaking the toxic familial cycles I was born into, which led me to building a relationship with God that would carry me through my darkest hours over the last twenty-one years.

Pain would continue to be a constant in my life and the grief of having several miscarriages and holding one of my dead babies in my hands was a kind of pain that felt like death itself. The cramping and hemorrhaging rendering me to let others take care of things. Asking for help was not easy for me. It made me feel unlovable, yet I was forced to slow down and let other people help me, which was a blessing and a lesson I still carry close.

I learned that letting the right people help me and being vulnerable with them could deepen friendships and it wasn't just me being weak or needy, it was the epitome of being human. I didn't walk alone, and others sharing their own stories of grief, consoled me and taught me that my willingness to be vulnerable opened the door for them to be as well. Such beautiful connections made during such immense grief.

When I received the call on my birthday that my mom had attempted suicide and driven off a cliff, time stood still. It was 2019. She'd been diagnosed with mental Illness over a decade prior and I had tried everything I could to help her for the past decade, to no avail. She'd refused treatment of any kind and the illnesses had continued to get worse to the point that she was a danger to my children. I'd set boundaries with the help of Doctors and Therapists, and she'd become irate and was threatening me so I told her unless she sought help, I would not continue to communicate with her. She disowned me. I hadn't spoken to her in close to two years when I received that fateful phone call.

She survived that attempt and would continue to OD multiple times ending up in the hospital and having her stomach pumped for the next four months. She reached a point where she wanted help, but she didn't qualify for insurance to cover her treatment, until finally after countless phone calls and at least 100 hours of research and conversations, I was able to get her into a treatment center that was covered by insurance.

Many people judged me for my firm boundaries with my parents, and I received a lot of push back, but I had learned in the many years of therapy I'd had at that point, we are sovereign beings. We deserve respect and love, bare minimum. Boundaries and support from trusted friends, family, acquaintances, coaches, teachers, whoever, are paramount. That familial shameful secrets do NOT need to be protected and we don't need to "sweep them under the rug down-playing them, saying, "It's just a little dysfunction." This is our story too. Our LIFE. We get to choose who is in it and what we will and won't allow.

Just because people are "family" does not mean we owe them something and it sure doesn't mean they can abuse us. Love does not hurt. Love is soft and soothing, like a gentle breeze on a perfect summer evening caressing your skin. Love elevates, protects and is in the details. Love is a verb, and when we feel true love, we KNOW it because it is safe.

Several years prior in 2015 my kid's dad kicked a hole in our daughter's wall and terrified me and all five of our children. I should have called the police but instead I kindly asked him to calm down and did everything I could to calm my children down, like I had done countless times before.

I spoke to a non-Mormon therapist and learned that even if someone has a good heart and comes by their own trauma honestly, we don't need to ever tolerate abuse or lie for them! Ever! They need to do their own inner work and seek treatment by themselves for themselves.

For ten years I had believed the lie that separation and divorce were not options. The first week we were married, he yelled at me and threw a VHS tape across the kitchen into the trash in a fit of rage. I'd never seen that side of him until then and that was only the beginning.

When the church disfellowshipped him, the leaders counseled me to stay with him and pray, love, support and help him. So, I did for sixteen years. Even his own mother gave me the same counsel when I tentatively mentioned the abuse.

My father just told my oldest son last month that he didn't understand why I divorced his dad, that he was a good provider. My father, who knows the bitter side of abuse and the hell we endured yet is still blinded by decades of the church teaching people to stay married come hell or high water.

I would spend years actively trying to educate the leaders of the church about the dangers of their counsel to me, to not report the abuse and endure to the end, because divorce surely would destroy my family. I was married in the temple after all. After countless meetings and my words falling on deaf ears it would become apparent that the church was in the business of protecting themselves and abusers. They didn't have any intention of listening to me or the countless other women with similar stories I had advocated for.

Separation and divorce are ALWAYS options ESPECIALLY if abuse is present. If someone tries to tell us otherwise, they are not looking out for our best interest. No one gets married to get divorced. Believe me, I know. If the boundaries we set are not respected then it's time to consult a therapist or someone we trust and as painful and scary as it can be, never sugarcoat what's happening. People can't help us if we aren't honest about the situation. Stockholm syndrome is real. Yet, another lesson…

About 8 years ago as a stay-at-home mama to 5 kids ages (ages 1-8), I was diagnosed with multiple Autoimmune Diseases, near adrenal failure, cellular dysfunction, having copious amounts of blood work done, put on hormone replacement therapy, supplements and prescriptions.

In total I was taking twenty-six pills a day, eating an AIP diet, suffering from chronic double pneumonia, chronic panic attacks, PTSD, was on 2 anti-anxiety/depression medications plus Xanax, Ambien and Klonopin as needed, and I was losing my hair.

I was bedridden with heavy fatigue for the majority of three years. At one appointment my Dr. looked me dead in the eyes and point blank said to me, "You are dying."

I was 35!! I couldn't die! My children needed me to LIVE! Not just, not DIE, but to LIVE, and live a life full of joy.

I TOOK MY LIFE BACK and in the end many years of consistent yoga practice, meditation, nature and sound therapy, DEEP inner work, 100s of hours of trauma therapy, leaving Mormonism and getting divorced have all led me too now.

My children are thriving, I take minimal medicine, I've lost 100 lbs. and I've learned a wealth of knowledge from it all.

Modern medicine and our current healthcare system failed me and has failed my family for generations.

That's why I became a Yoga Instructor, Intuitive Life Coach and Reiki Master.

In 2019 I walked away from Mormonism due to their double standards, history of protecting abusers, bigotry, racism, rigid beliefs and the silencing of the already oppressed. My standards are higher than that.

I was shunned by family and many in my inner circle that were still Mormon. I lost my entire belief system. Everything I thought I knew.

Was now in question. The dark night of the soul descended upon me with vengeance. Every major decision I had made was based upon Mormonism being true and so there I was. Once more picking up the pieces of my heart.

Some of my other silver linings are I learned that there is no ONE right way to do things. There is not only one way to heaven. It's okay to say no when we need to. It's okay to advocate for ourselves, to stand up for ourselves and we NEVER have to share a bed or a home with someone that is verbally, physically, emotionally, financially, mentally, sexually or spiritually abusing us.

I learned boundaries are a tool to protect us, to show people how we will accept being treated and if those boundaries are crossed there needs to be a consequence that we are willing to follow through with, otherwise we're just making requests.

Also, if our bodies don't feel safe somewhere including church, we DON'T have to be there. God is pure love and light and does not expect anyone to sacrifice their own well-being to go to church, ever. We can be close to God in many ways.

I've learned that people are messy. Many don't know themselves let alone love themselves and many times are subconsciously repeating patterns and programs that have gone on for generations. Causing trauma and cyclical pain to themselves and others.

In my decades of studying psychology the most profound work I have come across is the work of Dr. Amen. Dr. Amen has done over 83,000 brain scans and he says in his TedX Talk, "The single most important lesson that he and his colleagues have learned is that you can literally change people's brains and when you do, you change their life." He also said, "Psychiatrists are the only medical specialists that virtually never look at the organ they treat. That treatment needs to be tailored to individual brains, not clusters of symptoms and researchers have found that undiagnosed brain injuries are a major cause of homelessness, drug and alcohol abuse, depression, panic attacks, ADHD and suicide."

ABOUT ELLIE JONES

Ellie is a successful Yoga Instructor, Reiki Master and Intuitive Life Coach from New Mexico, USA.

She's been advocating for survivors of domestic violence for over 20 years and has healed herself from multiple Autoimmune Diseases, losing 100 lbs. in the process. In her own healing journey, she has worked with many Therapists, Coaches, Shamans and Healers. She believes healing isn't one size fits all and that one's healing journey is as unique as they are.

She combines Intuitive Life Coaching, Reiki, Sound & Crystal Healing, Breath Work, Water and Aroma Therapy, Hatha and Tantra Yoga, Meditation and Detoxification Methods in a variety of ways, offering her clients a menu to curate their own personalized healing experience in person and online.

Ellie is a single mama to five amazing children and two darling doggies. She enjoys baking with her kids, paddle boarding, being outdoors exploring & collecting rocks, coffee with friends and curling up with a good book.

Website: *www.ellieshealingarts.com*
LinkedIn: *www.linkedin.com/in/ellieshealingarts*
Instagram: *www.instagram.com/ellies_healing_arts*

16
EMILY DE LUZY

To the outside world, it looked like I had my life together; I seemed happy, I had nice materialistic things, and I was climbing the ladder at work. But inside I was battling with an invisible voice which nobody knew about. The voice I refer to as the 'gremlin.' From the moment I woke up, he was there, telling me how disgusting I was for letting my body become this big, fat mess. I was obese and the gremlin Monday through to Sunday never let me forget about it. The truth is I so deeply wanted to do something about my weight but I was scared to challenge my relationship with food. Why? Because food was the one thing that got me through my childhood and dealing with an alcoholic, drug-abusing father. I'd sit in his cabin in the middle of a field watching him pass out on the sofa, waiting for him to wake up and play with me. But when he did wake up, he wasn't interested in me, instead he just wanted to roll another joint and get his next beer, and that left such a huge void for me. At the time I couldn't understand it, being five years old, but little Emily knew she needed something to help her feel loved and that is when food became everything to me. The thing is, no woman chooses to be obese. You don't choose to gain all this weight. It happens because there are moments in your life when trauma leaves you no choice but to turn to food for comfort, and before you know it you've created a form of food addiction which feels impossible to break.

Little Emily remained with me through my teenage years and early twenties. I would be on a restrictive diet one minute and denying all responsibility the next, I'd shop in retail stores which were generous in their sizes so I didn't have to acknowledge going up a size. I removed my mirror on the inside of my wardrobe door so I didn't have to look at myself every time I needed to get dressed. This worked for five or so years but there was always going to be a moment when I had to face my reality and that moment well and truly came. It was a Tuesday afternoon at work, I bent down to pick up some files and my trousers ripped from front to back in front of everybody in the boardroom. I felt totally destroyed inside, seeing everybody looking at me not knowing what to say. I was a mess, my body was a mess and little did I know it at the time, but this moment was going to become my silver lining.

I left work that day and on that drive home I decided obesity was not going to win. I dedicated the next five years of my life to finding the path to conquering food addiction and my weight problem. I disregarded the one size fits all mainstream diets and instead tackled the deep-rooted issues behind my problems. I took the steps required to address and challenge my mindset towards food and learnt exactly how to work with my hormones to create long term, sustainable weight loss.

It has been my life's work to guide women out of the obesity trap and into their healthy identity. No matter how many diets you have done up to now or the grip food has over you, there is a way to create the body and life you desire, and I'm committed to showing you how. If you've read this today and you are at a total loss with your weight, I am providing you a safe, non-judgmental space to come and chat with me in my inbox. I will listen and guide you on what steps to take so you can step into the healthier woman you want to be.

Emily xx

ABOUT EMILY DE LUZY

Emily is the founder of FitQueen, which has guided over a thousand women to ditch diets, balance their hormones and find body image freedom.

Website: *www.fitqueen.co.uk*
Instagram: *www.instagram.com/emilydeluzy*
Facebook: *www.facebook.com/edeluzy*

17

HEATHER HARDY

THE SEAFARING SHIP

LAKE SUPERIOR

I **am an American.** I attended middle school and high school in Duluth, Minnesota, in the Land of 10,000 Lakes. Living right on the tip of Lake Superior, I knew the look of that giant lake in all seasons. I was familiar with the deep blue lake of summer, speckled with white caps from the waves and 1,000-foot rusty red cargo ships anchored close to shore ready to unload. I was well acquainted with the steel blue color of the water in autumn, with reds and yellow trees reflected in the water. In winter, I reveled in the silvery billows of steam that would rise from the lake when air temperatures plummeted suddenly well below zero next to the relatively warmer water. Pillars of clouds would rise in the clear, cloudless, morning sky as if there were giant pieces of dry ice floating in the lake sending the steam into the air. I always knew that the white icy waters would slowly but surely melt into a brown and then finally green and blue spring, and I knew by the sound of dripping water that temperatures were warm enough to put on shorts no matter the lingering piles of snow outside.

Living in the Great Lakes region of America also meant that I grew up singing "The Wreck of the Edmund Fitzgerald" by Gordon Lightfoot in school. We all knew the tragic story of the shipwreck. As history goes, the Edmund Fitzgerald was the largest freight ship on the Great Lakes in 1958 at the time it was built. Through its successful shipping years, it was nicknamed "The Big Fritz" or "The Mighty Fritz." Then, in November 1975, the ship left the port in Superior Wisconsin loaded with taconite, or iron ore, optimistic about its next voyage despite heading toward some troublesome stormy waters. But the storm just got worse. By the next day, it was reported to be some of the worst seas the captain had ever seen. The Edmund Fitzgerald received a small bit of damage in the stormy weather, and reported that damage to a nearby ship, but quickly said things were okay. Ten minutes later, the ship disappeared from nearby radar and nobody knew what had happened. All crew members were lost at sea. It wasn't until much later that the ship was found broken deep under Lake Superior's waters, about twenty miles from the nearest shelter.

MY SHIPWRECK

Just as the Edmund Fitzgerald was known as the biggest and best ship on the Great Lakes, optimistically delivering freight to and from the inland ports, I was optimistic and thriving in my 20s. By age twenty-five, I had completed my undergraduate degree in Piano Performance at BYU-Provo, served a full-time mission for the Church of Jesus Christ of Latter-day Saints in Berlin, Germany for 1.5 years, and returned to build up a thriving self-employed piano studio. I met, dated, and married my husband. We lived in Utah while he finished his masters degree in food science and I gave birth to our first baby. The challenges of life were difficult but manageable. By my husband's last semester, however, we knew we needed to make a decision. He was interviewing for full-time positions and had several good looking options that required us to move.

The option that seemed to call the most to him was working with his brothers at his family business in Canada. By the end of the search, this was clearly the best option for him. I was willing to follow him because I wanted him to be the primary breadwinner for our family. And besides, I thought. I could teach piano anywhere. And so, with all the courage we could muster, we decided to move to back to the small Alberta town where my husband was born and raised.

As a young mother, at age twenty-nine, I went with optimism along with my husband and our six-month-old baby, toward a new home in Southern Alberta. This was a small town with not even a stoplight, where I knew absolutely nobody except my husband's family. But I was optimistic. Anyway, things had always worked out if I just forgot about myself and pushed through. It turns out I was steering myself into some pretty turbulent emotional weather.

The first metaphorical crash for my ship was our arrival into town with the fully-loaded moving van. I didn't even realize that I had any expectations of a welcome wagon until we arrived from a full twelve-hour drive up to Canada. We pulled into the driveway and sat there in silence for a little bit. There was nobody to greet us. How could there be nobody here? I knew that whenever I had moved as a child, we had handfuls of people from our church congregation that would show up to move boxes and introduce themselves.

But here we were in our new Canadian town, and nobody was there to meet us. Not only that, but there was also not a single car in sight on a gravel road in a rural town. I turned to my husband to ask, "Isn't there anyone that is going to help us move our stuff into the house?" To which he replied, "Let's see if I can call my younger brother and nephew." He made the call, while I sat with my discomfort. Didn't he know that I wanted to connect with the actual community? People my own age and gender that would welcome me in and show me how to be a new Mom in a small rural town? Someone who I could see every day for fun? Someone who could validate my city skill set and see me as an important asset to this community.

I checked in with myself. Who did I expect to help us move in? After all, I completely failed to appoint members to my welcoming committee when we moved from the USA to Canada. I didn't know anyone, but weren't they supposed to show up somehow anyway? My thoughts turned to blame. I let myself believe that something was wrong with this town for not showing up to welcome us. Maybe there was something wrong with my husband for not setting things up with all the people he knew. Or my husband's family. It surely was everyone else's fault.. And I felt abandoned and lonely. I already felt that there would be nobody I could connect with. Nobody I could call on those days that were lonely and uneventful. Nobody would really notice me in this small place. During the days after that, I lived in a foggy loneliness, disconnected from my country, my immediate family, and my immediate community. I felt unseen. And I also felt like there wasn't much to see anyway.

My despair deepened when we decided to buy our first house. When my husband found an old house that needed lots of fixing up, I was hesitant to say the least. I wanted a house that would be beautiful and comfortable, but that's not what we bought.

This house was in rough shape. The kitchen had sparse cabinetry that was a light green seafoam color, the bedrooms had either shaggy orange carpet or light pink carpet. The walls in the livingroom were sheeted with the old light tan wooden vertical paneling. The whole interior needed to be torn down and rebuilt. With raging internal struggle, I consented to buy the house and agreed to put time and effort into renovating it.

This meant much more than I originally imagined. One particularly hard day I was with my four-year-old son, two-year-old daughter, driving them to Home Depot for the millionth time to pick up another part for our house renovation that we were so behind in. My frustration was that I didn't know how to do any renovations, so I was relying heavily on my husband, who was also working full time at his daytime job. I was frantically stressed about being so behind in the house work. I wanted to force it to get done.

I had both kids in the shopping cart asking energetically if they could get out. Gah. I was overwhelmed. I didn't want my kids crying in the cart, so I got them out. I told them to stay close to me while I looked at the tile for the kitchen backsplash. I didn't know what to buy. I fumbled around with my phone and tried to calculate the prices, while being distantly aware of my kids climbing on construction materials. With a bang, I was forced to pick up a crying child and then with the other hand, load up all of the pieces of tile that I thought I would need.

This was too much, I told myself. Everyone needed me too much. Where were the moments of happiness I was supposed to feel when raising my kids and working together with my husband to make a happy home? We were in fact living in my Mother-in-law's basement at the time, just trying to work on the house when we could.

I felt like I had reached another very low low. Things were not progressing and I realized I had very little control over this. I felt frustration and disconnect with my husband in our marriage, when actually I was craving more unity and connection. I felt like the only way I could have gotten this low was because everything that I had done leading up to this was a mistake. And I was doomed to live out all the terrible consequences.

THE CAPTAIN

"I'm ready for things to start going right," I said out loud in tears. I put my hands to my heart. I had always believed that there was a Great Creator, and that I was being helped along my journey. I thought I knew that God was in change, and that the Universe was conspiring in my favor. But did I really have that trust in God deep in my bones? My constant stress levels were wearing me out. I was frantically trying to force myself through this problem that I thought I had created and was eternally bound to.

I decided it was time to let go of all my stress and start trusting that things really would work out for me in the very best way possible. The stress was not necessary. God didn't say things will only go well for those who are stressed. As scripture teaches "All these things shall give thee experience and shall be for thy good… Therefore, hold on thy way." (Doctrine and Covenants 122:7, 9) Jesus Christ the healer of our souls can take all mistakes and transform them into something beautiful like butterflies. He is the reason for the transformation. He says that as we allow ourselves to hope for good things through Him, He "will consecrate thy performance unto thee, that thy performance may be for the welfare of thy soul." (2 Nephi 32:9) Nothing we do in that state of hope can be to our detriment. I could let go of my stress and lean more into trust. Trust that everything was indeed for my good. I was being held.

I originally thought that I had wanted to finish our house fast, and that being stressed and frantic would be helpful, but it ended up feeling terrible. Stress was not helpful. I had to surrender to the slow progress of our house. I also had to go back to the very basics of feeling my body moment to moment. I felt what it was like to feel stressed and resentful. I felt what it was like to feel love for myself and trust in God. This felt pleasing. This felt like pleasure. I began to see my path as a path of pleasure. And if I stray from the path of pleasure into stress or resentment, maybe I can just get back on the path of pleasure. I could turn my focus inward and find that love and trust.

And actually, maybe Jesus Christ could help me both see my beautiful desires, and get back on the path to experiencing love and trust. Desire is a powerful word because if you are in the position of desire, you don't possess the object yet. You are in want. You desire. And in the moment of wanting something that you don't have, which can be so painful, it's a powerful thing to give that desire to God and trust Him. And actually trust him that that desire is inevitably going to be fulfilled or something better will come in its place.

For my journey with our unfinished house, I decided I would focus on maintaining and keeping bright and cheery the parts of the house that were completed. I also:

1. I acknowledged my sad feelings about not having fully what I wanted,
2. I focused even more on the goodness of my desires. I wanted to experience delight and gratitude and ease. Those are beautiful values, and therefore, beautiful pieces of ME that felt the longings toward that. I could receive that piece of ME even if I didn't actually receive the results I wanted.

And actually, as I look back, I can experience sacred silver linings now for those difficult experiences that I had in the past. Moving to my rural Canadian town, I wanted support and connection. I wanted it so bad when we drove up to our empty house on an empty street in that empty driveway.

-Connection and support appeared in that first week when I had trouble setting up my cell phone. My beautiful Sister-in-law came rushing over to my house by herself to help me set up my phone instead of doing her family's dishes. She connected with me and supported me, and I'm forever thankful.

-Support appeared when my husband got stung by a wasp and needed to go to the hospital, my Father-in-law rushed over to drive him to the ER while I stayed with our baby son.

-Connection appeared when I spent my days home with my baby son belly-laughing when I got the hiccups and couldn't stop.

-Connection and support appeared when another sister-in-law invited me to dinner while our husbands were away. She complimented my soup making skills and I felt validated for making something yummy for us and our children to share.

-Support appeared when I had my second baby, my Mother-in-law came over to do my laundry for the first week. I was so grateful to feel supported in that way.

-Connection and support appeared for me when our older neighbor couple across the gravel road, after having my second baby, came out and offered empathy when they heard our baby suffered from colic.

When we bought our house, I wanted to experience relief, beauty, and enjoyment. With the house part way done and the difficulty of living life while renovating, I felt frustrated and despairing. But as I look back, I can experience these values from that time:

-I experienced relief and yes, enjoyment when my mother drove 3 days with me and my kids to Minnesota in a van that had a broken air conditioning. It was so hot and humid that I started praying to find a lake to jump in. As soon as I finished praying, I saw a turn off. We pulled off the highway right to a little lake beach for swimming. We all happily jumped in the lake and drove the last few hours in our wet clothes with the windows down.

-I experienced relief when my Mother-in-law invited us to live at her house while we worked on our renovations. We didn't have to rent another house while working on such a large home project ourselves. I am so grateful!

-I experienced enjoyment while living at my Mother-in-law's house, getting to be an intimate part of the "Hardy Headquarters" where siblings would come in and out frequently. When before I felt estranged from the family for marrying my husband so late, this gave me the sense of enjoyment from belonging that I so deeply wanted.

-I experienced beauty 1 year after moving into our still-not-finished house and my mother-in-law passed away from stage 4 pancreatic cancer. I was able to grieve losing her with the comfort of knowing that we spent as much time as we could have spent with her so close to the end of her life. I experienced beauty remembering eating dinner together, watching movies together, and singing church songs together. I knew the beauty of her handwriting from the way she would label leftover food in the refrigerator, I saw beauty in her work ethic by the way she would carefully scrub garden strawberries and clean off the green beans before processing them. I learned her love by the way she would carefully speak every child and grand-child's name and pray for them. I experienced so much beauty in that association.

And even now, while in the thick of disappointment with infertility, and being unable as yet to have more children despite trying for 5 years, I see beauty in my desire to experience enjoyment, family, and connection. I can look around and find opportunities to experience more enjoyment, family, and connection right now. I can look back and find evidence of experiencing enjoyment, family, and connection in the past. I can choose the values I experience, even if I can't control the way in which I experience them. I honor my desires and my feelings as beautiful, valuable parts of me.

The desires of my heart continue to lead me forward. My journey is not over. I continue to live in want. There are still many things that

I do not experience that I desire. But the unfulfillment of those desires is not what defines me. Those desires are indications of beauty within. And the realization of those desires in a beautiful and unexpected way is something I look forward to witnessing as I continue to sail my ship forward into the uncharted seas, relying and trusting that these good desires will inevitably be fulfilled in ways only God can design.

ABOUT HEATHER HARDY

Heather Anne Hardy is a multi-passionate woman with a rich educational background in music. She holds a bachelor's degree in Piano Performance from Brigham Young University-Provo, has taught piano lessons for twenty-one years, designed her own intro to piano course, and is currently launching a mentorship program called Whole Step Piano Teaching designed to support home-based piano teachers looking to improve teaching skills, business structure, and personal fulfillment in teaching music. Heather is a dedicated Christian and member of the Church of Jesus Christ of latter-day Saints. She is also a certified Light-Filled Astrologer and delights in reading astrology and human design charts to give others perspective and light and understanding for themselves and their relationships. Marital bliss is at the top of her interests. She is an advocate for passionate, strong, and deeply connected marriage relationships. She lives with her husband and two children in Raymond, Alberta.

Website: *www.heatherhardypiano.mymusicstaff.com*
Email: *heatherhardypiano@gmail.com*
Facebook: *www.facebook.com/heather.faerber.33*

18
KAYELEE ROSE

Sometimes, God speaks to me through numbers; sometimes, through babies. This is a story of how numbers and babies taught me to trust and be utterly honest with myself and the Divine, reconnect with my own inner knowing, and let go of illusions of perfection in order to more fully love myself and other people. I could write volumes about the lessons God has taught me through numbers and my own children, but this chapter will lead us ultimately to my experiences with one number—the number five—and the events surrounding the birth of one baby—my third child, Alea.

But first, we must begin with the number ***one***.

In my late childhood, I unconsciously believed that there was **one** clear path to happiness, safety, and a meaningful life: hyper-awareness of other people's emotional states and strategic suppression of my own nature and needs in order to please influential people. That version of me was far more nuanced and strong-willed than that description would suggest; however, managing other people's emotions and expectations permeated much of my reality throughout childhood and into adulthood.

Now for the number ***two***.

As a teenager, when it came to my religious and spiritual beliefs, I began to see **two** ways for me to walk in the world: integrity to self and my personal connection to God or obedience to other people's interpretations of doctrine. I understood on some level that the wisest, most fulfilling path forward for me would be one that incorporated *both* ways of approaching my spiritual and religious life, but fear of making mistakes still haunted me.

It wasn't until my mid-20s that I began to realize just how flawed and unnecessarily restrictive my interpretation of the gospel of Christ actually was. I *consciously* believed that Jesus Christ atoned for all of the sins and mistakes of every single person, but I *unconsciously* believed that the atonement didn't apply to me and that I had the impossible task of "earning my way to heaven" through not making mistakes (and punishing myself if I failed in that endeavor). I was near-endlessly kind to others; however, that kindness and consideration would often morph into unrealistic expectations, demoralizing self-talk, bouts of severe depression and crippling anxiety, and even occasional violence directed at myself.

By the time I was in my last year of university, I was grappling with depression that kept me from attending some of my classes, horrible nightmares, and spiritual attack-fueled insomnia. I would sit up at night, dread forming a heavy, black pit in my stomach and exhaustion clouding my eyes, hoping that somehow I'd be able to stay awake all night or finally be able to sleep undisturbed. The lack of sleep and the feelings of terror ate away at my attempts at being a "perfect" student, and my graduation from college was looking less and less certain.

I came to realize that I wasn't losing my mind; I really *was* being harassed by things I couldn't see, yet *undeniably* knew were there—but I was reluctant to seek help out of fear that someone else would question my sanity. I had been taught ways to cast out malevolent spirits, but no amount of casting out or faith-filled prayers was stopping the harassment I was experiencing. Daily, I begged God to release me from the pain and chaos, and I eventually spoke with an ecclesiastical leader who not only did not think I was crazy but also shared some additional ideas for how I could protect myself from spiritual attack.

Over the course of several months, these suggestions, much fasting and prayer, and the support of my then-boyfriend, Lige, led me to reduced spiritual attacks, more restful sleep, and, eventually, my on-time graduation.

This brings us to the number ***three***.

When I graduated from university in the spring of 2012, I knew **three** things:

First, my ability to sense and communicate with the world of spirits—an ability which I had largely been hiding since childhood—was now something I would have to face and develop if I didn't want to lose my mind. Slowly, almost without my noticing, my life-long receptivity to not only spirits and entities but also other people's emotions, the energy of generational patterns and beliefs, deception, and even the movements of planets and seasonal shifts was growing ever more apparent.

Second, I knew that I would be marrying Lige—one of my dearest friends from high school—a man who had demonstrated repeatedly that he loved me deeply, trusted my intuition, and would wholeheartedly support me in my efforts to undo the damage of decades of me believing deep down that I was fundamentally flawed. I did not know then that in **three** years, Lige would play a key role in the demolition and reconstruction of nearly everything I thought I knew about love, forgiveness, and myself.

And third, I knew that God had seen me through some soul-stretching, incredibly difficult experiences and had gently guided me to the life I was about to step into—a life I felt certain would be free of the pain and turmoil of previous years. I was marrying my best friend and stepping into the roles of wife and (hopefully within a few years) mother. I had been eagerly preparing most of my life for this. Surely, I had suffered enough. I did not know it then, but over the next few years, I would be tested beyond anything I imagined I could ever overcome. I would also discover how thoroughly and irrevocably grace could transform suffering into salvation.

While we were dating, Lige had told me about the unwanted pull he'd felt toward pornography since he was a pre-teen and his desire to overcome it, but I felt confident that we could quickly and relatively easily overcome what seemed to be a behavioral addiction with love, the help of God, and some healthy boundaries. Newly married me was so full of hope and joy that I buried my misgivings even when Lige continued to struggle with compulsive pornography usage, despite my best efforts to prevent his access and his best efforts to heal whatever part of him still craved the porn.

It's time for the number ***four***.

Fast forward to 2015. There were **four** of us living in an apartment—Lige, our two toddlers, and me. Though we would not have said so at the time, Lige and I were both pretending (even to ourselves) that everything was fine while each of us were trying to deny to ourselves that something was decidedly not right. I was pregnant with our third child, Alea. In some ways, life was genuinely breathtakingly beautiful; in other ways, there was a dank, festering underbelly of pain, shame, and deceit lurking under a polished facade of familial happiness.

Somewhere, somewhen along the passage of time from marriage to pregnancy with baby Alea, I lost part of myself. I became so caught up in whether Lige was hiding something from me or being honest and accountable—whether he was indulging in pornography or keeping his commitment to abstain and heal whatever kept him going back for more—that I sometimes had no clear idea who I was outside of our relationship, what I liked or disliked, or what I even wanted beyond the removal of any and all compulsive pornography consumption and dishonesty from my life.

I found myself over the course of my entire pregnancy having powerful spiritual experiences where I knew very clearly who I was on a soul level, conversed with God, and had positive interactions with spirits (including meeting Alea before I even knew I was pregnant with her) and having episodes of depression and panicky rage that had me once again questioning my sanity. I kept asking Lige if something was wrong, if he was hiding something from me, because I intuitively knew that something was very wrong and that I was most definitely not losing my mind.

As my pregnancy progressed, I began to have more and more interactions with both benevolent and malevolent spirits, though the benevolent ones would always make themselves known, while the malevolent ones were secretive and tried to hide their presence. I often mislabeled their influences as me just being silly or having mental health issues. With the increased interaction with spirits came nudges from God to start paying more attention to the numbers I noticed in my daily life.

Four digits began to show up, over and over again, in my awareness. 1234. 12:34 on the clock, $12.34 on receipts. Then I started seeing repeating number sequences. 111 and 1111. 222. 333. 444. Each time a number would jump out at me, God would lead me to a website or a book on number meanings and symbolism as a starting place for understanding the message I was supposed to receive. I would read a paragraph on a website or in a book, and then I would ask God, "What am I meant to learn or know from this?" Then I would hear clarifying words in my mind or have a sensation or emotional state confirm or further explain the message without words. As I honed my intuition and receptivity to Divine guidance, I received more and more messages through numbers.

In early December of 2015, I went into labor. Alea's birth was fast, powerfully primal, and felt much like a whirlwind. But if I thought her birth was intense, the delivery of her placenta was about to shatter my previous experiences with physical pain. Much of my memories of the minutes after Alea's birth are a hazy cacophony of voices and a blur of frenzied activity around me. Alea was healthy and safe, but I was losing enough blood that the doctor was considering taking me into surgery. My body was not delivering the placenta, and I was hemorrhaging severely.

In a last effort to avoid surgery, the doctor told Lige and I that he was going to have to "go in after the placenta," because pulling on the umbilical cord in this particular situation had a high risk of drastically speeding up the bleeding. So I found myself with a doctor elbow-deep up my vagina and into my uterus, trying to gather up all the components of my placenta and pull them out of my body. When I say it was the worst physical pain I have ever experienced in my life, I do not say it lightly. Waves of agony rippled through my body, and I could do little more than plead desperately for it to end. It wasn't until Lige prayed over me and asked for God to support and comfort me that I experienced a calm in my spirit that was utterly foreign to the pain and chaos racking my physical body and mind. But finally, the ordeal that seemed to me to be endless was over, and I had my precious baby in my arms.

By the time my sweet little Alea was a month old, I would discover that her birth was a symbolic representation of my own impending rebirth. The worst physical pain I have ever experienced came before the worst emotional pain I've ever experienced, and that physical pain taught me that I was far, far more resilient than I ever imagined, which was a lesson I would learn in greater depth, breadth, and clarity before Alea turned **four** months old.

Finally, we have reached the number ***five***.

Alea was born at 5:54 in the morning. 554…the number that—just as Alea's birth preceded my rebirth—immediately precedes the number 555. In the weeks leading up to Alea's birth, I had begun to see the number 555 often, just like I had seen 1234, 111, 222, 333, and 444. When I looked up the symbolic meaning of 555, I found a description that read, "Changes are rumbling throughout your entire life," and I felt God confirm that that was exactly the message I needed.

How perfectly apt that description would prove to be.

In the weeks after Alea's birth, I started seeing the number 555 every day, multiple times a day. How eerie was the frequency with which I saw that number; how strange were the situations where it appeared. I understood the message God was sending me; change was surely coming, but I had no idea how thoroughly I would change in the process.

When Alea was about a month old, my unrelenting intuitive sense that something was horribly wrong and the severity of the resultant mental health struggles I experienced whenever there was deceit in our relationship reached critical mass with Lige's deeply genuine desire to have an honest, truly vulnerable and healthy relationship with me. He finally overcame his shame and told me the truth about things he had been hiding from me since our first year of marriage. Lige's betrayal gutted me. The years of lies. The countless times I had expressed how painful and confidence-corroding his deceptions were, how traumatizing it was to feel a sense of violation knowing that I had been vulnerable emotionally, physically, and spiritually with him just to find out that he'd been lying to me.

I didn't know what to do. I questioned everything—my own intuition, my ability to understand God's guidance, the legitimacy of Lige's love for me. I hated Lige. I loved him. I hated myself for still loving him.

When the initial shock and devastation had abated enough for me to contemplate how to move forward, a dear friend and mentor suggested that I tell Lige to leave our apartment and have absolutely no contact with him for at least two weeks. She said that I had lost myself in trying to manage Lige and his compulsions and that I would never be able to see clearly enough to navigate things wisely unless I could distance myself enough from Lige to find myself again. So, I kicked Lige out of our apartment and cut off all communication, telling him I'd reach out to him when I was ready...only to have my mother unexpectedly tell me that she was divorcing my father.

I reeled with shock. My parents' marriage was ending. Mine seemed to be over. I felt utterly blindsided. Marriage and family—things I had cherished my whole life—seemed nothing but a farce designed to be a vehicle of pain, abuse, and hopelessness wrapped in a blanket of fake warmth and pseudo safety.

The following weeks of feeling my own deep rage and seemingly endless sorrow, alternately raging at God and pleading for Divine aid and guidance, and struggling to raise three young children alone was almost more than I could bear. It *was* more than I could bear. My body ached with sorrow. My soul was seared with agony. At the time, it felt like the suffering would never end.

Over time, with each nudge God gave me along the path of feeling and healing, I began to awaken to my Self and my own desires and needs again. I began to see how I was contributing to the dysfunction in my marriage, a dysfunction I had been determined to hide from myself. God showed me how I had shut down my intuition bit by bit and contributed to my own mental health crisis through wanting so badly for Lige's falsehoods to be true that I sacrificed true peace and safety for a fragile mirage of what my marriage was meant to be. My people-pleasing tendencies and hyper-awareness of other people's emotional states—fueled by a lack of conviction that I was deeply worthy and infinitely valuable regardless of how others treated me—had contributed to an environment where my best friend, my beloved husband had gaslit me into believing his deceptions, because I was already actively deceiving myself.

So, I got honest with myself. I felt what I honestly felt and stopped trying to run from reality. I got honest with God, sharing every ounce of rage, sorrow, and disappointment, every fleeting glimmer of peace, hope, and gratitude. I got honest with Lige. I told him that I hated him. I told him when I felt love for him again.

I gave myself space to feel broken. To heal. To acknowledge the pain that I had been running from my entire life. I learned how to trust myself again. How to trust God again. How to discern if and when to trust Lige again.

I walked through my own personal fires that seemed like hell but were really phoenix flames burning away the parts of me that needed to be reborn into something more real, more holy, and more honestly human and Divinely graced. As I did my own inner work and Lige went on his own journey of healing and radical self-honesty, God led us gradually back together, more healthy, more honest, and more vibrantly alive than we had ever been. Those experiences were harrowing, *and* they were necessary for me to learn to see myself with the kindness and compassion that I previously had reserved only for other people. I needed to let go of the lie of perfection and embrace the raw beauty of reality. I needed to see that I don't need to "earn" my way to heaven; God the Father, God the Mother, and Jesus Christ are cultivating heaven in me.

As a bonus, let's talk about the number ***six***.

Six months ago, I gave birth to our sixth child, Idalia. She was born in our home at 5:51 in the morning. Since her birth, I've been experiencing an upsurge in numbers that catch my eye, and God has been whispering, "pay attention." It started with 1234, 111, 222, 333, 444...but in the months since committing to writing this chapter, I've begun to see the number 555 with greater and greater frequency.

In all honesty, part of me quails, trembling at what that number may be signifying, but the part of me that trusts God and trusts myself is waiting with breathless anticipation and solemn gratitude for whatever transformation is unfolding.

ABOUT KAYELEE ROSE

There was a time in Kayelee's life when who she thought she was "supposed" to be largely defined her. She walked a confusing, precarious line between forcing herself into the most "respectable" mold possible and staying in alignment with her own deep knowing.

Eventually, Kayelee's desire for greater internal peace and stability led her on a journey of self-honesty, reality-checking, and embracing self-compassion. She has taken dark, painful experiences—as well as miraculous moments and Divine grace—as personal mentors.

Kayelee now works as an artist, pragmatic astrologer, professional intuitive, somatic educator, breathwork facilitator, and integration guide. She empowers Chain-breakers and Change-makers to foster safety, intuition, belonging, and emotional honesty in their inner world so they can show up more creatively, purposefully, and vibrantly in their outer world.

Kayelee lives in Idaho with her husband and six children, where they seek to love, learn, and grow through both light and shadow.

Website: *www.ourlunation.com*
Facebook: *www.facebook.com/groups/lunationlunarliving*
YouTube: *www.youtube.com/@OurLunation*

19

LEIGH JANE WOODGATE

There comes a time in your life when you stop protecting others under the guise of being a "good woman."

A distinct moment that sweeps over you, like the often not so gentle wind on your face, calling you into presence, inviting you to truly honour yourself by fully embodying all that which is true for you. Without apology, without permission, without choosing to place the reputation of those dear to your heart, above and before that which you stand for, any longer.

These moments in time, although distinct, are usually the sum of many discombobulating experiences over time, both mildly, and tragically so.

Layer upon layer.

Waiting, just beneath the surface, for the threshold of compounded discombobulation to be reached.

For some of us, it takes a few years to arrive at this point of allowing "the good woman" to die.

For others. A few more.

For me, sixteen was the magic number.

Up until that point I'd done well to keep my mouth shut. Uttering only a few words to my most trusted allies at the time, as I shared the depths of fear that I was experiencing in my own home, in the very rare moments when I felt safe to do so.

Prior to this unsettling existence in a small picturesque Northern Italian village in the Dolomites—with a population of just over 700 people—where I now found myself living and had become mother to my first and only son, after leaving Johannesburg, South Africa, my place of birth where I'd grown up for the first twenty years of my life. I followed the sun, hopping from one private yacht to the next, living the wildly dreamy life of a Yacht Stewardess aboard private and charter boats in the Baltic, Mediterranean, and Caribbean, over a period of five years in the early 2000s...

Where the Cannes Film Festival,

Monaco Grand Prix,

Luxurious South of France Summers,

Antiguan Yacht Shows,

An Eastern European Experience,

And the crossing of the Atlantic Ocean had become my new normal.

Yet no matter how extraordinary my surroundings and wildly dreamy my experiences, electric anxiety coursed through my veins. And in the years to follow, continued to amplify.

I was twenty-six years old, passionate about making a difference in the world for as long as I could remember. A feisty, fiery, highly intelligent, deeply sensitive young woman. Strong on the outside, shattered on the inside, yet a sufferer of fools, not glad to.

A woman in partnership with an Italian man of the mountains, the father of my newborn baby, my worst nightmare—a human being whom I did not feel safe with day to day.

At first, I thought it was just me, as I'd suffered with crippling anxiety for thirteen years prior, a state induced by my abusive mother and emotionally unavailable father, manifesting as a strong character with low self-worth, a lack of belonging, and a sense of unsafety in my own body.

Then, I thought that it was the circumstances that we were in.

I was wrong.

The first time I experienced this behaviour first hand was when we were on the second private yacht we worked on together in Turkey, one year prior.

The captain was off his chops.

The crew no less.

And the circumstances were highly stressful due to the lack of alchemy that existed on the boat and the pressures that filtered down from head office—two components that create an explosion of emotions in the close living quarters that yachts are well known for.

Though as time passed, I began to see and understand the cracks.

They weren't circumstantial,

And they weren't mine.

They were dysfunctional character traits, born from nature, nurture, and a lack of awareness.

Misogynistic,

Narcissistic,

And gaslighting tendencies, all guised as culturally normal.

Behaviours that shocked me to my core over and over and over again, yet somehow felt familiar.

Hands and voices raised.

Personal space invaded.

The victim-abuser cycle entered into, on repeat, for a decade and a half.

The four stages—tension, incident, reconciliation, and calm.

Nerve-racking, heart-breaking, mind-altering, soul-shaking.

A cycle I do not wish on anyone.

And as I sit here writing this chapter, I notice the lack of charge and emotion within me.

My nervous system no longer dysregulated.

My heart no longer aching.

My mind no longer racing with thoughts of disdain, disgust, and disbelief for a man to have treated me, the mother of his child, both whilst in utero and after giving birth, with the profoundly disturbing lack of respect with which he did.

Instead, I now sit here, forty-one years old, single, thriving, and at peace. Knowing that all is perfect as it is. Clear that we are merely part of the evolution of humanity. Here to be grateful to those who came before us, and acutely aware of the intentionality of the moves we are called to make, in order to positively influence, and exponentially raise the consciousness of self and those who come after us.

Soul-led, purpose-driven, embodied in my life's work—a High-Performance Leadership Mentor & Business Growth Advisor, here to enable wildly-dreamy-legacy-leaving leaders devoted to the transformation of humanity and the planet, to do so.

Unapologetic.

Zero *fcks* given.

And in deep gratitude for everything that this deeply present, incredibly reliable, undeniably committed, rock solid, yet heart-breakingly emotionally dysfunctional man has brought to my life.

The father of my now fifteen-year-old son.

A great father.

A strong man.

One however, who could not, will not, and continues to choose not to hold me in ways that honour my heart, mind, body and soul.

Highly energetic.

Emotionally closed.

Impatient in the most unexpected moments.

Yet incredibly loving and loyal.

And whilst I continue to allow the words to flow on to this page, immersed in the New Moon energy of this October Spring Month on the Central Coast of Australia, post an exquisite New Moon Smoking Ceremony held at the wild ocean beach that is Tudibarring, commonly known as Copacabana, led by an Aboriginal Wisdom Keeper, and supported by many of his bloodline. Where about a hundred humans gathered as we do monthly, to receive the cleansing gifts of smoke bath immersion and the powerful flickering warmth of fire, whilst the sun set with magical pink and purple hues in the sky, and a most perfect gentle breeze moving that which we chose to release, on and beyond, after cleansing our feet in the wild ocean womb of the Earth.

Pure heart connection,
Leaves of the season burnt,
Wood and liquid Earth gathered from Sacred Land,
The Spirit of nature embodied through dance,
The magic of intentional presence, enjoyed.

In perfect synchronicity with the first day of my bleed, a most aligned time to release and let go of all that which no longer serves me in order to create space for that which I, and we, are calling in through this next thirty day cycle.

> *"We are a continuum. Just as we reach back to our ancestors for our fundamental values, so we, as guardians of that legacy, must reach ahead to our children and their children. And we do so with a sense of sacredness in that reaching."*
>
> — PAUL TSONGAS

I have no desire to rehash the trauma of my marriage.

Or share the details of sixteen years that I will never get back.

There is no need to share the intricacies of why after two years of being spat at in my face by my husband, yelled at, and forced across our lounge room floor, the day after our wedding day—an intimate gathering of our nearest and dearest family and friends in Venice, Italy—that I finally found the courage to stand up for myself. A physical indicator of the warrior energy that lies dormant inside of me, ready to defend when needs must. A clear manifestation of my innate power, not to be antagonised.

The result of a line crossed too many times.

One where the victim becomes the defender.

And the abuser is put in their place.

I will however share twelve questions to ask yourself before making a potentially suffering-inducing decision.

1. Is this decision in alignment with my BRAND DNA?

BRAND DNA = your values + principles + mission + purpose + vision + virtues + brand essence.

2. Is this decision in alignment with my current FOUNDATIONAL GROWTH GOALS?...

FOUNDATIONAL GROWTH PILLARS = health + relationships + finances + self-expression.

HEALTH = Mental, emotional, physical, energetic, spiritual.

RELATIONSHIPS = with self, Earth, Spirit, family, lover(s) / friend(s) with benefits / beloved(s) / partner(s), friends, clients, suppliers / contractors, community members.

FINANCIAL = Salary / drawings, business, personal, savings, superannuation, investments.

SELF EXPRESSION = Authenticity, visibility.

3. Will this decision feed my WOUNDS?

WOUNDS = your vibrationally lowering patterns, programs, illusion stories, unhealthy thoughts and subconscious fears, debilitating feelings, unserving actions, unhealthy addictions, unnecessary proving of your already embodied high-value qualities, all developed in your formative years to keep you *"safe."*

4. Is this decision an act of SELF-SABOTAGE?

SABOTAGE = the act of consciously/unconsciously destroying the path you have created to realise your wildly dreamy dreams, whilst consciously/unconsciously taking action to descend into a wounded place, to access the past version of self, go to your familiar *"safe zone,"* experience your previous way of being and continue to *"play small,"* instead of choosing to be in the uncomfortability and unfamiliarity of the practice of embodying your next level of expansion.

5. Will this decision affect my levels of PRODUCTIVITY and VITALITY?

PRODUCTIVITY = The level of inspired, intentional, and courageous action you take to be in the process of realising your wildly dreamy dreams.

VITALITY = An embodied state of elevated consciousness.

6. Is the timing of this decision in alignment with my MENSTRUAL CYCLE & THE CYCLES OF THE SEASONS?

****for men reading this - skip the menstrual cycle, and pay attention to the seasons****

MENSTRUAL CYCLE = Follicular Phase + Ovulatory Phase + Luteal Phase + Menstruation Phase.

SEASONS = Spring + Summer + Autumn + Winter.

FOLLICULAR Phase (Spring): Set intentions. Plan new creative project(s). Think BIG. Say YES. Launch new products and/or services. Implement new ways of working internally.

OVULATORY Phase (Summer): Have important conversations. Connect and communicate with your community. Open yourself to receive. Focus on growth and prosperity.

LUTEAL Phase (Autumn): Complete your *"to do*'s.*"* Carve chunks of time out for project work. Organise. Focus. Complete. Prepare yourself to take time out to chill. Consolidate. And look for opportunities to optimise.

MENSTRUATION (Winter): Evaluate. Analyse. Rest, reflect, and optimise self, and systems and processes, to course correct.

7. Is the timing of this decision in alignment with the MOON CYCLE?

MOON CYCLE = Waxing Moon + Waning Moon + Full Moon + New Moon

WAXING Moon: A time to COMMUNICATE and SYSTEMISE.

FULL Moon: A time to CREATE and EXECUTE.
WANING Moon: A time to COMPLETE and CHILL.
NEW Moon: A time to DREAM and PLAN.

8. Is this decision in alignment with my current STAGE OF LIFE?

For the Women - as per various sources - in relation to the seasons:

STAGE OF LIFE = Maiden (Spring) - Mother (Summer) - Wild Woman (Autumn) - Crone (Winter)

MAIDEN: She is young at heart, full of optimism, energy, and a care-free nature. She embodies independence, strength and confidence.

MOTHER: She embodies creativity, nurturing (of the self and others), and attention.

WILD WOMAN: Also known as Medicine Woman, the Witch, or the Enchantress. The Wild Woman asks us to feel our pain and address the root of where it comes from, below the surface. Because this is the only way we can begin to truly heal. She asks us to stand still, reflect, accept, and alchemise our experiences. Because this is how we learn the lessons, grow, and move forward.

CRONE: Also known as the Wise Woman. She represents loss of fertility, external beauty, activity, and youth; the only things that our patriarchal society values in women. She is a community leader. She feels a need to slow down, physically and mentally. She becomes introspective, and sometimes more sensitive.

For the Men, as per Alison Armstrong, Creator of the Understanding Men & Women online series.

The stages' names are based on medieval terms:

- **Page:** Birth to puberty. "Wannabe Knights"; they want adventure on their (a child's) scale.
- **Knight:** Puberty until late twenties/early thirties. Characterised by a drive for adventure, fun, challenge, passion.

- **Prince:** Late twenties/early thirties through 40-45ish. Focus is on who he wants to be in his life, what he wants to accomplish, and goes about bringing that to bear, even at the neglect of his wife and family, even though he says (and truly believes) he is working this hard for their benefit.
- **King:** 40+. Kings are confident of who they are. They may not have acquired a lot of material wealth, but they are generous, whether with gifts, time, attention or affection.
- **Elder:** Later years, near the end of his life. Not all men become Elders. A man's life is complete. There is nothing to do but enjoy life, explore what he's curious about, appreciate his blessings and serve humanity.

There's also a *"state"*—not really a stage—called *"The Tunnel"* which most of us would label midlife crisis. This occurs during the transition between Prince and King. A man questions what he's achieved and become and can be dissatisfied at this point. He can then become withdrawn, difficult, uncommunicative, and a challenge to be around.

9. Is this decision the embodiment of my WEALTH CONSCIOUSNESS?

WEALTH CONSCIOUSNESS = Your role as a leader in the world.

10. Does this decision honour, and enable me to embody my HUMAN DESIGN?

HUMAN DESIGN = Your self-knowledge system combining astrology, the I Ching, Kabbalah and Vedic philosophy centered around your specific energy type to enable you to exchange energy with the world in a nourishing, nurturing, expansive, and sustainable way.

11. Does this decision enable me to honour and embody my GENE KEYS?

GENE KEYS = Your higher purpose influenced by your DNA.

12. Will this decision enable me to be of the HIGHEST SERVICE possible?

HIGHEST SERVICE = The expression of your innate gifts + Your ability to be in exchange with life and the world with unconditional love + Your sense of safety and security within self.

To learn more about how to embody the art of making decisions in alignment with your true self, head to my website *www.leighjanewoodgate.com/work-with-leigh*

Dear One,

Not every lesson needs to be a hard lesson learnt.

Not every energetic upgrade needs to be chaotic, stomach-turningly uncomfortable, or heart-wrenchingly scary.

You can simply just choose to be true to yourself.

Your standards.

To that which is important to you, in alignment with your values, principles, mission, purpose, mission, and essence.

No controlling or forcing necessary.

No reading someone else the riot act,

telling yourself that you're holding your standards when in fact all you're doing is avoiding taking responsibility for your own fear and undealt with trauma.

You can simply just choose compatibility over self-abandonment.

It's ok to choose the easier path.

The one of less suffering.

The one where you choose to say no before the *sht* hits the fan.

The one where you exit a situation before the seas get rough.

The one where you walk away before things turn sour, awkward, dangerous, and uncomfortable.

Suffering is a choice,

I've come to learn,

After multiple decades of healing.

Immersing yourself in pain,

when you can clearly feel that the thing or the person or the situation or the opportunity is not compatible with where you're at,

is a choice.

When you are clear on your standards,

You've dealt with your wounding,

You know who you are,

and are centred and grounded in yourself,

You don't need to wait for the activation or trigger to occur, to disengage.

Growth can occur WITHOUT suffering,

It's not always a roller coaster *shtshow* of shredded red flags on a pile of what the *fck* just happened there?!

It can just be a *"oh cool, this is not a vibe for me, enjoy the rest of your life, I'm out, much love, thanks for momentarily crossing my path to remind me of what it looks like to choose suffering, wishing you peace, bye, Ima just be over here enjoying the path of least resistance. See ya"*

To get there however,

You are required to attune yourself to the frequency of ease and flow.

And in order to do so,

You're required to give up your addiction to suffering, by asking yourself the above twelve questions that enable you to stay on your path, in alignment with who you truly are, in order to grow with ease and flow, instead of destruction and suffering.

And if you've momentarily forgotten what's possible for you.

Here's your reminder…

It gets to be easier,

And even more enjoyable,

For no other reason,

other than,

you choose it to be so.

And as for other people's level of intelligence; intellectual, emotional, physical, energetic and spiritual.

That has nothing to do with you.

What others are able to understand and hold is not your responsibility.

Whether something that you have clarity of intention on lands for others or not has nothing to do with you.

You are here to embody your mission and purpose on planet earth, soul-led and devoted, in alignment with your own personal ethical framework.

You are not here to make yourself smaller to morph into other people's smallness.

Those who don't "get you."

Are not an indicator that you are not "gettable."

And those who are for you will never pass you by—both light and dark.

All is welcome.

All is necessary.

All is in perfect order.

All showing up to show you where your work is and where you are being invited to celebrate where you've landed due to all the commitment you have poured into being quintessentially you.

The journey of being an embodied leader.

ETHICAL. PROSPEROUS. GENEROUS. INTUITIVE. AND IN YOUR PERSONAL POWER.

Where your unshakeable capacity to hold duality is non-negotiable.

And a reminder that if you don't have the capacity to hold both the *"good and the bad,"* the *"right and the wrong,"* the *"darkness and the light,"* the *"understanding and the misunderstanding."*

There isn't space for harmonised high-performing soul-led purpose-driven leadership.

Because the truth is, stuff that happens at *"the top"* and *"behind closed doors"* isn't all roses.

It's not all perfect.

It's not all a walk in the park.

It requires grit.

Resilience.

Centredness.

Groundedness.

Compassion.

Empathy.

Understanding.

And the capacity to RECEIVE all of it.

As there is no space for being precious.

Taking things personally.

Defensiveness.

Ego-driven nonsense.

Embodied Ethical Leadership requires taking full responsibility for every move you make.

And dealing with the consequences of those moves, with integrity.

The higher you climb, the more you are shown who your true friends are.

Who your true ride or dies are.

Who your true audience is.

Who your true allies are.

The more you expand.

The more space you are required to create for those who are ready to expand at the level that you are choosing to expand at.

Me?

I am personally not here to pussyfoot around anything or anyone.

You're either devoted to rising at the expansiveness at which I desire to move at or you're not.

Those who are,

Choose to be in my life, and I choose to be in theirs.

And those who choose to be supported by me,

Often work with me for many consecutive years.

Those who are not,

reach their point of growth,

go off into the world to apply what they've learnt,

embody it,

and create the wildly dreamy results that they desired to create when working with me.

Some come back to then take their next big leaps at a later stage.

Some don't.

The level at which others choose to operate in life and business is not your responsibility.

Your only responsibility is to have clarity on who you are, what you stand for, and what you're devoted to creating and contributing to.

The rest…

Is not of your concern.

You are who you are.

I am who I am.

We are the sum of our Ancestors, both light and dark.

They have passed down to us our strengths and have shown us our weaknesses.

It is up to us to acknowledge such. And when we have taken a turn out of alignment with that which enables us to be of the highest service possible to self, and others—supported by the above twelve effective decision-making questions, aka *The Refined Wealth Creation Mapping Assessment [head to my website to access the online assessment]*—we are invited to course correct, with love, dignity, honour, humility, and respect.

"Parenting has nothing to do with perfection. Perfection isn't even the goal, not for us, not for our children. Learning together to live well in an imperfect world, loving each other despite or even because of our imperfections, and growing as humans while we grow our little humans, those are the goals of gentle parenting. So don't ask yourself at the end of the day if you did everything right. Ask yourself what you learned and how well you loved, then grow from your answer. That is perfect parenting."

— L.R. KNOST, AUTHOR

My marriage was a disaster.

As was our ceremonial five-week *"European Divorliday"* together with our son, intended to celebrate our divorce, which was finalised on 13 March 2023, after eight and a half years of separation, during which time harmony had been meticulously cultivated within our non-conventional family unit, and within five weeks, absolutely obliterated.

The Sacred Silver Lining?

We are parents to one of the most extraordinary human beings I know.

Our son—a young man of honour, dignity, empathy, wisdom, joy, and the most incredible sense of 'beyond his years' humour and intelligence; intellectual, emotional, physical, energetic, and spiritual.

And for this I am deeply grateful, beyond blessed, and constantly challenged to be better.

He is the sum of all our parts, of those who came before him, before us, and the parts that will contribute to the evolution of those who come after him.

Here to add another layer of uplevelment to our humanity and gently destroy that which no longer serves us. As only the next generation knows how.

ABOUT LEIGH JANE WOODGATE

Leigh Jane Woodgate is a High-Performance Leadership Mentor, Business Growth Advisor, Human Optimiser, Author of two #1 international bestselling books *"Trailblazers"* and *"Awakening,"* host of *Business, Sex & Being Human, the Podcast,* and the Founder of Inategy Business School, an online business school and leadership collective for soul-led business owners, purpose-driven entrepreneurs and conscious leaders, creatives, consultants, advisors, healers and therapists to optimise themselves for sustainable personal and business growth.

For over twenty-three years she has built and grown successful global businesses alongside influential entrepreneurs and CEOs.

Her passion?

Enabling the boundary challengers, disrupters, change-makers, social advocates, purpose-driven entrepreneurs and conscious leaders to slow down to speed up, create wealth in the Feminine Leadership Flow State ©, and create greater social impact without having to compromise who they truly are to achieve their wildly dreamy legacy-leaving dreams.

Born in Johannesburg. Raised in South Africa by her Father. Mother to her fifteen-year-old son. She lives on the East Coast of Australia.

Website: *www.leighjanewoodgate.com*
Instagram: *www.instagram.com/leighjanewoodgate*

20

MICHELLE SAWARD

THIS DETROIT AIN'T HUSTLING HARDER

I have twenty-three years in the real estate business, and over 2000 career sales. As of this publication, I have an organization of over 1600 real estate agents who have aligned with me. Yes, it's a lot of hustle. This real estate accomplishment comes by moving at a very fast pace, and the repeated action required to establish a great business. All in all, I've created a pretty good life for myself through real estate and I have no regrets. Yes, it earned me the trophies, the adrenaline rush of recognition, my name in lights, a place in Maui, great vacations, a million-dollar home, and free and clear rental properties.

My childhood took place just outside of Detroit. You may have seen the T-shirts that say, "Detroit Hustles Harder." Let me tell you, the hustle started very young for me. I was surrounded by friends on the block, kids were everything to me. They were all a year older than me, honor-roll students, and had nicer clothes and things than me. Because I didn't have the things others had, and I wasn't as old as the other kids, I felt that I was never equivalent, nor could I even compete with these older kids. From such a young age I was left with a feeling of less than. As I matured and got into the work field, I realized I could always work harder and faster than the people around me, and that was how I could get ahead. I used to see those T-shirts and be filled with pride in my hard work ethic thinking, "Yes! Detroit hustles harder!" Now, I see that slogan and feel a little nauseous.

Creating this business has done a lot for me, but it also meant no time for personal relationships and no time for my marriage. I have invoices from three different marriage counselors, and not a moment left to create balance and an even smaller circle of friends. There's a time and a place to hustle and a time and a place to sacrifice and hustling has afforded me some great luxuries. However, I sacrificed a lot for my business. I have come to realize that it is important to invest in myself to create the future of my dreams.

THE PAUSE

I've had a heck of a year in 2023; I cut my sales from over 200 transactions in 2022 to ending this year with just over 100, cutting my business in half. I did that with intention and purpose, and it did not come the way that I thought it would. It certainly didn't look the way that I thought it would look. When I found myself mentally, physically, emotionally, and completely drained after running hard for twenty-three years in real estate, I was in dire need of a break. After years of running, it was so easy for me to get sucked back into the adrenaline rush of the deal, feeling needed by clients, and the high of the go, go, go. The introduction to my overdue and much-needed rest came with the resignation of my manager. We had a lot of differences in opinions about how things should be run. When he resigned, I laughed out loud. It felt so right! I had an instant insight that this was the answer. Within days of his resignation, another key team member also resigned. I could have and should have made some of these decisions for myself, but instead, they were made for me. And with that, I had the choice to rebuild it or not. I was exhausted yet still willing to try. The fear of falling back into old "business survival patterns" haunted me… I had a real fear of defaulting back & working in the way that is familiar. "Hustling Harder" was not going to work this time. I wanted something different.

I knew that moving forward required serious contemplation. I had to get my head straight. So I decided to do something radical and take a twelve -hour walk in Maui— no phone, no music, just me and myself walking for twelve hours, sometimes along long stretches of beaches alone. When I needed to sit down and take a break, I would sit down and take a break. I even took a nap on the beach. I was just gone for a full twelve hours. I was walking where my heart led me and after twelve hours, I finally got some clarity. It allowed me to decide how I wanted to build this, and it was crystal clear that I no longer wanted to do it the way I did it before. I was so tired of people-pleasing. I had given so much of myself. I felt the way I had run my business and my life before was like the erosion of a beach. Every wave that comes in takes a little bit of sand away from the beach, wave after wave. And one day you wake up only to realize there's no beach left. You wonder, "What happened to my beach?! It was a beautiful, amazing beach!" I was just like that beach. How I ran my life and business eroded me until I was almost gone.

PUTTING MY FEET ON THE FLOOR

Have you ever run in a race, or watched a sport when the score was nearly a tie? It's so interesting to note how people respond. Spectators applaud near the end or at the halfway pivotal moments. They don't applaud athletes when they put their freaking feet on the floor in the morning. They don't applaud at the beginning of the game. No one was applauding the downsize of my company. I had to stop caring about what anyone else thought and begin to care more for myself. I had to reclaim and find my power. I began by making small commitments to myself and decided no matter what, I would do something that filled my heart with joy every day. I began to take things off my checklist and make space for myself and my heart's desires. I removed things from my list that did not fill my heart, bring me joy, or feel intentional. It was a great start to making deposits in myself. I was giving myself "my beach back." And I started to feel pride, deep fulfillment, and clarity that I was doing the right things to realign with my true self. I have received such insight this year about how to live life by my new definition of better and create tremendous success in my life. I know I am on the right path.

SHOULDING ON MYSELF

I learned if you don't take a pause for yourself and if you don't take a stand for your business and set some boundaries, you will find yourself burning to the floor, and burning out faster than you would have otherwise. I ran hard in business for twenty-three years. I don't know how I made it that long. I lived in reaction mode, was playing whack-a-mole real estate beating down things as they popped up (as many business owners do) and was not operating from a space of putting myself first. I was reacting, reacting, reacting. Over time, I found myself lying awake in bed, for far too many nights, shoulding all over myself. Shoulding is when you are constantly living in the state of, "I should have done this," "I should be moving into this future," or "I should be delivering more of what they need." I would lie awake in bed at night thinking about my organization, the groups of people that I'm leading, and my clients and how I could make it all better. It became obsessive. The thoughts over and over of, "Am I doing enough to serve? If I can't serve, what value do I have as a human being? How many more people can I help? How many more lives can I touch? Am I doing the right thing? Are my systems good enough? What more are people expecting of me? How can I deliver?" It was a big question about the value that I hold as a human being. These obsessive thoughts brought me right back to being a little girl, trying to keep up with the other kids on the block, never quite measuring up. Damn, I am now forty-seven years old and this takes me right back to feelings of unworthiness and leading to obsessive future self-destruction. When you are running around like a crazy person with your hair on fire, your desk is full of to-do lists and you're playing whack-a-mole with your life, you're living an unconscious life. You don't have time to create value for yourself. Unfortunately, the power of an unconscious life can feel so effing good; that rush of "Go, go, go." Adrenaline is a great addictive feeling that gives you the belief that you're winning at life. The financial rewards hustling brings can be seen as a false win. Left with a fleeting feeling, because the win came without conscious intentional creation, it leaves you always wanting more.

The hardest part about finding real fulfillment is that it requires letting go of several things; letting go of the need to get an adrenaline rush, the need for approval, and caring about what others need, think, feel, or want. You have to take a stand and set some boundaries to feel wholeness and to feel proud of yourself at the end of the day. Surrender sleepless nights l ying in bed wondering what else you should have, could have, may do in the future, or how better you can serve and instead take time to pause and meditate. You need to go into the silence. No one else can do this for you. No guru, no coach, no mentor, no trainer. Just YOU. It requires going into your stillness and your darkness. Remember that the darkness of your past is here to help you equally as much as your light. All that stuff that you're doing that is keeping you living in avoidance and reaction will not lead you to build a positive future, it will only lead you to repeat the unworkable past. Without self-awareness and self-reflection, you will come back to the same emotional past hoping to create a new future— you cannot put a bandage over a broken bone and expect it to heal just right. Tapping into unconscious behaviors requires deep reflection and meditation. It is setting the bone. Might be painful, yet necessary to get back to wholeness. In the stillness, think about what is holding you back. When you tap into the root of the thought, you can build upon it (or remove it) to guide yourself back and create a positive future for yourself.

BREAKDOWN OR BREAKTHROUGH?

In 2023, with less to manage, I found myself in a great space to have time to bring back daily reflection and meditation; the one important thing that had fallen off my self care list made its way back on the list. I made meditation a priority for myself and with that came massive clarity. It was with that massive clarity that I found I was able to create way more money, with fewer people to manage or wo. about. I created a life with fewer moving parts, and with more peac and simplicity. The old me has been shed. No more adding more to the business without an intentional reason; I'm now operating with fewer systems and cleaner processes. I traded less for more, reaping the benefits of peace and ease.

I've heard this phrase many, many times over my career, "Only through a breakdown can you have a breakthrough." It's true. And does it suck at the moment? Sure. Oh yeah. It sucks. The people on my team, some of whom I considered real friends, had been with me for well over a decade. They are now all gone. When I simplified, it became easy to see the mistakes I made.

I assumed business relationships were also personal friendships. I assumed the work I was responsible for was essential to keeping the business going. I assumed they appreciated my effort. I assumed I was responsible as a business owner to keep people happy.

HARD CONVERSATIONS AND LABELS

There were so many days that I would avoid tough conversations. I learned that you have to have hard conversations with yourself and with the people in your world to have peace. Tough conversation with a significant other, with a business partner, with myself... It's so much easier to stay in the hustle and grind and to do, do, do, and go, go, go than to take a moment and have that hard conversation. It seems so much easier to avoid it, keep moving, and sweep everything under the rug. Well, I did that for a long time. It got to the point where the pile under my rug created an obvious bulge and a trip hazard. It was out of hand and needed housekeeping. I had to create space in my life to tackle the big hard things and move into those hard conversations. It took courage. I had to come to a place where I valued authenticity in my life, in my business and myself. Being in integrity with myself, became my highest priority. I valued that more than I valued what anyone thought of me.

ry e .ıt mean you're weak. Likewise, if you're moving .an that you're strong. When people were leaving my .d I wasn't going to label it good or bad. I just stopped .ıbel on it. I decided that I was going to let these cards play . see what happened with this hand I was dealt and play the .s as they lay. Pain lives in labeling the past, and labeling what ou've experienced as good or bad. Pain also lives in labeling the unknown future, worrying about a future that you don't know if it will manifest or not. The power is in this present moment, right here, right now. Give yourself the gift of no labels and witness and watch how things will unfold.

GROWTH REQUIRES CHANGE

Your personal growth can never exceed your income. It is impossible. We are limitless beings with the ability to create positive futures and growth opportunities for ourselves beyond measure. This is a limitless conversation. This is a conversation about the limits you are putting on yourself.

Steve Jobs said, "Simple can be harder than complex. You have to work to get your thinking clean, to make it simple. But it's worth it in the end because once you get there, you can move mountains." What can you create when you give yourself time to make choices about your life? If you are choosing to change nothing, that is also a choice. Deciding to stay the same is a choice. Ask yourself these questions: Will staying the same do you more good than harm? Making a change will be a little scary, but can you do scary? Are you willing to take the chance and see what that outcome may look like on the other side? Is it worth it? Are you worth it? If you look at your life and go deep enough, you will find something that would benefit from change. Whatever you're doing that's got you to this level of success so far likely won't get you to that next level of growth. So where do you want to be this time next year or in five years?

Growth has to start with detachment from things you have been holding onto that may have worked for you in the past but are no longer serving. Trusting the free fall and letting go is part of the process. Holding onto the way it was, not changing creates a false sense of peace, for the hope of "one day" fosters a lack mentality. Whether you're trying to lose weight, cleaning out your closet, revamping your business or your life, have a bigger conversation with yourself. Mourn what you will be letting go of and prepare to emotionally detach. Let go to allow more in.

MAKE BOLD MOVES:

The only way to create a new story is to make bold moves. One way to do this is to wipe out your calendar, like I did. I eliminated community events I had been a part of for twenty-three years, I canceled classes I was teaching, I removed anything from my calendar that felt obligatory. Anything that felt like I should do it because someone else wanted it, or like a have-to, or like I wasn't benefiting in any way, shape, or form. I stopped having conversations that felt one-sided or like they were falling on deaf ears. I took an eraser to my whole calendar, wiped it out, and found myself with freedom. With a free calendar, I found space to build back into my life with intention. I created new, more interesting, and consciously crafted decisions adding back only the things that felt good to me. Asking myself questions like; What is serving me now? What is filling my cup? What is bringing me joy? How do I want this life of MINE to go? If you could take an eraser to your business, what would you take out? What is worthy of your time, energy, talents, and resources? What makes you feel good? What would you add if you had the time? Those are the questions that you need to ask yourself. The better you feel, the more successful you are going to become. Energy begets energy. Give yourself the gift of space to design a life that makes you happy for yourself.

The future of my dreams allows for more authenticity and is about living my truth with more open-heartedness. I will continue to build a higher level of income but it's about hustling differently. This hustle is a spiritual hustle. I will move forward in a grounded and conscious way with focus and intention. I am actively living out my goals. No "one day or someday." I am no longer willing to personal vision, goals and dreams for the benefit of ave no intention to end this life feeling empty-handed. fulfillment is my highest goal. When I die, I want to go out a feeling of fulfillment, a life well lived.

Everything you do is either at a cost or benefit to yourself. Be mindful of how you're spending your time, energy, and resources. Trying harder, going faster, and adding more to your life, you calendar, your obligation list, is not the answer. In the words of **Edward Abbey**, "Growth for the sake of growth is the ideology of the cancer cell." Be mindful of what you are putting in your calendar and who is in your calendar, because you do have options.

Through this experience, I have found time to create my personal manifesto and identify my values. I invite you to use it to create your own, perfectly suited to you.

- I run my own race and move at my own pace. My external accomplishments no longer define me. I only need to feel pleased with myself.
- Peace, joy, and productivity are my highest values. I honor my body, mind, and heart.
- I give unto myself first. I create my own boundaries. I am obligated to no one.
- I put my dreams at the top of the list. I decide upon the things that may enter my life.
- I work because it brings me joy. I work with people I like and appreciate and with people who like and appreciate me.
- I trust myself and my instincts.
- Life is happening for me, not to me. Tough situations and conversations are here to help me grow as a human. I am not in control of others' thoughts or feelings.
- I share my knowledge and abundance with people who appreciate my offering. I am skilled at identifying those people. They fill me up and encourage me to continue in my work.

- I face things head-on. I am known for saying, "Every outcome I desire, is on the other side of a conversation."
- I am separate from my business. The decisions I make as a business owner are separate from me as a person. I am not my business. My business is an extension of me. I take a stand for what is right.
- My darkness is here to help me just as much as my light.
- My joy comes from within; it is not found outside of me.
- My value comes from being alive on this planet. I am here to experience my soul's evolution, to create, to grow, and to die fulfilled.
- My peace is found in the present moment. Pain comes from thinking about the past or thinking about the future. Life is not to be experienced in the past or the future, it is to be experienced right here, right now.

...UT MICHELLE SAWARD

Michelle is a twenty-three-year veteran of the industry, and in 2018, she opened an EXP office in Trenton MI and has grown from a personal sales team of three to an organization that exceeds 1,600 agents. She and her team have closed over 2000 career sales.

Michelle is committed to the growth and the betterment of others and has a strong track record for developing and elevating the careers of many who have aligned with her. She is known for:

"Opening doors to a better future"

Michelle lives with her husband of eighteen years, is a dog mom, a boater, and lover of travel and island life.

Entrepreneur

Investor

Public speaker

Success Coach

Team Leader

6x Icon agent award winner

Chairman's Award for Circle of Excellence

Southeastern Michigan Regional Chamber of Commerce Women of Achievement Award

Website: *www.michellesaward.com*

ABOUT AMA PUBLISHING

AMA PUBLISHING

AMA Publishing is an international, award winning publishing company that champions the stories of entrepreneurs who are trailblazers, innovators, and instigators.

Forbes has said that, *"AMA Publishing is helping women reshape the future of publishing."*

We would love to help you tell your story. We have helped thousands of people become international, bestselling authors through our courses, multi-author books, and as solo authors.

Your story, it's ready to be told.

Website: *www.amapublishing.co*

Made in the USA
Las Vegas, NV
18 November 2023

81086892R00118